The Context of Casuistry

Moral Traditions & Moral Arguments

A SERIES EDITED BY JAMES F. KEENAN, S.J.

The Evolution of Altruism and the Ordering of Love
STEPHEN J. POPE

Love, Human and Divine: The Heart of Christian Ethics
EDWARD COLLINS VACEK, S.J.

Bridging the Sacred and the Secular:
Selected Writings of John Courtney Murray, S.J.
J. LEON HOOPER, S.J., editor

The Context of Casuistry

EDITED BY
JAMES F. KEENAN, S.J.,
AND
THOMAS A. SHANNON

GEORGETOWN UNIVERSITY PRESS/WASHINGTON, D.C.

Georgetown University Press, Washington, D.C.

Printed in the United States of America
10 9 8 7 6 5 4 3 2 1 1995
THIS VOLUME IS PRINTED ON ACID-FREE ∞ OFFSET BOOK PAPER

Library of Congress Cataloging-in-Publication Data
The context of casuistry / James F. Keenan and Thomas A. Shannon, editors.
p. cm. — (Moral traditions and moral arguments)
Includes bibliographical references.
1. Casuistry. I. Keenan, James F. II. Shannon, Thomas A.
III. Series: Moral traditions & moral arguments.
BJ1441.C66 1995
241—dc20 95-7775
ISBN 0-87840-585-2 (alk. paper).
ISBN 0-87840-586-0 (pbk. : alk. paper)

To Our Teachers and Mentors
Josef Fuchs, S.J.
and
Zachary Hayes, O.F.M.
with deepest gratitude and affection.

The following articles have been used with the permission of the proper copyright holders:

Marilyn McCord Adams. "The Structure of Ockham's Moral Theory." *Franciscan Studies* 46 (1968): 1–35

James F. Keenan. "The Casuistry of John Major, Nominalist Professor of Paris (1506–1531)." *Annual of Society of Christian Ethics,* (1993): 205–222.

John T. Noonan, Jr., "Development in Moral Doctrine." *Theological Studies* 54 (1993): 662-677.

Thomas A. Shannon. "Method in Ethics: A Scotistic Contribution." *Theological Studies* 54 (1993): 272–293.

Contents

Foreword

Stephen Toulmin and I wrote *The Abuse of Casuistry* in the hope of refurbishing the reputation of casuistry as a form of moral reasoning. That reputation, hard earned over some five centuries of work in the Christian church (to say nothing of its counterparts in Judaism and Islam) was unfairly trashed by Blaise Pascal, a genius in mathematics and physics, but a brilliantly prejudiced theologian. After his *Lettres Provinciales* (1656), one of the world's great satires, anyone seriously practicing or defending casuistry would be laughed out of academe or church or wherever moral debate was held. We entitled our book *The Abuse of Casuistry* because another defender of casuistry, the late Anglican Bishop Kenneth Kirk, had noted, in his 1927 book, *Conscience and Its Problems*, "the abuse of casuistry is properly directed, not against all casuistry, but only against its abuse." (p.127). Toulmin and I believed that and felt that it was time to investigate those abuses, both by Pascal and by the historical casuists themselves, in hopes of finding the roots of a method of moral reasoning that had flourished so long and in so many cultures.

Our book succeeded to some extent. If we did not entirely revive the good reputation, we aroused enough curiosity about casuistry to stimulate a new debate over its utility. A flock of neo-casuists appeared, eager to use this method (or recognizing, like Moliere's Monsieur Jourdain who was surprised to learn he had been speaking prose all his life, that they had been crypto-casuists in their approach to ethics). At the same time, a swarm of contra-casuists also hove on the horizon. These critics of neo-casuistry, like post-modern Pascals, are skeptical of the power of casuistry to perform the hard work of moral reasoning. And so, in the six years since *Abuse* appeared, the word "casuistry," hitherto banished except as a dyslogism from moral philosophy, has appeared in the titles of many a scholarly article.

The debate, however, centers on several very practical questions about the nature of moral discourse. The counter-casuists assert that, because casuistry has so tenuous a link to moral theory, it must inevitably become a rootless relativism. They also assert that, because casuistry works with maxims and paradigms that are culture bound, it cannot viably survive in a pluralistic and individualistic culture such as we post-moderns inhabit. Neo-casuists counter these critiques in a variety of ways. They reinterpret the role of moral theory, seeing it less as the premise for deductive reasoning and more as a broad background against which looser and richer moral reasoning takes place. They acknowledge that its maxims and paradigms are colored by the communities in which they arise, but believe that, more often than not, they will be recognized in disguise in other communities. This debate is a moving one, since the critics stimulate the neo-casuists to examine the method of case reasoning more deeply and to become themselves more critical of the method they hope will serve moral reasoning well.

The very practical points of the current debate have not generally returned to the historical casuistry that Toulmin and I described in *Abuse*. I have been disappointed, for example, that no article that I've seen has commented on the three chapters in which we discuss the history of three specific cases, usury, equivocation and self-defense. Toulmin and I particularly enjoyed researching and writing those chapters and thought they shed interesting light on the method itself. So far, no one has seemed to notice. Another scholarly volume, *Conscience and Casuistry in Early Modern Europe*, that appeared almost simultaneously with *Abuse*, also attempted to set this form of moral reasoning in its historic context: it has rarely been referenced in the debate. It may be symptomatic of the a-historicism of many philosophers that they head directly for the theoretical arguments, with scant or any attention to the historical expositions.

I do believe, however, that the current debate about casuistic method and the relation of case reasoning to ethical theory can benefit from a closer study of the history. Abuse swept through twenty-three centuries of moral philosophy and theology, stopping only briefly at Aristotle and Cicero and dwelling most leisurely in the century of "high casuistry," which we decreed to be 1556-1656. Around that century, and even within it, much more history remains to be uncovered. *The Context of Casuistry* contributes importantly to this discovery. It looks at authors in the 13th, 14th and 15th centuries who began to lay foundations for high casuistry and at several authors during the era of high casuistry whom Toulmin and I discussed too briefly. It studies how an author of the 19th century who inherited the casuistic tradition, but used it, not according to its genius, but as an instrument of a very different way of viewing moral reasoning.

Why should this set of historical essays, or any further exposition of the history of casuistical reasoning, illuminate the current methodological debate? Rather than answering with a theoretical argument, let me go to a case. The case will be a literary one, indeed, a fictitious one. This collection of essays begins with a section entitled "Franciscan

Roots" and contains an essay on Duns Scotus and another on William of Ockham. My literary case is the one analyzed by Friar William of Baskerville, himself a Franciscan of the 14th century, who refers to his "friend from Occam." The case, of course, consists of "the wondrous and terrible events . . . that took place in the abbey whose name it is only right and pious now to omit, toward the end of the year of our Lord 1327" and recounted for us by Umberto Eco in his extraordinarily popular novel, *The Name of the Rose*.

I was inspired to use this medieval murder mystery to make my point about the value of historical casuistry while reading an essay by my colleague at the University of Washington, the brilliant historian of ideas, John Toews. In his essay, "The historian in the labyrinth of signs," (*Semiotica* 83 (1991), 351-384), he invokes "William of Baskerville as an ideal semiotic practitioner." Throughout the novel, the friar-detective reads and interprets the signs—we would say the clues—that lead him to identify the monk-murderer. He reminds his young scribe, Adso, that the "world speaks to us like a great book," both in obscure fashion about ultimate things and as a more "talkative text about closer things." In the latter mode, it is "a starting point for the construction of limited, terrestrial, immanent truths about the perceivable relationships among the palpable things in the natural and historical realms of human experience." (Toews, p. 353, Eco, 23-24). Toews notes that "success in the latter form of immanent sign-reading involves mental self-discipline, a bracketing of the metaphysical question of ultimate cause, an ironical distancing from the metaphysical yearning for absolute answers, a focused attentiveness to particular detail . . . and hands-on thinking." The fascination of the novel (though few of its many readers were likely to have been explicitly aware of this) was that "as William tries to uncover some kind of limited order among the multiple possibilities of the signs . . . he is confronted at every turn by opponents and false friends ready to read all signs in a univocal fashion on the basis of a single, closed system of meanings authorized by self-confident faith in a transcendent truth." (Toews, p. 355).

It is remarkable that the authors of this present volume seek the origins of casuistry in the theology and philosophy of Scotus and Ockham, figures whose mode of thought William of Baskerville obviously appreciates and emulates. Their subtle thought, later swept into the general category of "nominalism," attempted to break down the massive intellectual systems of scholasticism and press the mind into the work of making sense of the visible, empirical world. Scotus, called by his admirer Gerald Manley Hopkins, "of reality rarest-veined unraveller," Ockham, his Franciscan brother and erstwhile disciple, and their later follower, John Mair "greatly influenced modern logic and the rise of modern science" says Karl Rahner (*Theological Dictionary*. New York: Herder, 1966, p.321) and, similarly, they greatly influenced casuistic moral thinking.

The authors of the essays on those figures will explain how and why the nominalists were precursors of casuistry. I will note only one feature of their thought that can, I believe, illuminate the current debate. Nominalists were also, again in Karl Rahner's words, "more existentialist" than the other great scholastics of their era ("Scotism," p.439). This existentialism is not the popular philosophy that swept France and washed up in America in the 1950s. Rather it anticipates Rahner's own approach to ethics, articulated in an essay, "On the Question of a Formal Existential Ethics," in which he struggled to define the relationship between the concrete particularity of individual choices in specific circumstances and the general and universal form of ethical principles and rules. Nominalism itself insisted on the primacy of the single and unique individual in the natural, social and personal world and strove to explain how human thought and language could express this singularity in conceptual terms. While their solutions may be, in many ways, inadequate and misleading, their formulation of the problem, whether in epistemology or theology, is compelling.

Casuistry, at its deepest, follows this formulation of the problem. Ethics begins with the irreducibly private and personal acts of conscience, as they weave norms and circumstances and opinions together into a strand of will and understanding called a judgment of right action. As it advances from this base into moral philosophy, it unweaves this strand bit by bit, examining the strength and weaknesses of each filament. When the acts of conscience are untangled, moral philosophy, at the highest level of theory, wonders how to plait them together again, perhaps in a different pattern and toward a different result.

As this reflection goes on, it quickly moves from the irreducible private act of conscience to the setting of that act in the midst of circumstances: the who, what, when, where, why and how of the casuists and rhetoricians. At that point, the essential problem of an existential ethic appears: how can one best express the multitude of internal and external facts and opinions that influence the acts of conscience. Must these not be stated at some level of generality in order to be intelligible? This is the place of "the case," the confluence of persons, places, times and things about which arguments must be made and decisions taken. It is the peculiar skill of casuistry to identify these elements and to construct and examine arguments about them. Traditionally, the logic of identifying and arguing about concrete particulars has been the province, not of dialectic but of rhetoric. Toulmin and I discuss too briefly the importance of rhetorical reasoning for casuistry. This volume advances that discussion by pointing to one form of rhetoric, homiletics, that influenced casuistic reasoning. We would hope to see further studies about the relationship between preaching and confessional practice.

The case, then, is a convergence of many "signs," clues that, if carefully followed, allow for the interpretation of the case. But interpretation always leads away from the case to larger contexts. Friar William recognized that each murder was marked with symbolism of the Apocalypse, taking him from the horror of the moment to the terror of the scriptural last judgment, placing an act of bloody mayhem in a theological context. That theological context itself includes other cases: the internecine strife over the poverty of Christ and the poverty of the Church. William's mind moves back and forth between concrete circumstances and broad visions. This is the second move of good casuistry: after describing the case in terms both general and proximate to the singular, reflection oscillates between fact and theory. It refuses to allow itself to be trapped in the attractive but rigid confines of a theory, as William refused to be lured into the dogmatic explanations of the antagonists of the mystery. At each oscillation between fact and theory, fact is seen in a different light and theory is challenged.

The question, however, is how widely do the oscillations swing. A case is embedded in many contexts: Friar William's case takes place within a Benedictine Monastery, a strife-torn Empire, a schism-rent Church, an ideological rift within and among religious orders, and many others. There are also ideal contexts: a tranquil monastery, a peaceful Empire, a unified and holy Church, fraternal religious orders, and others. How do these many contexts open up interpretation of the murders? Are any of them normatively final, allowing for closure of the case? Casuistry, as such, does not answer those questions: it searches through all the contexts, as did Friar William, for partial illuminations that, in the end, make up a probable interpretation. That is the path that the nominalists started to tread and the casuists, sometimes unknowingly, followed. Now much overgrown with ethical theory, the neo-casuists attempt to open it again.

A moral case is not, of course, a murder mystery. There are many and significant differences, among them the major one: we know that the murder was wrong and we only seek the evil perpetrator. In a moral case, we are asking whether the act at the center of the case is wrong or not. The counter-casuists wish to find the answer outside the case; the neo-casuists seek it in the reciprocity between circumstances and broader vision. The counter-casuists want a sure answer; the neo-casuists are satisfied with a plausible one. The neo-casuists insist that the circumstances of the case bear genuine moral meaning, even if they are not the 'locus of moral certitude'; for the counter-casuists the color of moral meaning comes to the case only from the light of principle and theory. These are not new debates; they are perennial divergences. A return to their historical expression, as in *The Context of Casuistry*, refreshes our memory and gives us hints about how these perennial questions might be reframed.

ALBERT R. JONSEN

Introduction

JAMES F. KEENAN, S.J. AND THOMAS A. SHANNON

In her essay, "The Structure of Ockham's Moral Theory," Marilyn McCord Adams cites Étienne Gilson: "The science which Ockham considers one of the safest and best established (that) we may naturally acquire is ethics." Gilson's statement about surety is ironic in light of our general associations with the More than Subtle Doctor's nominalist claims. But it is even more ironic in this collection of essays on casuistry, for casuistry is conceived in doubt, born in turmoil, and lives in constant search of resolution. Only in coming to terms with its very indeterminacy and lack of certitude does casuistry find its proper context and correct resolutions.

This collection of essays is like its topic: open-ended, reexamining older insights with new empirical and historical data, while deciphering emerging trends and patterns. In a word, it is a heuristic work and, thus, not a work of retrieval; it does not attempt to reconstruct casuistry's method. It acknowledges, immediately, that there is much we do not know—historically, philosophically, or theologically—about casuistry's origins and sources, its popularity and utility, as well as its infamy and abuses. We, the editors, want to expand the inquiry into the nature of casuistry by providing a broader sampling of individuals who, while not normally associated with high European casuistry, either cleared the path for or actually used cases to find practical truth in their contemporary, concrete situations. From this amplified context of casuistry, three particular influences emerge: the rise of nominalism in the academy, the importance of preaching in Renaissance and Reformation Europe, and the distinctive contribution of Franciscan sources.[1]

Our work, *The Context of Casuistry*, is a deliberate response to Albert Jonsen and Stephen Toulmin's *The Abuse of Casuistry*.[2] We recognize their claim concerning the distinctiveness of high casuistry: that is, the method of moral reflection practiced in the sixteenth through eighteenth centuries was considerably different from the science associated with the "manuals" of nineteenth- and twentieth-century Catholic thought. To equate modern attempts at solving moral problems with the moral reasoning method of the sixteenth century, the authors argue, is mistaken.

Their claim has prompted other scholars to study a variety of casuists, as well as their precursors. This collection is prompted by an occasion in which several such interested persons gathered. At the Annual Conference of the Society of Christian Ethics (January 1993), one of the editors, James Keenan, presented the paper included here on John Mair. Keenan explored the roots of high casuistry by looking at the most popular professor at the University of Paris from 1505–1530 and argued that Mair's nominalism was not incidental to his casuistry. Keenan's assertion was not completely new. For years, the noted historian of moral theology Louis Vereecke argued that the roots of casuistry are found in nominalism.[3]

In the audience were four others associated with this volume—Thomas A. Shannon, Charles Curran, Richard Miller, and John Samples, the publisher of Georgetown University Press. These individuals were independently pursuing their own scholarship, focusing on similar issues and insights. At the conclusion of this meeting, we began planning this book.

In large measure, interest in casuistry is prompted by the fact that the scope of the dilemmas facing the sixteenth century is not unlike the contemporary horizon: the explosion of new data from an expanded vision of the world; a turn to the subject as singularly responsible to account for one's actions both religiously and ethically; the failure of existing principles to resolve satisfactorily urgent issues; and the inability to achieve consensus among moral thinkers, church and political leaders, and the general population.

Specifically, in the sixteenth century two major issues prompted casuistry and in both instances nominalism's claim on the particular made that turn to casuistry easy. The first was profoundly social: the explorations of the New World, the trade with the East, and the evangelization that accompanied both. As Jonsen and Toulmin note, existing moral structures were not able to keep pace with European expansionism. Questions of ownership, governance, political autonomy, and financing came to the fore in a dramatically new fashion. Age-old moral rules were unable to entertain the new and unfamiliar circumstances being introduced by explorers, tradesmen, and missionaries. The center was collapsing.

The challenge to create new structures for moral guidance and resolution became, for academicians, worthy as well as necessary. As John Mair noted, "Has not Amerigo Vespucci discovered lands unknown to Ptolemy, Pliny and other geographers up to the present? Why cannot the same happen in other spheres?"[4] To do this, many scholars turned to the immediate and the practical, nearly abandoning methodological, speculative, and metaphysical concerns. In a word, they turned to the cases at hand.

The second major issue was profoundly personal: the state of one's soul before God. For all Christians, the sixteenth century was especially noted for extensive evangelization that called for personal renewal and transformation. For Catholics that renewal was met through the confession of one's sins on a regular basis. As both Thomas Tentler in *Sin and Confession on the Eve of the Reformation*[5] and John O'Malley in *The First Jesuits*[6] note, the confessional was the place where Christians of the sixteenth century could encounter the consolation of God. For reformers, the renewal was made through the acknowledgment that one in faith was saved. The reformers' claim of *sola fide* prompted them to replace the confessional with the individual's conscience as the locus for encountering the redemptive love of God. But both the overworked Catholic confessor and the anxious Protestant conscience needed correct moral guidance for living out the issues of the day.

As academicians of the sixteenth century relied on nominalism to face the uniqueness of these many particular cases, contemporary religious leaders relied on the institution of preaching to engage affectively the concerns of all members. The preacher's ability to captivate the listeners' imaginations, not with speculative theory but with the practicalities of daily life, aroused not only the interests of ordinary Catholics and Protestants, but more specifically those of the casuists themselves. The rhetoric of the sermon gave the casuists a vehicle that was seductive and instructive. It lured the reader into resonating with the particularities of the case, and it instructed the reader to find solutions to the case by drawing analogies from similar cases.

Finally, while the advocates of high casuistry are Dominicans and Jesuits, the precursors of the case method have distinctive Franciscan sources in the latter's preaching and nominalism. Moreover, their religious charism prized the primacy of the will, both human and divine. For Franciscans, the human will encounters the immediacy of choice in the face of urgent contradictories. Human choice is not limited to the first and fundamental one (Deuteronomy 30.15, "Today I offer you the choice of life and good, or death and evil.") but is made throughout life. Through these choices, the person determines oneself as either responding to or rejecting the invitation of God. To begin to understand the human will as self-expressive, then, is to get a glimpse of the will of the Creator, which expresses God's self as radically and absolutely free. God's choices *ad extra* then are always free, never necessary, but rather contingent. When Franciscan writers apply this insight to the act of creation and describe it as contingent and not imminently necessary, they (like the nominalists) erode the essentialism of much scholastic natural law.

In sum, the world is the place where both the human makes her or his choices daily and God chooses to reveal God's self. The world is both God's text and stage, where we can read the signs of God's creative love and encounter God through our moral action. God is not encountered in the abstract or the remote, but in the concrete and the immediate. Our daily choices become choices about God.

This Franciscan insight into the will and its place in the world complements a Franciscan understanding of the virtue of obedience, which rejects a legalistic sanction of blind submission and depends upon an abiding trust in God's creative love. Wonder, not fear, is the beginning of wisdom found in obedience. Obeying God's will is, then, understood through two centrally expressed presuppositions. First, creation is an expression of God's love and beneficence; obedience to God is confidence in the present and in an even more benevolent future. Second, our rational nature is an expression of God's will and, therefore, of the proper mode of reading the text of God's world. Human reason is not lost, then, in the Franciscan context; it is guaranteed its dignity and place.[7]

SPECIFIC CONTRIBUTIONS

The book is divided into five historical parts, with the first and final parts being more theoretical than the middle three. The first part examines the Franciscan sources of casuistry, with its emphasis on human freedom. Thomas A. Shannon's "Method in Ethics: A Scotistic Contribution" recognizes, on the one hand, that Scotus operates within a recognizable scholastic framework. On the other hand, his emphasis on divine and human contingency led him to claim that the world's final cause derives from no necessary discernible plan or archetype, but simply from God's free will. Rather than positing some necessary metaphysical purpose, Scotus drops final causality and turns both to the contingency of efficient causality to find the intention of human action and to right reason to establish the standard for correct behavior. The moral act is only understood and measured then through the particulars of circumstances: the specific end, the manner of performance, time, and place. The moral act is measured for its fittingness in the here and now of this willing Christian.

Marilyn McCord Adams' "The Structure of Ockham's Moral Theory" challenges the assumption of many academicians that Ockham's ethical theory can be reduced to a simplistic divine command ethics. On the contrary, she proposes that a correct reading of Ockham conveys a "modified right reason theory," which encourages us to determine the morally right according to the standards of reason. Moreover, Ockham's Franciscan vision of God as gracious and generous presumes that the God who commands is the same God who invites the thinking Christian into a relationship of mutuality, not blind subservience.

The second part treats two precursors of casuistry whose cases are distinguished by their respective vocations: the preacher and the academician. Unlike the first, this part focuses on these individuals' specific use of cases.

Franco Mormando's "To Persuade Is a Victory: Rhetoric and Moral Reasoning in the Sermons of Bernardino of Siena" models the methodology of casuistry. Mormando locates the sermons in a particular time and place and illustrates Bernardino at work: engaging a plethora of circumstances, arousing the hearers' affections, and challenging the audience with the Franciscan call to conversion. There is an immediacy here which presents practical insights imaginatively through the use of anecdotes, fables, and vignettes. Interestingly, Mormando notes that while Bernardino's sermons are faithful to the "rhetorical principles of the Middle Ages," he can find no cohesive ethical theory that gives order or structure to Bernardino's moral sermons. Practical moral instruction and exhortation, not theory, is the foundation of Bernardino's preaching and reflects another Franciscan emphasis.

James Keenan's "The Casuistry of John Mair, Nominalist Professor of Paris (1506–1531)" studies the Paris logician's nominalism and its denial of the negation of essential objects and universals. Mair led a shift in moral thinking away from an "object" of moral activity and toward the role or vocation of the moral agent who approaches new social contexts and new moral problems. Without such objects and their attendant universal principles, Mair turns from deductive (or geometric) logic to inductive (or taxonomic) logic to resolve the uncertainties facing the new situation of the sixteenth century. Still, though Mair engaged more ordinary matters of ordinary citizens than any of his predecessors, he remained the arbiter of moral decision making, and his casuistry was no more accessible to the lay person than the moral theory of his predecessors.

Though three of the figures in the first two parts enjoy British ancestry, their influence extended deep into Continental thought. In the third part, however, the influence of the two casuists is restricted primarily to Great Britain and, later, to the United States. In order to get a broader view of high casuistry, rather than examine the Catholic Continental figures generally associated with the period (as Jonsen and Toulmin as well as Mahoney have done), we present the work of two reformed British casuists.

James Keenan, in "William Perkins (1558–1602) and the Birth of British Casuistry," turns to the distinctiveness of British reformed casuistry by underlining its audience and its notion of authority. While Continental casuists wrote for policy makers and confessors, British reformers wrote for everyone, especially the laity. Furthermore, their central preoccupation was not the Catholic issue of sinfulness, but the reformed one of the assurance of salvation. This search for assurance engaged the individual's conscience and intensified the previously noted shift to the subject by making that individual's conscience not only confident of its election in faith but also able to arbitrate all subsequent moral decisions. But Keenan highlights that the distinctive root for Perkins' casuistry was based in the profound perplexities, terrible anxieties, and overwhelming ignorance that his congregation felt. British casuistry, like its Continental forerunner, was born as ministry to those in doubt.

Richard Miller's "Moral Sources, Ordinary Life, and Truth-telling in Jeremy Taylor's Casuistry" turns to the end of the era of British reformed casuistry by studying the Doctor of Doubts. His doubts had two origins: first, the questions surrounding the ordinary activities of ordinary life; and second, the tension between conventional morality and the new needs of society and individuals. Taylor finds human reason somewhat unreliable and therefore does not "look to the order of creation, but to the sovereign agency of God as recorded in the Bible." In examining this Scripture-based ethics, Miller studies the important case of truth-telling to illustrate both Taylor's casuistry and his commitment to a "morality of modest expectations" that addresses the issues of daily life.

The fourth part treats the aftermath of casuistry in terms of the development of both the moral manuals in the nineteenth century and moral doctrine itself. In Charles Curran's "The Manual and Casuistry of Aloysius Sabetti" we find the methodology of the Neapolitan Jesuit who taught at Woodstock College, Maryland. Along with his contemporaries, Sabetti reversed the method of high casuistry; first, he developed rules from principles that are known for their certitude and, second, he applied these rules to cases in order to prescribe proper courses of action.

For Mair and Perkins the case was the measure of reality; in manual thinking the case was measured by the rule. This clear shift to deontological thought which enjoyed an apparent confidence in the certitude of principles manifested a bias for legalistic thought. Sabetti as a manualist was more a presenter of legislated thought than an inquiring theologian, more a writer who demonstrated than one who argued. Only when there was room for speculation, when the principle did not clearly solve the case or the Catholic magisterial authority had not "determined" the solution—that is, only when there was uncertainty—did Sabetti entertain an inductive case method, as he did with the case of ectopic pregnancy.

John T. Noonan, Jr., in "Development in Moral Doctrine" presents four case studies to show that significant change has occurred in the moral teaching of the Catholic Church. He does this by applying Cardinal Newman's insight into doctrinal development to the history of moral theology: "It is the warfare of ideas under their varying aspects. . . ." Noonan studies the mutations of old rules affected by both new social circumstances and the dynamic presence of the Holy Spirit. In order to respond to the great commandments of love of God and neighbor, while being governed by the principles of justice and charity, moral communities have been forced to examine the adequacy of traditional moral rules for contemporary life. In such a context, change, though threatening, has been and continues to be morally demanded and positive.

Part five turns to a contemporary context for casuistry. These essays, like the first two, are more theoretical than practical. Thomas Kopfensteiner in "Science, Metaphor, and Moral Casuistry" studies the hermeneutics of moral decision making. This hermeneutics is developmental: its contours are spiral, not circular. Kopfensteiner makes his case by reflecting not on early casuistry but rather on its later expression in the manualist tradition and specifically examines the object of moral activity as the manualists used it. While he acknowledges that an essentialist metaphysics of human nature has often defined this object, he proposes instead a personalistic metaphysics. The result is that, since "the world is mediated through language," we need a "metaphorical structure of normativity." For Kopfensteiner, "moral casuistry is a hermeneutical art."

The final essay concerns the "Contexts of Casuistry: Historical and Contemporary." Our investigations into the historical context of casuistry show that casuistry is not as context neutral as Jonsen and Toulmin state. They argue that casuistry is an instrument that can be used independent of context. For instance, they contend that the diverse backgrounds of the bioethics commissioners were not substantively engaged in the moral resolutions of the dilemmas that they faced. Instead, they claim that casuistry resolved the dilemmas independent of or even in spite of their differing moral presuppositions and beliefs. But our findings show that casuistry absorbs the context in which it is employed; the casuistry of a Sienese preacher differs from his Puritan counterpart, just as a Scottish logician's differs from a Neapolitan theologian's. The presuppositions operative in the context in which casuistry is used enter into the casuistic logic. Thus, even the casuistry of that bioethics commission was probably much more culturally bound than the authors admit. Casuistry is always ladened with the moral assumptions of the culture in which it functions.

We conclude that essay by proposing certain conditions for a context in which some (but not all) insights from high casuistry might operate in contemporary decision making. Foremost among these are the need for a personalistic metaphysics of human nature that appreciates the development of moral character and a theology of love that assumes the positive role of change. These conditions suggest the possibility of turning to the virtues as an appropriate context for the practice of casuistry. Historically, the virtues have acknowledged the priority of prudence, the effectiveness of human agency, and the centrality of personal and social circumstances. Their fundamental teleological orientation offers both a dynamic structure and a solid anthropological foundation that counters the endemic relativism and philosophical agnosticism of our times. That context could provide the contemporary believer with an opportunity to see the Scriptures as practically relevant for daily life in the concrete world, through both the sermons of preachers and the cases of ethicists.

James F. Keenan, S.J.
Thomas A. Shannon

NOTES

1. For a general background, see Kenan B. Osborne, ed., *The History of Franciscan Theology* (Saint Bonaventure, New York: Bonaventure University, 1994).

2. Albert Jonsen and Stephen Toulmin, *The Abuse of Casuistry* (Berkeley: University of California, 1988).

3. A partial collection of his essays appear in Louis Vereecke, *De Guillaume d'Ockham a Saint Alphonse de Liguori: Etudes d'histoire de la theologie morale moderne, 1300–1787* (Rome: Alfonsianum, 1986).

4. John Mair, *Commentary of the Fourth Book of the Sentences,* quoted in John Durkan, "John Major: After 400 Years" *The Innes Review* 5 (1954) 131–157, at 135.

5. Thomas Tentler, *Sin and Confession on the Eve of the Reformation* (Princeton: Princeton University, 1977).

6. John O'Malley, *The First Jesuits* (Cambridge: Harvard University, 1993).

7. See a similar discussion in John Mahoney, *The Making of Moral Theology* (Oxford: Clarendon Press, 1987) pp. 224–258.

Part One

FRANCISCAN ROOTS

Method in Ethics: A Scotistic Contribution

THOMAS A. SHANNON

INTRODUCTION

When Vatican Council II noted that "the human race has passed from a rather static concept of reality to a more dynamic, evolutionary one,"[1] few may have appreciated the profound impact this would have on moral theology. Contained in this phrase is an implicit challenge to the tradition of moral theology, particularly as received through the manualist tradition of the past two centuries.

This tradition was founded on a vision of natural law derived from a cosmology that is static and fixed, a reality in which certain physical functions and acts have been assigned a role by the Creator. Morality consists in knowing these functions and conforming oneself to this order established by God. As Pope John Paul II himself stated in an early work: "The whole order of nature has its origin in God, since it rests directly on the essences (or nature) of existing creatures from which arise all dependencies, relationships and connections between them. . . . Man is just towards God the Creator when he recognizes the order of nature and conforms to it in his actions."[2]

In the manualist tradition, nature is an hierarchically structured order in which each being has its proper place assigned to it by the eternal law and discovered through reason, which constitutes the norm of the moral law. That is, the norm of morality is the inbuilt order of nature manifested in fixed natures, designed and created by God. These fixed natures then serve as the foundation for establishing both the objectivity of moral norms and the claim that some acts are intrinsically good or evil.

To affirm, then, that reality is dynamic and evolutionary, as Vatican II did, is to challenge the received order and apparently to undermine the objective nature of morality. How could an act be intrinsically evil in an evolving world? Two trends emerged. One sought to maintain the tradition as received by continuing to locate the norms of morality in the order of nature, as for example in the Instruction

Donum vitae, which condemned various forms of artificial reproduction because they are against nature. The other, represented by proportionalism, sought to develop a new basis for moral norms.

KEY CONCEPTS IN SCOTUS'S ETHICAL THOUGHT

Freedom

One core element in freedom is contingency. Whenever we will something, Scotus argues, we also know that we could just as well have not willed it. This analysis also extends to the goods or values we experience. We can be offered a good, know it is a good, and yet refuse it. At the core of each of these acts is the experience that "at the very moment that it wills or causes something, it [the will] could equally well will the contrary. A decision of the will never takes away its potentiality to act in the opposite way."[3] And for those still not convinced of the contingency of our acts, Scotus suggests that "those who deny that some being is contingent should be exposed to torments until they concede that it is possible for them not to be tormented."[4]

A second dimension of freedom is an implication of God's love of himself. Scotus knew, as the other schoolmen did, that God loves himself necessarily because there is no other possible being for God to love appropriately. Scotus preserves freedom in this situation through his doctrine of *firmitas,* "the will's ability to adhere to that in which consists its perfection."[5] This perspective comes from Augustine through Anselm, who declared: "Whoever has what is appropriate and advantageous in such a way that it cannot be lost is freer than he who has this in such a way that it can be lost."[6]

Thus infinite freedom is characterized as "the ability to continually adhere to the unlimited perfecting object."[7] Finite freedom, on the other hand, is the ability "not to limit oneself to limitedly perfecting objects."[8] Thus Scotus's understanding of freedom, whether infinite or finite, shifts the ground for thinking about the significance of the fact of choice. To be sure there must be minimally one choice, but the more important reality is that the will "self-determinately possesses a willable object through its action and such that the resultant act possesses a degree of perfection."[9]

As finite humans, our choices are not infinitely perfect. This means that we will experience freedom primarily as choice. That is, we are aware that we could have chosen otherwise and that such a choice would have given us a different degree of perfection. Thus, "choice is simply basic freedom in inferior conditions."[10] In choosing, our will is never fully actual, for it is contingent. Yet for all that, we can approach our perfection through our steadfastness or constancy in cleaving to the object of our love. "The perfection of freedom connotes a perseverance and stability in the will's adherence to the good."[11]

As a further elaboration of the notion of freedom, Scotus contrasts a nature to a will. A nature is a principle of activity by which an entity acts out or actualizes its reality and is the reason why an entity acts as it does. Or, as he says, "The potency of itself is determined to act, so that so far as itself is concerned, it cannot fail to act when not impeded from without."[12] A nature is essentially the reason why an entity acts as it does. A will, on the other hand, "is not of itself so determined, but can perform either this act or its opposite, or can either act or not act at all."[13] Thus the reason why this act was done as opposed to another is that the will can elicit an act in opposite ways.

Scotus, following Anselm, distinguishes two movements in the will: the *affectio commodi,* the inclination to seek what is advantageous or the good for one's self; and the *affectio justitiae,* the inclination to seek the good in itself. The *affectio commodi* leads us to do what is to our advantage, perfection, or welfare. It is a nature seeking its own fulfillment. For Scotus, the *affectio commodi* is not an elicited act. Rather, it is a natural appetite necessarily seeking its own perfection:

> That it does so necessarily is obvious, because a nature could not remain a nature without being inclined to its own perfection. Take away this inclination and you destroy the nature. But this natural appetite is nothing other than an inclination of this sort to its proper perfection; therefore the will as nature necessarily wills its perfection, which consists above all in happiness, and it desires such by its natural appetite.[14]

The *affectio justitiae,* on the other hand, is the source of true freedom or liberty of the will, as well as a restraint on the *affectio commodi.* The *affectio justitiae* allows us to transcend nature and go beyond ourselves and our individually defined good. The *affectio justitiae* is the capacity to see the value of another being. "To want an act to be perfect, so that by means of it one may better love some object for its own sake, is something that stems from the affection for justice, for when I love something good in itself, then I will something in itself."[15]

Allan B. Wolter, O.F.M., notes four characteristics of the *affectio justitiae.* First, it gives us the capacity to love a being in itself rather than for what it can do for us. Second, it enables us to love God for who God is rather than for the consequence of God's love for us. Third, the *affectio justitiae* allows us to love our neighbor as ourselves, thereby recognizing the equal value of each individual. Finally, seeking for the good in itself leads to a desire to have this good beloved by all, rather than being held to oneself.[16] This leads Wolter to the conclusion that the *affectio justitiae* amounts to a "freedom *from* nature and a freedom *for* values."[17] Or, as Scotus puts it: "From the fact that it is able to temper or control the inclination for what is advantageous, it follows that it is obligated to do so in accordance with the rule of justice that it has received from a higher will."[18]

Such an understanding of will as *affectio justitiae* frees the will from the necessity of a nature's act of self-realization or the seeking of its own good. Paradoxically then, if a free agent acts according to nature it acts "unnaturally," since to seek what is "*bonum in se* is not to seek something that 'realizes the potential of a rational nature.' It is somehow to transcend 'the natural' and thus to have a mode of operation that sets the rational agent apart from all other agencies."[19]

This understanding of will grounds our capacity to transcend our own self-interest. This is where Scotus's discounting of the fact of choice plays a critical role. In keeping with his mentors Augustine and Anselm, Scotus views freedom as "a positive bias or inclination to love things objectively or as right reason dictates."[20] That is, the proper focus of moral analysis is not the individual act or choice, but the inclination as a whole. And such an inclination focuses on fidelity to the good in itself, not the specific act of choosing that good nor the necessary appreciation of what is good for the fulfillment of the nature of the agent. Moral analysis is not, therefore, centered on the individual act but on the good to which we wish to adhere and which is manifest in this particular act.

Natural Law

Duns Scotus divides natural law into strict and extended. Natural law in the strict sense is "one whose truth value can be ascertained from its terms (in which case it is a principle of natural law, even as in theoretical matters a principle is known from its terms) or else one that follows from the knowledge of such truth (in which case it is a demonstrated conclusion in the practical order)."[21]

These laws of nature in the strict sense possess "necessary truth. Therefore, God himself cannot make them false."[22] Thus in the strict sense such truths are either "first practical principles known from their terms or as conclusions necessarily entailed by them."[23]

A law of nature in the extended sense is "a practical truth recognized by all to be in accord with such a law."[24] Such truths are "not practical principles that are necessary in an unqualified sense, nor are they simply necessary conclusions from such."[25] Of critical importance is the fact that the precepts of the natural law in the extended sense do not necessarily follow from the first practical principles of natural law strictly understood. They are, however, in harmony with such principles.

Following the customary practice of dividing the Decalogue into two tables—the first three commandments referring to God, and the final seven referring to our neighbor—and taking the Decalogue as a summary of the natural law, Scotus asks whether all the commandments of the Decalogue belong to the natural law. Using his distinction, Scotus argues in the following way.

With respect to the first table of the Decalogue, the practical principles known from it

> belong to the natural law in the strictest sense, and there can be no dispensation in their regard . . . . It is to these that the cannon of the *Decrees of Gratian* refers, where it is said that the "natural law begins from the very beginnings of rational creatures, nor does time change it, but it is immutably permanent"—and this I concede.[26]

Additionally, the commands of the first table "regard God immediately as an object."[27] Therefore, since God alone is to be loved as God and since nothing else must be worshiped as God, it follows that "God could not dispense in regard to these so that someone could do the opposite of what this or that prohibits."[28]

Such indispensability or immutability does not apply to the second table, although these commandments are surely in harmony with the first table. Among the various arguments Scotus presents for this position, two are key. First, in addition to the fact that the second table contains no necessary conclusions from the principles of the first table, Scotus argues that the second table

> contains no goodness such as is necessarily prescribable for attaining the goodness of the ultimate end, nor in what is forbidden is there such malice as would turn one away necessarily from the last end, for even if the good found in these maxims were not commanded, the last end [of man as union with God] could still be loved and attained, whereas if the evil proscribed

> by them were not forbidden, it would still be consistent with the acquisition of the ultimate end.[29]

Second, Scotus argues that a consideration of the divine will shows that the commandments of the second table do not pertain strictly to the natural law. Anything other than God is willed freely and contingently, for "that alone is necessarily willed without which that cannot stand which is willed with regard to an end."[30] Since God is the only necessary being, God exists even if nothing else exists. "Therefore, in His volition, He wills nothing other than Himself necessarily."[31] As for commands not referring to God as their immediate object, "by reason of the very nature of God's willing, a certain contingency must be present in these precepts."[32]

Scotus's argument is both logical and metaphysical. The logic of the argument says that the commands of the second table cannot be derived necessarily from those of the first table. Since they are not necessary, they are contingent. Metaphysically, since God could in fact have created another order of reality—and, therefore, the present order is contingent—the rules governing this present order are not necessary because the order itself is not necessary. Therefore, though the commands of the second table are congruent with the first table and are harmonious with the actual existing order, they are contingent and could change with a changing reality. Robert Prentice summarizes this position in a clear and powerful statement:

> [T]hose precepts have been chosen by God's will from all the possibilities that are presented to it through the abundance of God's essence. By means of them He has freely chosen how to orient man towards his last end in this particular way. But from His abundance He could also have arranged such other means by which this could have been achieved. . . . If, therefore, there is an element of freedom in the very institution of the precepts, there cannot be any absolute, indispensable and inherent necessity in them.[33]

SCOTUS'S ETHICAL METHOD

Efficient Causality

Scotus argues that God's activities *ad extra* are free, and that therefore such acts and their consequences are contingent. He further argues that neither can we distinctly know our ultimate end from natural things nor are we capable of knowing those things which lead to our ultimate end. To argue such would suggest necessity in the order of creation. Thus, for Scotus there is no necessary connection between an act and our final end. While such an act may indeed be appropriate to our final end, such appropriateness is contingent.

Therefore if the end is the principle of action, then for Scotus, there is no such end that is naturally known that can constitute the necessary appropriateness of human actions. This further means, as Mary Elizabeth Ingham states, that "the end or object of the act appears within the will, as the reason or intention."[34] This Scotistic turn to efficient causality removes final causality as a key element in moral theory because it "appears to necessitate moral goodness and to remove self-determination from the will."[35]

Moral Goodness

"Moral goodness is the integrity of all conditions and circumstances, under the direction of right reason."[36] This definition of moral goodness is yet another consequence of Scotus's turn to efficient causality. Moral goodness comes from the dictates of right reason, not from conformity to the final end or because the act is a means to a good end.

Scotus distinguishes three levels of goodness. The first is metaphysical or transcendental goodness. This is essentially a function of being, since only insofar as a being exists "could anything be an object of desire or love. Not to be in this uninteresting and trivial sense is simply not to be at all."[37]

Second is natural goodness. An act is "naturally good when it has all that becomes it insofar as these things are concerned that are suited by nature to concur in constituting it naturally."[38] Important here is Wolter's observation that natural goodness is related to the will as nature (the *affectio commodi*) and that this goodness is necessarily pursued in the fulfillment of the agent's nature.

Third is moral goodness or the moral goodness of an act, as defined here and as further described by Scotus as "a combination of all that becomes the act, not in an absolute sense, as if it were constitutive of its very nature as an act, but in the sense that according to right reason it is becoming to the act."[39] Yet another way that Scotus describes the moral goodness of an act is to compare it to an aesthetic judgment. One could say that just as beauty is not some absolute quality in a beautiful body, but a combination of all that is in harmony with such a body (such as size, figure, and color), and a combination of all aspects (that pertain to all that is agreeable to such a body and are in harmony with one another), so the moral goodness of an act is a kind of decoration it has, including a combination of due proportion of all to which it should be proportioned (such as potency, the object, the end, the time, the place, and the manner), and this especially as right reason dictates.[40]

Right Reason

Ingham formulates the significance and centrality of right reason for Scotus: "Moral behavior is dependent upon the power of the agent to control his action through the operation of right reason, not upon the ultimate goal nor upon the agent's understanding of the deeper significance of the norms to be followed."[41] For Scotus, since his critique of natural knowledge implies an inability to know our final end, "right reason replaces objective finality as the measure of moral goodness."[42]

Right reason establishes a standard of behavior rather than identifies a goal in a teleological sense: "It is necessary for the moral goodness of the moral act that the complete dictate of right reason precede it, to which dictate it conforms as measured to measure."[43] Also, right reason is the source of the "practical principle by which rational judgment is made and the act is accomplished."[44] Right reason's task, therefore, is to evaluate and judge appropriate circumstances. In the absence of any teleological goal which typically constitutes objective moral goodness, Scotus identifies moral goodness "with the intention of the agent and not a real aspect of the act as such."[45]

The moral goodness of an act "consists in its having all that the agent's right reason declares must pertain to the act or the agent in acting."[46] At the outset, then, right reason is present as the judge of the appropriateness of the circumstances of an act. Additionally, the individual "must actually pass judgment upon the act and carry it out in accordance with that judgment."[47] Thus for the act to be morally good, there must be an act constituted by reason, an agent capable of acting, and the appropriateness or harmony of the circumstances.

Note particularly that the good now operates as an integral efficient cause, with the consequence that the end "has no objective existence exterior to the will."[48] Ingham observes that Scotus has made an interesting parallel here, in that he "presents the rational, finite will as constitutive of moral goodness in a way similar to that of the divine will as creative of goodness."[49] Thus for Scotus, agents with intellectual knowledge are suited by nature to judge the appropriateness of their actions and thus have "an intrinsic rule of rectitude for their actions."[50]

Structure of the Moral Act

In addition to the nature of the agent, which makes it possible to adjudicate the appropriateness of the act, Scotus argues that two more elements are necessary for a moral act. First we must determine the object of the act which brings it under the generic heading of moral. This does not determine its moral species but rather opens the act "to further moral determination, for when an act has an appropriate object, it is capable of further moral specification in view of the circumstances in which it is performed."[51]

Second, the goodness of the act is further defined by the circumstances. First is the circumstance of the end, "for given the nature of the agent, of the action, and of the object, one immediately concludes that such an action ought to be performed by the agent for such an end, and that it ought to be chosen and wanted for the sake of such an end."[52] Second is the "manner in which the action is performed."[53] This is determined through prudence, right reason, and the suitability of that act in relation to the nature of the actor. Third is the circumstance of appropriate time. An act is appropriate "only when the act can be directed to or can attain such an end."[54] Thus the timing of the act which contributes to its moral success is critical in establishing its morality. Finally is the circumstance of place, which Scotus does not regard as significant for many acts. One can see, though, that an act which is morally appropriate in private may take on a different moral tone in public.

Scotus discusses how these circumstances morally qualify an act by arguing that some acts are "performed under circumstances that are not all they should be [to make the act good], yet neither are they so improper that they ought not to be there."[55] In this case the act is directed neither to an appropriate end nor to an inappropriate one. Such an act is bad "privately,"[56] presenting a lack of suitability, "the absence of what ought to be there."[57] Also, an act can be bad "contrarily," when it "is performed for some unlawful purpose"[58] or is "the contrary of goodness."[59]

With the exception of two acts—the act of loving God, which is the only one that is intrinsically good, and the act of hating God, which is the only one that is intrinsically evil—all acts must be contextualized for them to receive their full moral status. While the object is significant in establishing the natural goodness of the act, one must still situate the act with respect to its end, manner, time, and place for it to be truly a moral act. Scotus summarizes his position:

> This delimitation introduced by the object first brings the act under the generic heading of moral. Not that the nature of its object determines its moral species; rather it opens it to further moral determination, for when an act has an appropriate object, it is capable of further moral specification in view of the circumstances in which it is performed. That is why an act is said to receive its generic goodness from its object, for just as genus is potential with respect to differences, so the goodness derived from its object first puts it into the generic class of moral acts. Only goodness of nature is presupposed. And once it has generic goodness, the way is open to all the additional moral specifications.[60]

SCOTUS'S ANALYSIS OF SPECIFIC MORAL PROBLEMS

In this section I present examples of how Scotus reasons through several ethical problems. But two caveats are in order. First, these examples occur within the context of a different mode of reading biblical texts than we use. Second, the discussion of marriage does not reflect the coequality of the two ends of marriage. Yet given these critical differences between Scotus's time and ours, his mode of analysis is both interesting and illuminating. For he demonstrates clearly the implications of the contingency of the second table of the Decalogue as well as the necessity of contextualizing an act. Thus although the content of his argument may be dated, his method is extremely relevant to the concerns of the proportionalists, particularly the distinction between premoral and moral values and disvalues and the debate over whether some acts are intrinsically evil.

Bigamy and Polygamy

Scotus discusses this question as one of commutative justice within the ends of the marriage contract.

> In the case of the matrimonial contract, there are two reasons for the exchange: one, the procreation of offspring; the other, a remedy against fornication. As regards the first purpose, the male body is of more value than the female, for the same could fecundate several women during the time it takes for the same woman to conceive through men. . . . As for the second purpose, which

> only held good for the state of fallen nature, namely, to avoid fornication, the bodies of man and woman are of equal value.[61]

Given this assumption of the primacy of reproduction, Scotus argues that one man might, at a time when there were few humans, share his body with many women, either in order to increase the number of humans or to increase the number available to participate in the worship of God.[62] Since at the time he was writing, the population was of ample size and children received a religious education and participated in worship, Scotus argued that bigamy would be prohibited because "the principal end [of marriage] does not require it at present."[63]

However, Scotus continues to argue that "when it is extremely necessary that the primary end be attained, this must be done, in which case the secondary end should be neglected, as it were."[64] Scotus argues that one can favor the primary end, even if this qualifies the secondary end, without doing injustice to the marriage contract.

> And so it is clear how there is justice for both parties in the marital contract, because each ought to be willing, according to right reason, to surrender something he or she has a right to as regards the less important end, in view of the fact that each receives an equal good as regards the more important end—an end that should be desired more, even if one party should have to sacrifice something in exchange to obtain it. And at times it would be necessary to do so, namely, when one is obligated to make such a sacrifice.[65]

Scotus provides several examples of circumstances in which such obligations might arise. One might be commanded by God, as Abraham and Hagar were. Or many men might be lost through war, the sword, or pestilence; in such circumstances, there being few men and many women, bigamy would be licit. For the good of the species, justice in marriage would be served by having the primary end take precedence over the secondary end, one male impregnating many women. "According to right reason, a woman should be willing that her man be joined to another woman that childbearing may occur."[66] Again, Scotus argues that the present circumstances do not warrant such a conclusion, but that "it does not follow that in a special case the opposite could not be licit, or even in some cases necessary."[67]

Divorce

The issue is whether, under Mosaic law or the natural law, a man could licitly divorce his wife. Scotus does not address divorce with respect to marriage as a sacrament. Rather, his argument refers to the natural law. It reflects standard male bias, insofar as it considers a wife's displeasing her husband as an adequate basis for divorce.

> To avoid an evil which outweighs the good of wedlock's indissolubility, God can dispense from it so that the marriage holds good until such a time as the woman may come to displease her husband. And in such a contract justice is preserved to some extent. For not only to obtain a greater good, but also to avoid a greater evil, the parties marrying may want to give themselves to each other in this fashion. Now, uxoricide is a greater evil than indissolubility is a good because it includes not only the serious evil suffered by the woman killed but also the grave evil of the guilty killer. Uxoricide would also be a serious evil for the whole country, because it would be an occasion for continual discord and fighting by reason of the ire of the wife's parents toward her murderer and this would tend to break down the family, because if the man were killed by his adversaries or by the law, it would destroy his family and the education of his child.[68]

Scotus explicitly does not use this argument to support the wife's divorcing of the husband because he thinks "the sex difference prevents the woman from taking such vengeance as a man is wont to do."[69] One can assume that, exposed to our contemporary experience, Scotus would reverse his position.

However, his larger point is that divorce is not against the law of nature in the strict sense, is not against any self-evident principle of natural law or the education of children. "For God could have arranged another plan for the education of children, but one not as convenient as this is, and then even though one of the goods of marriage is in harmony with the law of nature, namely indissolubility, God could have dispensed with this in order to avoid a greater evil."[70]

Lying

Lying is a particularly interesting example because, in discussing it, Scotus argues that circumstances can remove the badness which an act has *per se* by reason of this object.[71] He gives several arguments.

First, "false beliefs are not more inappropriate or illicit matter for speech than is the innocent killing of a human being for the benefit of the state."[72] Given the correct conditions, Scotus argues, killing can become licit or even meritorious should the command be revoked; similarly with lying. Second, since what holds good for a lesser excusing reason also holds good for a greater, the precept of not deceiving our neighbor is not more binding than the precept of not killing: "Indeed one's neighbor loses less if occasionally given a false view or if deprived of our true opinion then he would if deprived of bodily life; in fact there is no comparison here."[73] Third, and critical in relation to the other two examples, lying "does not immediately remove one from God, just as the opposite action [i.e., telling the truth] about some indifferent matter does not have to do with God as its immediate object."[74] Thus the prohibition on lying is a natural law only in the extended sense and is, therefore, contingent.

But Scotus provides another argument which is extremely interesting, first, in that it describes the structure of the moral act, and second, because it provides an intriguing description of the act in relation to the actor's intentions.

> Although the positive act and its malice do not represent anything that is one *per se*, a name can still be imposed which signifies not just the act or its deformity, but the whole combination at once. The name "adultery" is imposed to signify not just the undertaking of this thing, but also the illegal appropriation of what belongs to another against his will or that of any higher owner. It does not seem that the sort of combination signified by such names could possibly be good, though it is possible for the underlying act to exist without the deformity, for instance, the act of intercourse or that of appropriating such a thing. Such is the case here. Although the utterance of such and such words with or without such significance could be sinless, nevertheless, to utter them knowing the opposite to be the case, and hence with the intention of deceiving, could not occur without sin, because it implies that in addition to the underlying act there are such circumstances as necessarily deform it.[75]

Scotus's argument is that, in addition to the act itself, further specification is needed to ascertain its moral status. That is, the act needs to be specified or measured by intention and circumstances through the use of right reason to determine how the act is to be morally categorized. Words or speech do not constitute a lie, therefore, until they are further specified by intention and circumstance.

Summary

Although monogamy, indissolubility, and truth telling are congruent with the extended sense of the natural law and in the present dispensation are to be observed, nonetheless specific circumstances can qualify such laws and morally mandate another set of behaviors. And right reason is sufficient to discern when these circumstances are altered so as to change the binding nature of natural law. Finally, and most importantly, for Scotus it is necessary to look beyond the act itself to categorize it morally. That is, one needs to consider the circumstances and intention before an act can be morally evaluated in its totality. As Scotus noted, the underlying act can be considered without deformity; it is the circumstances and intentions, not its physical structure, that constitute its moral status.

SCOTUS AND CONTEMPORARY ISSUES

By way of conclusion, I shall highlight what I take to be the critical contributions of Scotus to contemporary debates on method in moral theology, grouping these contributions under four general headings.

Classical Natural Law

The point at issue here is the static, Newtonian cosmos in which the classical theory of natural law came to be expressed, particularly in the manual tradition, and the manner in which such a framework sets up the problem of the naturalistic fallacy. In this classical framework, ethical obligations are derived from the ontological structure of the universe, in that natural law is the human perception of the eternal law in the mind of God expressed in creation. This order grounds the ontological foundation for objective moral norms, in that they are reflections of the given order of the cosmos. One derives one's "ought" from the "is" of the cosmos, which in turn justifies the objectivity of the "ought."

Given the loss of this classical, Newtonian view of the world and given a new cosmos constructed on evolution, quantum physics, and historical consciousness, new questions are posed for theology and moral theology in particular. The Scotistic emphasis on contingency is of particular help in responding to this paradigm shift.

Since Scotus himself is a citizen of the classical world, one cannot bootleg a theory of evolution into his metaphysics or cosmology. But one can argue from Scotus's perspective of contingency that the present cosmos is *a* cosmos, not *the* cosmos, much less the best of all possible ones. That is, even though this cosmos exists, even though it is created by God, and even though what is present in this cosmos is appropriate, physically and morally, for human existence, nonetheless one cannot derive a logical, necessary ethical "ought" from such a world, because this world, actual though it is, is neither a necessary world nor the only possible world. For Scotus, values will be drawn from an ontology, but, given the radical contingency of any ontology, one cannot argue that these values lead to an ethical conclusion that is necessary.

Scotus's contribution is that of a metaphysical openness to a myriad of ontologies as well as scientific theories to articulate the world in which we live. Thus while Scotus himself assumed the classical cosmos, his affirmation of the radical contingency of all that is, other than God, renders his thought uniquely open to a variety of understandings of the cosmos. This philosophical position gives us an epistemological way to understand that a different cosmos is possible and to construct a new method of ethics to respond to this new paradigm.

A second contribution derivative from the contingency of created reality is that no act (other than love of God) is intrinsically good and no act (other than hatred of God) is intrinsically evil. Love of God is intrinsically good because such an act of necessity relates us to our final end. But between any other act and one's final end there is no such necessary connection because all such relations are contingent. To argue otherwise, for Scotus, would introduce necessity into the act of creation. While Scotus does not argue that acts commanded or prohibited by the second table of the Decalogue are not to be obeyed or are inappropriate for this time and place, he does argue that such commanded or prohibited acts, because of their inherent contingency, are not and cannot be either good or evil intrinsically.

The Locus of Moral Judgment

One feature of traditional moral theology is its focus on the individual act as the locus of moral judgment. While it is clear that many of the examples cited from Scotus also look to individual acts, nonetheless his perspective discerns the moral meaning of the act in its context or through a consistent manner of acting.

While neither denying nor denigrating choice or the significance of the act as a consequence of a choice, Scotus's emphasis on steadfastness or *firmitas* highlights what we would term developmental continuity. This leads to an emphasis on the inherent, though contingent, value of the beloved and the ensuing perfection that comes from continued adherence to it. Scotus's concept of *firmitas* gives us a way of affirming the moral significance of the act, but more importantly of appreciating the transformative possibilities that emerge from the continual adherence to the particular good.

Freedom understood as *firmitas* leads us beyond the individual act to a deeper examination of the good at stake and to an evaluation of the individual act in relation to the whole of one's life. That is, the individual act receives its meaning and significance from its relation to the project of one's life which is characterized by steadfast adherence to the good, not the isolated act apart from the totality of one's commitment. One's moral intention comes from one's steadfastness in the good (*firmitas*) rather than from an individual, isolated act.

Anthropological Perspectives

Scotus's thought also presents an interesting grounding for the experience of self-transcendence. This is based on his distinction between the *affectio commodi*, the inclination to do what is to my advantage, and the *affectio justitiae*, the inclination to do justice to the intrinsic reality of a particular being or situation. In the former, we have nature seeking its self-perfection, whether in the individual or the species. Seeking what is to one's advantage is seeking to actualize the potential instilled in it by virtue of what the being is. Seen from the viewpoint of a nature, this quest for perfection is a good because it fulfills the nature by enabling it to become what it is.

The affection for justice is the capacity to love something or someone for their own selves, regardless of whether this happens to be a good for me or not. As Wolter phrases it, this is a "freedom from nature and a freedom for values."[76] This leads to the paradox that

> what differentiates the will's perfection as nature from the perfection of all other natural agents is that it can never be attained if it be sought primarily or exclusively: only by using its freedom to

> transcend the demands of its nature, as it were, can the will satisfy completely its natural inclination.[77]

Scotus here affirms that we have the capacity to value an entity for its own sake, independent of its personal or social utility. As Scotus would phrase it, we have the ability to transcend the capacity to do justice to ourselves by doing justice to the good itself. The strong claim is that we are capable of recognizing the good and choosing it, even though such a choice may run counter to our personal self-interest or what does justice to our own nature.

> The will by freely moderating these natural and necessary tendencies to happiness and self-perfection is able to transcend its nature and choose Being and Goodness for their own sake. . . . Thus the free will is not confined to objects or goods that perfect self, but is capable of an act of love. . . . [L]ove is the most free of all acts and the one that most perfectly expresses the will's freedom to determine itself as it pleases.[78]

The conclusion is that one can distinguish at least a good and a better in human life. What is good in human life is a life that perfects us, that brings our being to a greater actualization. This is the realization of the *affectio commodi.* But what is better is the transcendence of self, either to appreciate what is good or even to curb our legitimate interest in self-perfection in order to seek the good of others for their own sakes. This is the realization of the *affectio justitiae.* Put existentially:

> A free choice then is the meaning of existence and the total initiative is left to man to rightly moderate his natural tendencies in the pursuit of being for its own sake. And in this sense one's causal initiative is an ultimate response to Being or Nothingness.[79]

Put ethically:

> Right reason also recognizes that our self-perfection, even through union with God in love, is not of supreme value. It enables man, in short, to recognize that the drive for self-perfection paradoxically must not go unbridled if it is to achieve its goal, but must be channeled lest it destroy the harmony of the universe intended by God.[80]

What is most helpful about this perspective is that, while it affirms self-perfection, such perfection is not ultimately an end in itself. To really "be all that we can be," we must step beyond the confines of self and actualize that most free of all acts, an act of love. Only then do we find ourself open to the depths of reality. And in the steadfast adherence to that beloved, we realize the fullness of freedom.

Ethical Method

Scotus's ethical method, as described, contains several elements that are of particular significance for contemporary discussions of methodology. The critical features of Scotus's method are open to modern consciousness and allow access to and conversation with contemporary debates. Additionally, these elements give us a way to escape the constraints of the traditional natural law discussions. That is, Scotus's method helps us redefine the terms of the debate.

First, Scotus's affirmation of the contingency of the second table of the Decalogue makes a critical argument that the physical structure of an act is not sufficient to determine its morality. Since Scotus argues that the love of God is the only act morally good under all circumstances (and conversely the hatred of God is the only act morally evil under all circumstances), he also argues that an act has to be contextualized before a judgment can be made about its morality. To put this in a contemporary idiom, the premoral goods or evils of an act are neither exclusively nor normatively determinative of the act's morality but require further determination in terms of intention and circumstances to determine the specific moral dimension of the act.

Second, given his turn to efficient causality, objective morality is constituted not by the act's defining the intention but by the *intention's defining the act*. This is so because it is not the case that "the nature of its object determines its moral species: rather it opens it to further moral determination."[81] As Scotus argues, while one would think that the type of act signified by the terms adultery and theft could not possibly be good, "it is possible for the underlying act to exist without the deformity, for instance, the act of intercourse or that of appropriating such a thing."[82] Thus from Scotus's perspective, a statement about or a description of the physical act as such is not sufficient to establish the morality of the act.

Third, three elements are needed to determine the moral suitability of a specific act for a specific agent: (1) the nature of the agent "to act by virtue of intellectual knowledge, which alone is able to pass judgment;"[83] (2) the nature of the agent, which is the ability actually to "pass judgment upon the act and carry it out in accord with that judgment;"[84] and (3) the essential notion of the act itself, which comes from a consideration of the circumstances of end, manner, time, and place.

Scotus says that the "moral goodness of an act consists in its having all that the agent's right reason declares must pertain to the act or the agent in acting."[85] This is fulfilled when "these three notions are given [since] no other knowledge is needed to judge whether or not this particular act is suited to this agent and this faculty."[86]

Those seeking a grounding for the revisionist theories of moral theology would do well to study carefully these and other elements in Scotus's thought. His ethical method, derived from his metaphysics, offers a way to address current methodological problems in moral theology that avoids the problems of trying to harmonize contemporary insights with specific historical texts. His thought also provides a way to break through the logjam created by the debate over intrinsically evil acts and the analysis of individual acts. Finally, Scotus's analogy between a moral judgment and an aesthetic judgment opens a fresh way to appreciate both the structure of the moral act and its many nuances, as well as the types of skills necessary to make good moral judgments. If we follow the Franciscan's lead here we will also see that there is variation and development as well as continuity with respect to both personal moral growth and methodology in moral theology.

NOTES

1. *Gaudium et spes* no. 5, cited in David J. O'Brien and Thomas A. Shannon, eds., *Catholic Social Thought: The Documentary Heritage* (Maryknoll, N.Y.: Orbis, 1992) 168.

2. Karol Wojtyla, *Love and Responsibility,* trans. H.T. Willetts (New York: Farrar, Straus, Giroux, 1991) 246.

3. J.R. Creswell, "Duns Scotus on the Will," *Franciscan Studies* 13 (1953) 147–58, at 148–49.

4. *Reportatio* I, Prol. q.3, a.1 (quoted from *John Duns Scotus: Philosophical Writings,* trans. Allan B. Wolter, O.F.M. [Indianapolis: Hackett, 1987] 9).

5. William A. Frank, "Duns Scotus' Concept of Willing Freely: What Divine Freedom Beyond Choice Teaches Us," *Franciscan Studies* 42 (1982) 68–89, at 80.

6. Q.16, a.2, n.8; quoted from John Duns Scotus, *God and Creatures: The Quodlibetal Questions,* trans. and ed. Felix Alluntis, O.F.M., and Allan B. Wolter, O.F.M. (Princeton Univ., 1975) 378.

7. Frank, "Willing Freely" 82 (italics in the original).
8. Ibid. 82
9. Ibid. 85
10. Ibid. 87
11. Ibid. 78
12. *Quaestiones in Metaphysicam* 1, q.15, a.2 (quoted in Allan B. Wolter, O.F.M., *Duns Scotus on the Will and Morality* [Washington: Catholic Univ. of America, 1986] 151). This is the most accessible collection of Scotus's texts on morality; most citations will be from this work, which presents the text both in Latin and in English translation.
13. *Quaestiones in Metaphysicam* 1, q.15, a.15 (Wolter, *Will and Morality* 151).
14. *Ordinatio* 4, suppl., d.49, qq. 9–10 (Wolter, *Will and Morality* 185).
15. *Ordinatio* 4, suppl., d.49, qq. 9–10 (477).
16. Allan B. Wolter, O.F.M., "Native Freedom of the Will as a Key to the Ethics of Scotus," in his *The Philosophical Theology of John Duns Scotus*, ed. Marilyn McCord Adams (Ithaca, NY: Cornell Univ., 1990) 151.
17. Wolter, "Native Freedom" 152.
18. *Reportatio Parisiensis* 2, d.6, q.2, n.9 (quoted in Wolter, "Native Freedom" 152).
19. John Bowler, "The Moral Psychology of Duns Scotus: Some Preliminary Questions," *Franciscan Studies*, forthcoming.
20. Wolter, "Native Freedom" 152.
21. Ordinatio 3, d.17 (*Wolter, Will and Morality* 263).
22. Ordinatio 3, suppl. d.37 (271).
23. Ibid. 277.
24. Ibid. 263.
25. Ibid. 277.
26. Ibid. 277.
27. Ibid. 277.
28. Ibid. 277.
29. Ibid. 277.
30. Robert Prentice, O.F.M., "The Contingent Element Governing the Natural Law on the Last Seven Precepts of the Decalogue according to Duns Scotus," *Antonianum* 42 (1967) 258–92, at 285.
31. Ibid. 285.
32. Ibid. 286.
33. Ibid. 287–88
34. Mary Elizabeth Ingham, C.S.J., *Ethics and Freedom: An Historical-Critical Investigation of Scotist Ethical Thought* (Lanham: Md.: Univ. Press of America, 1989) 162.
35. Ibid. 167.
36. Ibid. 155.
37. Wolter, "Native Freedom" 154.
38. *Ordinatio* 2, d.40 (Wolter, *Will and Morality* 227).
39. Ibid. 227.
40. *Ordinatio* 1, d.17, no. 62, quoted in Ingham 154.
41. Ingham 163.

42. Ibid. 163.
43. *Ordinatio* 1, no.92 (Ingham 157).
44. Ingham 160
45. Ibid. 162
46. *Quodlibet* 18, no.3 (Ingham 158).
47. *Quodlibet* 18, no.4 (Ingham 159).
48. Ingham 162.
49. Ibid. 162.
50. *Quodlibet*, q.9 (Wolter, *Will and Morality* 211).
51. Ibid. 213.
52. Ibid. 215
53. Ibid. 215
54. Ibid. 217.
55. Ibid. 217.
56. Ibid. 217.
57. Ibid. 219.
58. Ibid. 219.
59. Ibid. 219.
60. Ibid. 215.
61. *Ordinatio* 4, d.33, q.1, a.2 (Wolter, *Will and Morality* 219).
62. Ibid. 293.
63. Ibid. 295.
64. Ibid. 293.
65. Ibid. 293.
66. Ibid. 295.
67. Ibid. 297.
68. *Ordinatio* 4, d.33, q.1, a.4 (303–4).
69. Ibid. 311.
70. *Ordinatio* 4, d.33, q.3, argumenta principalia 309.

71. Thus Scotus would differ here from Johnson's presentation of Thomas in *Quodlibetum* 9, where there are acts that have a deformity inseparably linked to them and, therefore, can never be done well. The examples Thomas gives are fornication and adultery. Lying was typically included in this category. These are examples of acts considered intrinsically evil. It is interesting to compare Scotus's analysis to Johnson's presentation of Aquinas. Mark Johnson, "Proportionalism and a Text of Young Aquinas: *Quodlibetum*, Q. 7, A. 2.," *Theological Studies* 53(1992): 691.

72. *Ordinatio* 3, suppl., d. 38, a.1 (Wolter, *Will and Morality* 485).
73. Ibid. 485.
74. Ibid. 485.

75. Ibid. 487. Here Scotus clearly joins the issue raised by Aquinas and commented on by Johnson with respect to the nature of certain acts (i.e., those with a certain deformity inseparably linked with them). In Aquinas's words: "*Quaedam enim sunt quae habent deformitatem inseparabiliter annexam, ut formicatio, adulterium, et alia huiusmodi, quae nullo modo bene fieri possunt*" (Johnson, "Proportionalism and Aquinas" 691, n.22). For Scotus, one also needs intention and circumstances in addition to the act to specify it morally.

76. Wolter, "Native Freedom" 152.

77. Ibid. 184.

78. Valerius Messerich, O.F.M., "The Awareness of Causal Initiative and Existential Responsibility in the Thought of Duns Scotus," in *De Doctrina Ioannis Duns Scoti 2:Problemata Philosophica* (Rome: Acta Congressus Scotistici Internat., 1968) 629–44, at 630–31.

79. Messerich, "Causal Initative" 631.

80. Wolter, "Native Freedom" 153.

81. *Quodlibet*, q.18 (Wolter, *Will and Morality* 215).

82. *Ordinatio* 3, suppl., d.38, a.2 (Wolter, *Will and Morality* 487). Again note the critical difference between this text of Scotus and that of Aquinas in Quodlibetum 9: "Quaedam enim sunt quae habent deformitatem inseparabiliter annexam, ut fornicatio, adulterium, at alia huismodi, quae nullo modo bene fieri possunt" (Johnson, "Proportionalism and Aquinas" 691, n.22).

83. *Ordinatio* 1, q.18 (Wolter, *Will and Morality* 213).

84. Ibid. 213.

85. Ibid. 211.

86. Ibid. 213.

The Structure of Ockham's Moral Theory

MARILYN MCCORD ADAMS

INTRODUCTION

Ockham's moral theory, like his nominalism, finds its place among the most notorious, and yet widely misunderstood, doctrines of medieval philosophy. (a) Many take Ockham's as the paradigm of "divine command morality," according to which moral norms are entirely a function of the arbitrary choices of the free will of an omnipotent God. Paul Helm's recent comment is merely representative when he writes,

> What can be labeled an Ockhamist Divine Command Theory holds that morality is founded upon a free divine choice. If God commands fornication, then fornication is obligatory, and it is within God's power to do so. He could establish another moral order than the one he has in fact established and he could at any time order what he has actually forbidden.[1]

Maurice De Wulf had characterized Ockham's moral theory the same way at the beginning of the century:

> Applied to the Deity, this absolute autonomy of volition makes the Free Will of God the sovereign arbiter of moral good and evil. But if nothing is *of itself* morally good or evil, this study of nature can teach us nothing about morality.[2]

Likewise, Armand Maurer sees Ockham's doctrines of divine omnipotence and free will so converging as to rob morality of its footing in nature. For he observes,

> Because God is omnipotent and absolutely free, he is not bound to impose a given set of laws upon men. We should not imagine him as ruled by an eternal or divine law from which human laws flow as necessary conclusions from premises. The laws he imposes on men are completely arbitrary, so that he can change or annul them at will.[3]

Maurer concludes that the moral code which binds humans is "not rooted in human nature."[4] Again, Dom David Knowles contends,

> The methodological use of the absolute power of God is corollary of the emphasis on the absolute freedom of God first emphasized in a tendentious manner by Scotus. Ockham followed Duns here, stressing the primacy of the will and the concept of freedom both in God and man. . . . Acts are not good or bad of themselves, but solely because they are commanded or prohibited by God. Not only murder and adultery, but even hatred of God could become ethically good actions at God's commands.[5]

(b) Some felt the epistemological corollary of such divine command ethics to be skepticism about our natural knowledge of moral truths. Thus, De Wulf complains that, for Ockham, "intelligence is powerless to instruct us on the requirements of the Divine Law. . . ."[6] Lamenting "Ockham's view of God's absolute power" and his use of it "with devastating effect to show the impossibility of discussing matters of faith," Leff protests that given "the sheer unrestricted limits of His omnipotence" and radical freedom, "anything was possible, and so there could be no means of knowing what He might will."[7] Knowles, also, joins this chorus:

> [a]s we know nothing by pure reason of God's attributes or way of acting, and as the first article of the creed is an assertion of the omnipotence of God, ethics becomes entirely dependent upon revelation, which is the only channel by which God's will becomes known to us.[8]

So, too, Helm:

> From this position Ockham could consistently only regard ethics as a matter of special divine revelation in Scripture or elsewhere, and not a matter of natural law discerned through reason or conscience.[9]

(c) The principal difficulty with this interpretation is that it overlooks Ockham's repeated reference to right reason in his most concentrated discussions of moral philosophy. Gilson highlights the More than Subtle Doctor's outright contradiction of moral skepticism when he notes that "the science which Ockham considers one of the safest and best established we may naturally acquire is ethics."[10] Maurer cleverly tries to adjust these texts to his original interpretation, with the suggestion that if—for Ockham—divine commands replace natural human tendencies as the norm of morality, nevertheless, the dictates of conscience are a medium through which God makes His commands known.[11] Copleston squarely faces the bulk of the divine command texts, on the one hand, and the right reason texts, on the other, and is puzzled that

> . . . we are faced with what amounts to two moral theories in Ockham's philosophy. On the one hand, there is his authoritarian conception of the moral law. It would appear to follow from this conception that there can be only a revealed moral code. . . . On the other hand, there is Ockham's insistence on right reason, which would seem to imply that reason can discern what is right and what is wrong.[12]

At one point, Copleston hypothesizes that the former is offered by Ockham *qua* theologian, inasmuch as it expresses his "conviction of the freedom and omnipotence of God as they are revealed in Christianity," whereas he advances the latter *qua* philosopher under Aristotelian influence.[13] On balance, however, Copleston cannot tear himself away from the idea that "the authoritarian," "ultrapersonal" strand so dominates Ockham's moral theory as to be the superstructure, leaving the Aristotelian emphasis on right reason as the substructure.[14] But if the real norm is the commands of a free and omnipotent God, it seems that right reason is not a sure guide: "What can be known apart from revelation is simply a provisional *code of morality,* based on nontheological considerations."[15]

As with other topics, the representations of Ockham's theory in the secondary literature contain some elements of truth. For example, (*i*) Ockham does recognize the commands of a free and omnipotent God as a norm of morality, and (*ii*) he does follow Aristotle in assigning the dictates of right reason a normative role as well. Again, I believe (*iii*) Copleston is on to something when he discerns more than one layer in Ockham's value theory. So far as the epistemology of morals is concerned, (*iv*) Ockham does believe that revelation plays a necessary role in informing us of the moral content of divine commands, and (*v*) denies that moral norms can be read off of necessitating human natural tendencies. These concessions notwithstanding, (*vi*) Gilson is correct to say that for Ockham some moral precepts can be known naturally through right reason, in such a way that moral science is indeed the surest and safest that we posses. But the overall picture is distorted by a fixation on the idea (*vii*) that Ockham sees morality primarily as a matter of doing what is necessary to avoid the sanctions of an arbitrary omnipotent tyrant by obeying his commands.

In my judgment, Ockham's moral theory is subtle, interesting, and worthy of consideration by Christian philosophers. In what follows, my effort will be to refocus well-known texts to expose its structure. Like Lucan Freppert, whose doctoral dissertation contains the best and most complete account of Ockham's moral theory to date,[16] I take as my interpretive key the often noted but poorly exploited facts that Ockham was, first of all, a *Franciscan* philosopher, and that he worked out his own value theory in reaction to that of his most eminent Franciscan predecessor, Duns Scotus. My working hypothesis is that Ockham, like Scotus, presents us with a value theory best understood in terms of the interplay between its three-tiered structure and a high doctrine of freedom of the will.

NATURAL GOODNESS AND THE FREEDOM OF THE WILL

Natural Goodness as the Baseline of Value Theory

Scotus and Ockham merely join the medieval consensus when they make natural goodness the baseline of value theory. Scotus explains that where transcendental goodness converts with being, natural goodness pertains to the perfection of a thing (e.g., a three-legged horse would have transcendental goodness but be deficient in natural goodness, because horses normally have four legs);[17] yet both are directly proportional to degree of being.[18] And Scotus follows Anselm's intuition that some natures are better and nobler than others, to argue for the existence of God as the most eminent being.[19] So, too, Ockham takes it for granted that some natures are nobler and better than others: An angel is more perfect than a man; a man than a donkey;[20] the human intellectual soul than the human sensory soul.[21] Likewise, substances are nobler and better than their inherent accidents;[22] a more intense degree of whiteness than a less intense one.[23] With Scotus, Ockham deploys a no-infinite-regress principle to demonstrate that there is a nature than which none is nobler and better. And, while he rejects the Subtle Doctor's attempt to *prove* that there is only one such nature, Ockham holds by faith that the divine essence is the noblest nature, the highest being, and the highest good,[24] the most desirable and worthy of honor.[25]

The Freedom of the Will

Moral goodness concerns itself with the acts of the best natures (human, angelic, and divine), whose special function is to operate by intellect and free will. Distinctive to Scotus and Ockham are their high but contrasting doctrines of free will.

Ockham argues that (*i*) the created will is—by its very nature—a self-determining power for opposites and hence an "Aristotelian" rational power. But rejecting Scotus' doctrine of instants of nature, Ockham construes the will's power in terms of the "evident" capacity for opposites and dismisses the "nonevident" capacity as spurious.[26] God's freedom is insured by special features of the intentionality of divine mental acts,[27] and an angel's choice is contingent at the first instant of its creation in the reduced sense that it can, apart from any outside interference, cease from that act or omission in the next instant.[28] Likewise, dismissing Scotus' formal distinction, Ockham insists that intellect and will are really the same as each other and as the intellectual soul; the difference lies not in the reality of the powers but in the different connotations of the terms 'intellect' and 'will' (of acts of intellect and will, respectively).[29]

Further, Ockham is as comfortable with causal models in action theory as in epistemology. Accordingly, he does not share (*ii*) Scotus' apprehension about assigning things other than the will an efficient causal role in the production of the will's acts. To be sure, he maintains that the will's action requires only the activity of the will itself, the intellectual apprehension of the object, and the general concurrence of God upholding the general order of creation.[30] And he agrees that the will is not naturally determined to choose in accordance with any such intellectual cognitions nor by any sensory acts; if it were, its actions would not be within its power.[31] Nevertheless, Ockham is quite happy to admit intellectual and sensory acts among the efficient *partial* causes of acts of will.[32]

Nor does he draw Scotus' conclusion (*iii*) that the will is not the kind of thing whose acts can be necessitated. While insisting that the will is self-determining when it acts freely, Ockham observes that conclusion *iii* admits of counterexamples in both theology and the natural order. (*a*) For the divine will necessarily wills the procession of the Holy Spirit and freely and contingently wills to produce creatures.[33] (*b*) Further, within the created order, Ockham recognizes that some mental acts are incompossible with others. Distinguishing between "formally imperative acts" (by which the will wills for or against something unconditionally) from "equivalently imperative acts" (by which the object is willed conditionally upon obstacle removal or the right circumstance),[34] he maintains that a created will's general formally imperative act (e.g., a volition to do whatever is required for health) together with the relevant information (e.g., the intellectual recognition that drinking bitter medicine is required) can necessitate the particular volition (e.g., to drink the bitter potion), although the latter volition could be elicited freely and contingently by the same will in another context.[35]

Likewise, when the will wills to do whatever right reason dictates and then acquires the belief that right reason dictates a particular act, the will will be necessitated to will accordingly.[36] Again, if the will has so willed against fornication that it will not do it for the sake of anything contrary to right reason, and the intellect recognizes prison to be the cost of not fornicating, the will will necessarily will to go to prison.[37] And if charity inclines and I love God and everything that God wills me to love, and my intellect recognizes that God wills me to love John, then given the general volition and the two cognitions, necessarily I have to love John.[38] In these cases, however, the volition is indirectly within the will's power, because it is always within the will's power to revoke the general volition.

(*c*) Finally, God, whose omnipotence enables Him to produce all by Himself whatever He can produce in cooperation with others, can intervene to be the total efficient cause of a created volition.[39] Thus, the happiness of the blessed[40] and the misery of the damned[41] are insured by the fact that God is the total efficient cause of a whole-hearted love of God in the former and a willing against punishment and a volition for happiness in the latter. Of course, there will be no liberty in such acts[42] because they are necessitated (so that it is not within the agent's "power to act or not to act, to suffer or not to suffer, to receive or not to receive"[43]) by the irresistible divine will.

Ockham agrees with Scotus on the general point (*iv*) that the created will has built-in, nonnecessitating inclinations. These are "natural" in the broad sense that they pertain to the will in and of itself, but not in the strict sense of Aristotelian physics, because they are not naturally necessitating and because action contrary to them does not count as "violent."[44] And if the will's inclinations are not natural, strictly speaking, the will cannot be coerced, strictly speaking, because coercion is a matter of something's being forced to act contrary to its natural inclinations.[45]

Ockham puzzles over the will's quasi-natural inclination to choose what leads to sensory pleasure (*delectatio*) and to will against what leads to displeasure or sorrow (*dolor*),[46] which can be so strong that choices against them are counted heroic.[47] By contrast, he barely mentions the Anselmian double affections for the advantageous and for justice, and then only to say that corresponding to the inclination to will (*velle*) the advantageous, there is one to will against (*nolle*) the disadvantageous (*incommodum*), and to the inclination to will (*velle*) the just there is one to will against (*nolle*) the unjust, and to observe that the will acts thus when it follows the dictates of reason.[48]

Most importantly, Ockham does not follow Scotus' lead (*v*) in trying to construct the will's freedom out of its twofold inclination for good and against evil. On the contrary, Ockham believes himself to be following philosophical tradition when he contends that the will's liberty is that of indifference and contingency.[49] This means that with regard to any given object, the will's options are not merely action versus inaction, but also willing (*velle*) versus nilling (*nolle*); and it has all three options, no matter what right reason might dictate.[50]

From this general thesis, Ockham counts the ways a free will can will against (*nolle*) the good: (*a*) the will can choose to hate God;[51] (*b*) the will apart from divine interference can will against (*nolle*) enjoyment, even when the divine essence is clearly seen;[52] (*c*) the will can will against its own happiness and will its own misery;[53] (*d*) the will can will against its ultimate end, whether because of ignorance (as when it mistakenly thinks it has no ultimate end or that its ultimate end is not happiness[54]) or simply because as a free power it can will against any object;[55] (*e*) the will can will against the good in general.[56] And with equal detail, he spells out how the free will can will (*velle*) evils: (*f*) the will can do the opposite of what right reason dictates;[57] (*g*) the will can do unjust deeds precisely because they are unjust, dishonest, and contrary to right reason;[58] and (*h*) the will can will evil under the aspect of evil.[59]

Scotus had tried to rule out such startling consequences as (*a*)–(*h*) with the argument that just as there is a natural suitability and unsuitability of objects for acts of various sensory powers—e.g., colors in the range from yellow to purple but not infrared or X-rays for human vision—so it is where acts of will are concerned. Thus, he concludes, "misery is not suited by nature to be an object of volition," nor is "happiness naturally suited to be an object of willing against (*nolle*)."[60] But goodness under the aspect of goodness can be properly sought by the will.[61] Ockham admits that right reason, as the internal regulator of the will, does pronounce the latter objects unsuitable to willing and willing against, respectively. But he contends that such suitability is relevant to the morality of such acts, not to the scope of the will's power.

Like Scotus, Ockham also recognizes habits to be really distinct mental qualities inherent in the soul that incline, without necessitating, the will to go for or against a given course of action.[62] Differentiated into species in part by their intentional objects, acquired habits are caused by their corresponding acts.[63] Moral virtues are acquired habits that incline the will to moral acts (see the following section),[64] while the theological virtues of faith, hope, and charity are infused by divine agency in accordance with the sacramental system of the Church.[65]

MORALS: BROAD SENSE AND NARROW

Ockham's placement of morals relative to their foundation in natural goodness can be clearly seen from his explicit taxonomy of moral science. In the prologue to his *Sentence*-commentary, Ockham explains that 'moral science' one way is "precisely about mores (*moribus*) which are within our power."[66] Philosophical and theological textbooks on morals contain a lot of metaphysics and philosophy of mind, but in the strict sense moral science is practical and has to do precisely with what is within our power.[67] In the *Quodl.*, among the latest of his nonpolitical works, Ockham explicitly divides the subject into two parts: (*i*) "Non-positive moral science" "directs human acts apart from any precept of a superior" or authority.[68] It includes all evident practical principles, whether known per se—e.g., "Every intrinsic good (*honestum*) should be sought," "Every intrinsic evil (*inhonestum*) should be avoided," "The will should conform itself to right reason," "Every benefactor deserves to be benefited," etc.[69]—or from experience—e.g., "An angry person is to be soothed with soft words"[70]—or inferable therefrom. Ockham observes that this is the subject matter carved out by Aristotle in his moral philosophy.[71] (*ii*) By contrast,

> positive moral science is that which contains divine and human laws which oblige one to pursue or avoid those things which are neither good nor evil except because they are prohibited or commanded by a superior to whom it belongs to make (*statuere*) laws.[72]

It includes the science and jurisprudence where human laws are concerned,[73] and sacramental theology and perhaps canon law, which study divine precepts. Both provinces are united in their focus on acts that are within our power. The former has to do with the principles of rational self-government and so is a subject area shared with Aristotle and other pagan philosophers. The latter includes, besides the common field of political philosophy, the special area of religious obligations imposed by a sovereign and personal God. The precepts of nonpositive morality have the authority of the agent's own reason underlying them; those of the latter bind by virtue of some external authority.

In his treatise *"The Connection of the Virtues"*, Ockham likewise construes nonpositive morality along generally Aristotelian lines, in terms of rational self-government. Morally virtuous action has two components; as Ockham declares, "No one acts virtuously unless he acts with knowledge and freedom."[74] (*i*) On the one hand, an agent is bound to make his own value judgments and to do so correctly so far as this lies within his power.[75] Neither the act done mindlessly, nor that done in slavish obedience to another can be morally virtuous. For an agent acts morally only insofar as he follows his own conscience;[76] indeed, according to Ockham, a dictate of the agent's own intellect must be an efficient partial cause of any virtuous act,[77] and if God were to preserve the act of intellect and suspend its casual efficacy with respect to the volition, the act would not be virtuous.[78] But no one is blameworthy for ignorance that it is not within his power to overcome.[79] On the other hand, conquerable ignorance doubles the crime. For either the agent acts in accord with the dictates of his own intellect or he does not. If he does, and the intellect is in error, then he is culpable for not having avoided the erroneous judgment, as well as for eliciting an act contrary to right reason. And if he does not follow his own conscience but the correct dictate of someone else, he is still to blame for his own ignorance, and he compounds the error by showing "contempt for what ought to be his rule in acting" [viz., his own conscience].[80] (*ii*) But no act is morally virtuous unless it is imputable, and none is imputable to an agent unless it lies within and is produced by the efficient causality of the will, which can act in accordance with right reason or not.[81] If God were to suspend the activity of the will regarding one of its acts, the act would become not-virtuous negatively (neither virtuous nor vicious).[82]

That morally virtuous action involves the free coordination of choice with right reason likewise appears in Ockham's catalogue of the degrees of virtue. For, he explains, (*i*) a person has first-degree moral virtue

> when someone wills to do just deeds (*a*) in conformity with right reason dictating that such deeds should be done, (*b*) according to the required circumstances for precisely this deed, and (*c*) for the sake of the end of the intrinsic value (*honestatem*) of the deed itself.[83]

For example,

> the intellect dictates that such a just work should be done at such a place and time for the sake of the intrinsic worth of the deed or for the sake of peace or some such thing, and the will elicits an act of willing such deeds in conformity with the dictates of the intellect.[84]

Thus, in virtuous action of the first degree, the agent's intellect dictates the what, how, and why of the deed, and the will conforms to it. (*ii*) Second-degree virtue differs from the first in determination or perseverance, and is exemplified

> when the will wills to do just works according to the above-mentioned correct dictates, and besides this [does so] with the intention of in no way abandoning such deeds for the sake of anything contrary to right reason —not even because of death, if right reason were to dictate that such a deed should not be abandoned even to avoid death.[85]

Suppose right reason dictates that one should honor one's country and not give up doing so even in the face of death. One who conforms to such a dictatc and wills by an equivalently imperative act to honor his country even at the cost of death, manifests virtue in the second degree.[86] (*iii*) Third-degree virtue differs from the previous two as regards the end of action: viz., here the materially correct action and circumstances are willed precisely because right reason has commanded it.[87] Beyond these three, Ockham recognizes (*iv*) a species of heroic virtue, according to which the materially correct act is efficaciously willed (by a formally imperative act) for the sake of right reason, and hence the extraordinary perseverance contrary to our quasi-natural inclinations (to seek sensory pleasure and avoid sensory pain).[88] In third-degree virtue, conformity with right reason emerges as an ultimate end or bottom-line reason for choosing one action over another. It is from this function as end that right reason derives the authority (referred to in the first two degrees of virtue) to dictate the material content of the action to be willed. The moral hero adheres to such conformity uncompromisingly and sacrificially. In all this, Ockham finds himself in agreement with Aristotle and other pagan philosophers.[89]

MERIT

Merit and demerit define a category of value relating free creatures to their eternal destinies, and reflect a creature's free coordination (opposition) of his choices with (to) what is pleasing to God. According to fourteenth-century stipulation,

> (*i*) '*x* is predestinate' entails '*x* will receive eternal blessedness from God on Judgment Day'
>
> (*ii*) '*x* is reprobate' entails '*x* will receive eternal punishment from God on Judgment Day'
>
> (*iii*) 'Action *a* is accepted by God' = df. '*a* is so pleasing to God that if *x* performed *a* and died immediately thereafter, *x* would receive eternal blessedness on Judgment Day'
>
> (*iv*) '*x* sins mortally' = df. '*x* freely commits an act which is so displeasing to God that if *x* were to die in that state, *x* would receive eternal punishment from God on Judgment Day'[90]
>
> (*v*) 'Action *a* of agent *x* is meritorious' = df. '*x* does *a* freely and *a* is accepted by God'[91]

Roughly speaking, merit is a property that renders the possessor (or its agent) prima facie worthy of eternal life; demerit, prima facie worthy of eternal punishment.

Following Scotus and in opposition to Aureol and Lutterell, Ockham insists that merit and demerit constitute a category of positive morality, created by free and contingent divine statutes.[92] If, according to Ockham, nonpositive morality cannot "get off the ground" unless some act is intrinsically and essentially moral,[93] he contends that

> (*vi*) No creature is necessarily and intrinsically acceptable (unacceptable); none is necessarily or intrinsically worthy of eternal life (eternal punishment);

rather,

(*vii*) if anything is acceptable (unacceptable), worthy of eternal life (punishment), it is so through a relation to an extrinsic cause—the divine will issuing certain statutes.[94]

For nothing in creatures is either a logically necessary[95] or a logically sufficient condition[96] of either eternal blessedness or eternal punishment. (*a*) Metaphysically, this is clear because eternal blessedness involves the future inherence of a created mental quality or qualities (e.g., a steadfast act of wholehearted love of God) in the soul; likewise, eternal punishment (e.g., a steadfast act of hating God and/or willing against punishment). But the existence of a creature with certain acts or habits now is logically independent of the future existence of that or any other creatures later. It is within the scope of God's omnipotence, for example, simply to annihilate any free creature after death.[97] And since God, like humans and angels, has the liberty of contingency and indifference, He can exercise this power any way He chooses, whether to will for (*velle*) or to will against (*nolle*) or not to act regarding any created objects or states of affairs.

(*b*) Further, Ockham maintains, God is a debtor to no one.[98] Since He has no obligation to violate, He cannot act unjustly or sin no matter what He does. In governing creation, God is not bound (*i*) to follow "Ockham's Razor" and refrain from doing with more what could be done with fewer.[99] (*ii*) He has no obligation to continue creatures in existence or to give any creature eternal blessedness or eternal punishment. (*iii*) Again, God would do no wrong if He distributed blessedness and misery to, bestowed or withheld a beatific vision of Himself on free creatures on some basis other than their free acts—say, eye color, gender, or national origin.[100] But because merit is a subcategory of morals, and morality generically pertains to acts that are within the agent's power, divine laws instituting such apportionments would not define the values of merit and demerit.[101] These categories exist only if God so legislates as to attach eternal rewards and punishments to some feature of created acts performed freely and with knowledge.[102] (*iv*) But even if God regards the free choices of creatures, He is under no obligation to line up eternal rewards and punishments with any particular feature of free acts. For example, (*iva*) He will do no wrong if he treats like cases differently, as He allegedly did in the case of Esau and Jacob.[103] (*ivb*) Nor would God be unjust if he not only failed to return the love of someone who loved Him above all and for His own sake,[104] but rendered him eternal punishment instead.[105] (*ivc*) Further, He is under no obligation to accept morally virtuous acts or to reject morally vicious ones. Scotus had already maintained that the second table of the Decalogue, having to do with neighbor-love, did not belong to the natural law strictly speaking, and hence that God could dispense from its precepts.[106] By contrast, Scotus maintained that the first table with its injunction to a wholehearted and exclusive love of God above all—or, if the existence of God is not obvious without attention to speculative reasoning, at least the negative ('Do not hate God')[107] or conditional ('If God exists, He alone must be loved as God')[108] pertains to the natural law from which God cannot dispense.[109] So far as the second table is concerned, Ockham holds that God in His freedom could positively command the opposite of the acts which we now call "theft," "adultery,"[110] and "fornication."[111] (Logician that he is, Ockham notes that if God were to enjoin such acts, they would no longer receive these labels, the nominal definitions of which connote that God has forbidden acts of this type.) Bolder still is Ockham's declaration that God is not bound to legislate the first table either. God could command us to hate Him both in this life and the next.[112] (*v*) So far as ecclesiology is concerned, God was under no obligation to tie merit and demerit to the sacramental system of the church,[113] nor was He required to link the reception of the sacraments with the infusion of the theological virtues.[114]

If merit and demerit neither pertain to free created acts intrinsically and necessarily, nor arise from any structure of obligations that God bears to creatures nor from any internal necessity in God to do things "the most reasonable way," that there is any such category of worthiness for one eternal destiny rather than another must have its sources in God's love and generosity. Thus, Ockham declares, "It is not necessary for God to love from any motive; rather He liberally and freely loves whom He loves."[115] Rather, "by His sheer grace, He will give with liberality to whom He will give. . . ."[116] "Whatever He does for us, He does by grace alone."[117]

In fact, God has so ordained and legislated that these properties of merit and demerit conform both to the dictates of right reason—since God commands created agents to obey the dictates of nonculpable reason—and to the sacramental system of the church. According to the former, a person in fact merits and is acceptable when he loves God above all and for His own sake, loves whatever God wills him to love, and hates whatever God wills him to hate. And he sins mortally when he hates God or loves or hates something contrary to divine precept.[118] Where relevant, God has aligned merit and demerit with moral virtue and vice in such a way that being morally virtuous is a necessary condition for merit; morally vicious, a sufficient condition for demerit. Nevertheless, because extant divine legislation in fact ties merit and demerit to infused theological virtues (most importantly, charity) dispensed in accordance with the sacramental system, moral virtue is not sufficient for merit. Indeed, many pagans perform virtuous acts apart from any infused habits.[119] Thus, according to the New Covenant, (*v*) no one will receive the Holy Spirit[120] or (*vi*) elicit a meritorious act apart from infused charity.[121] Similarly, (*vii*) guilt is not taken away apart from an infusion of grace,[122] but (*viii*) whoever dies with an infused habit of grace or charity inhering in him will receive eternal life.[123]

MORALS AND MERIT: MUTUALLY OVERLAPPING

Morals Encroaching on Merit

A perfectly virtuous act is one that is completely conformed to right reason.[124] But what an agent's intellect will dictate depends on what information it has at hand. As noted in the section on natural goodness, Ockham holds that unaided natural reason can demonstrate the existence of a nature than which none is nobler and better, although it cannot take the further steps of proving that there is only one such;[125] that it is personal and hence acts through intellect and will; that it is free; that it issues commands or what precisely its precepts are. Thus, unaided right reason will dictate that God (= a nature than which none is nobler and better) ought to be loved in the highest degree.[126] It could reason further that if there were only one such and He were personal, then wholehearted love of Him would be expressed in trying to please Him in every way, by loving Him and what He wills to be loved, not willing what He wills not to be willed, and willing against what He wants to be willed against.[127] Accordingly, Ockham contends, the negative dictate "No one should be led to do anything contrary to the precept of his God"[128] is known *per se*. Reason informed by revelation as to the unity of God, His nature, and the content of His commands would go further to issue the positive dictates—that "whatever is pleasing to God ought to be done,"[129] that His will regarding creatures should be fulfilled,[130] that the created agent should love God and what He wills to be loved and hate what He wills to be hated,[131] and that these things ought to be done for God's sake[132]—as well.

The upshot is that when suitably informed by speculation and revelation, right reason, the internal regulator of the agent's willing, finds another rule in divine commands. Thus, there is a double criterion of a morally virtuous act—the dictates of right reason, on the one hand, and divine precepts on the other. But within the sphere of nonpositive morality, the latter derives its authority from the former. Ockham repeatedly gives expression to this perspective in his examples. He cites "the will to pray for the sake of God's honor and because it is commanded by God, according to right reason, etc." as an act "intrinsically morally good," by contrast with "the will to pray for the sake of vain glory and because it is contrary to God's precepts and contrary to right reason," which is "intrinsically evil and vicious."[133] Again, he envisions three vicious-making conditions of an act of loving a human being: viz., doing it "because it displeases God or because he is a sinner or because of another bad end and contrary to right reason."[134] And he declares that "rightness is nothing absolute or relative other than the act itself, which should be elicited according to right reason and God's will."[135]

Indeed, Ockham goes so far as to recognize a fourth degree of moral virtue, which is exemplified "when someone wills to do such a deed" in conformity with right reason as to which deed should be done, as well as when, where, and how it should be done, and as to the end for which it should be done—viz., because right reason dictates it—"and additionally" wills to do such a deed "precisely for the love of God."[136] Fourth-degree virtuous acts are like third-degree virtuous acts except that they have a double end—they are done because right reason dictates them and for the love of God (alternatively, because God commands them). Since their intentional objects thus differ, Ockham concludes that fourth-degree virtues and their corresponding acts differ in species from the third-degree virtues and acts recognized by Aristotle and the other pagan philosophers.[137] And just as there is a heroic version of third-degree virtue, so also of fourth.[138]

To the question how such a virtue can be a moral virtue when it has a theological object, Ockham replies that it is a moral virtue because it proceeds from moral acts—viz., acts which are within our power and so allegedly intrinsically imputable.[139] And Ockham insists that only acts of the fourth degree are "perfectly" virtuous: e.g., willing "to love that human being for God's sake, according to right reason and to all other required circumstances," or willing "to eat for God's sake and according to right reason and other circumstances."[140] Likewise, it is probably against this background picture—of right reason making divine precepts criterial for nonpositive morality—that Ockham sees Eleazar's refusal to eat pork in violation of the old positive divine law prohibiting it as a heroic refusal to do anything "contrary to right reason" and a heroic willingness to "sustain death according to the dictate of right reason."[141]

Merit Reverts to Morals

In the category of merit and demerit, defined as they are by what is pleasing and displeasing to God, divine precept is the baseline criterion.[142] As free and omnipotent, God's only limitation is that He cannot will contradictories.[143] Nevertheless, as we saw in the introduction to this section, wherever relevant, divine legislation in fact maps the categories of merit and demerit onto those of nonpositive moral virtue and vice. Thus, God in fact wills that we follow the dictates of nonculpable reason[144] and so—except in cases of invincible ignorance—elicit acts in conformity with the dictates of our own right reason.[145] And Ockham remarks that while sin is a matter of doing what is contrary to divine precepts, we are now obliged to elicit acts that conform to right reason.[146]

The result is once again a double criterion, but this time divine precept is primary and yields right reason as a partial and derivative but internal rule regarding merit and demerit. Given actual legislation, conformity to the dictates of right reason will be a necessary condition of merit. It will not be sufficient, because—as we saw—merit requires infused theological virtues dispensed in accord with the existing sacramental system as well. Thus Ockham explains that a sin of commission occurs when "the will elicits an act which it is bound not to elicit, because it elicits an act contrary to right reason and God's precepts."[147] Again, he infers that "not every sin of commission is an act of hating God. For someone can will to do unjust deeds contrary to right reason and neither love nor hate God."[148]

PUZZLES AND PARADOXES

We have seen that for Ockham right reason and divine precepts are the twin criteria for (nonpositive) moral virtue and merit alike. A theory may do no harm in positing two logically necessary and sufficient conditions of the same thing, provided they yield extensionally equivalent results. But given Ockham's characterization of the liberty of indifference, human and divine, in this case "it ain't necessarily so." And this brings us back to the paradoxes and puzzles so notorious in the secondary literature.

Divine Commands Versus Right Reason in Nonpositive Morality

Ockham explicitly affirms the possibility that God in His freedom could command us to perform acts of the species now labeled "hatred of God,"[149] "fornication,"[150] "adultery," and "theft."[151] And whether or not—from Ockham's point of view—right reason, of itself and apart from any divine or human positive law, would prohibit the latter three types of acts, he does see it as handing down the dictum "God ought to be loved in the highest degree."[152] At the same time, Ockham holds that "No one should be led to do anything contrary to the precept of his God" is known *per se*.[153] Further, since God exists and is personal necessarily, and truly does issue commands, fully informed right reason will issue the further dictate that "Whatever is pleasing to God ought to be done."[154] Thus, if God were to command free creatures to hate Him, rightly informed practical reasoning would lead to the contradictory conclusion that God is to be loved above all and hated at one and the same time.

One might think this difficulty easy to quarantine. For practical reason does not necessarily dictate whatever follows from its dictates. Hence, it does not in general follow that, because right reason leads to contradictory prescriptions and anything whatever follows from a contradiction, therefore right reason dictates anything whatever. Thus, a command from God to hate Him would not necessarily interfere with first- and second-degree virtuous acts. Suppose, for example, that right reason were to dictate that, at a particular point in arms negotiations, the diplomat should offer to reduce his country's arms production, and that right reason dictates nothing to the contrary regarding this particular matter. If the negotiator willed to make the offer at the moment indicated, and willed it for the sake of peace, his act would be morally virtuous in the first degree. If he willed it with such perseverance that he would not abandon the act for the sake of anything contrary to right reason, he would elicit an act of second-degree moral virtue.

Nevertheless, a divine command to hate God would infect the crown of the moral life. For third- and fourth-degree virtuous acts are to be done for the sake of right reason, or for the sake of right reason and for the love of God above all. Against those who hold that a volition can have only one object, Ockham contends that one and the same volition—like a single act of understanding—may have many partial objects: a generic object (e.g., to go to church), together with partial objects pertaining to the circumstances (e.g., at this particular time and place in this manner), as well as the end or principal object. Thus, the same act may be variously labeled from the diversity of objects.[155] Thus, a volition to do *A* for the sake of right reason and/or for the love of God above all is, according to Ockham, correctly describable as "a volition to do *A*," "a volition to do whatever right reason dictates," and/or "a volition to do whatever God commands."[156] Thus, it follows that every third- or fourth-degree virtuous act would be in part a general volition to conform to all the dictates of right reason and/or divine commands. But Ockham thinks that this general volition, together with the belief that right reason dictates *p* or that God commands *q*, will be sufficient to cause a particular act of willing *p* or willing *q*, respectively.

Further, Ockham maintains that contradictories cannot be wittingly willed, whether by God or by creatures. Thus, the former acts—of willing *A* for the sake of right reason and/or the love of God above all—would be incompossible with the belief that right reason had dictated contradictories or the conviction that God had commanded creatures to hate Him. God's freedom to command creatures to hate Him, or to dictate that they act contrary to right reason either in general or in particular, would be the freedom to make third- and fourth-degree virtuous acts impossible for the well-informed. Under such divine legislation, the ideal of third- and fourth-degree morally virtuous life as the good or happy life would break down.

Divine Commands and the Category of Merit

The situation is different in the category of merit. For, as noted, Ockham holds that no one can wittingly will contradictories by a formally imperative act. An omniscient God can never be ignorant. Accordingly, He can neither efficaciously will nor command contradictories.[157] In fact, God has commanded creatures to follow nonculpable reason and to love Him above all and for His own sake. Under the present legislation, God is most pleased by heroic virtue of the fourth degree. As Ockham observes,

> . . . given existing divine precepts for the opposite [of hatred, theft, adultery, etc.], no one can do such acts meritoriously or well, because they could be done meritoriously or well only if they fell under the divine precept.[158]

Likewise, as things stand,

> the created will is obliged by God's precept to love God, and therefore given that precept cannot do well to hate God or to cause an act of hatred. Nor given the first precept can God command him the opposite.[159]

Nevertheless, in His liberty of indifference, God could command the acts now labeled "hatred," "theft," "adultery," etc.; He could dictate that creatures hate Him; and He could find such hatred so pleasing as to reward it with eternal life, and be so revolted by wholehearted love of Himself as to meet it with eternal punishment. And doing so, He would revoke present legislation, because—according to Ockham—divine commands cannot lead in contradictory directions. Thus, under that constitution, acts now labeled "hatred," "theft," "adultery," etc., "could even be done meritoriously by a pilgrim."[160] After he left dangling, in *Scriptum in I Sent.*, d. 42, q. un., the issue of whether "someone could without demerit, even meritoriously, hate God,"[161] Ockham finally lays his cards on the table in *Quaest. in IV Sent.*, q. 16. Regarding the scope of the created will, he argues:

> Further, every will can conform itself to the divine precept. But God could command that the created will hate Him. Therefore, the created will could do it.[162]

Behind this reasoning lies Ockham's doctrine that both divine and created wills have the liberty of indifference, by which each can will not merely good under the aspect of good, but also evil under the aspect of evil (see the section on the freedom of the will above). Regarding the evaluation of such acts, he further contends that

> whatever could be a right act here below, could also be a right act in the Fatherland (= heaven). But hating God can be a right act here below; therefore likewise in the Fatherland.[163]

Ockham does not mean here that hatred of God could be morally virtuous, but rather that—under the logically possible divine statutes hypothesized—it would be meritorious, in the sense that it would be pleasing to God and rewarded by Him with eternal life.

Some will charge that the category of merit/demerit is not so easily vouchsafed. For do not Scotus and Ockham build merit on top of morals? Ockham in particular repeatedly asserts that while God is in no way *obliged* to anyone, rational free creatures are *obligated* to Him, *bound* to obey His commands.[164] But what foundation has the More than Subtle Doctor laid for this authority, if not that such obedience is dictated by right reason? If the walls of nonpositive morality "crumble" by virtue of yielding contradictory dictates, will not the penthouse of merit/demerit come crashing down with it?

As we have seen (in the section on the Divine commands), the authority of divine commands within the sphere of nonpositive morality *does* rest on that of right reason, whereas in the category of merit/demerit divine commands are fundamental. Ockham does not articulate his understanding of God's authority in this sphere of positive morality. When he remarks that its values are defined by a "superior" who has the authority to legislate its contents,[165] he has politico–legal models in mind. Like Scotus, he continues the metaphor in his discussion of absolute versus ordered divine power, where he compares God's role as legislator of the sacramental system with the pope's rule of the church;[166] the authority of temporal monarchs would provide the other medieval analogy. These comparisons are of limited utility, however, to the extent that Ockham sees such ecclesiastical and temporal authority as delegated by God. So far as I know, Ockham nowhere gives the answer that modern commentators (perhaps inspired by St. Paul's image of the potter and the clay) have hastened to supply: that divine authority to command other persons rests on the fact that He is their creator and owner, and so has the right to dispose of them as He chooses.[167] Nor does he explicitly trace the authority of divine legislation back to divine power.[168] On the other hand, Ockham could be taking either or both answers for granted.

CONCLUSION

The picture of Ockham's moral theory drawn by his cultured detractors finds its principle distortion in their failure to keep his treatments of nonpositive and positive morality distinct.

Regarding the former, which corresponds to the subject matter of philosophical ethics, Ockham upholds the Aristotelian ideal of rational self-government. A pagan, thoroughly committed to the life of reason—to believing only what unaided natural reason can prove, and to conforming himself to right reason in every way—will be able thereby to discover all he needs to know to live a life heroically virtuous in the third degree. The data regarding what is suitable/unsuitable for humans is ever ready-to-hand. That is why Ockham declares narrow-sense morality the surest of all the sciences. Enlightened by revelation, right reason will go further and enjoin obedience to God's commands, and the obedience will carry the agent to fourth-degree moral virtue, which does everything for the sake both of right reason and of God Himself.

For Ockham, it is a necessary truth that divine commands are a derivative norm in nonpositive morality, but that does not make his theory an authoritarian "divine command ethics." For in theories of the latter type, the obligation of the commanded person to obey comes from without and binds the individual so to act even against his own reason and deepest inclinations. In Ockham's account of nonpositive morality, this is not so; rather, the virtuous person commands himself to make his fullest self-development an offering of love to the infinite being. Nor does the encroachment of morals into the category of merit/demerit turn Ockham's moral theory into a "modified divine command theory"; for in these theories, divine commands are the fundamental norm, but function as such only on the condition that God commands what is good for human beings. Otherwise—if God does not exist or if His commands run counter to human interest—morality "breaks down."[169] Because Ockham's ethics begins with right reason and is led thereby to divine commands, with the consequence that nonpositive morality can "break down" in the event that they don't agree, his theory might be better labeled "modified right reason theory."

It is within a subdivision of positive morality—that of merit and demerit—that divine commands are fundamental. There God has in fact used His authority to make—through legislation—things that are intrinsically deserving of neither eternal life nor eternal punishment, meritorious or demeritorious, respectively. Here, in principle, God could tie acts to consequences in such a way that created persons would have to act contrary to reason or inclination to collect the reward of eternal life. Thus, Ockham could be said to endorse a "divine command theory of eternal destiny."

These corrections notwithstanding, Ockham's opponents may still feel vindicated. For even his "modified right reason ethics" combines with his doctrine of freedom to open the possibility that morality might break down, leaving creatures in heteronomous subjection to a free and omnipotent tyrant, who could—on pain of eternal punishment—enjoin the frustration of created personhood. Was it not better, in metaphysics, to deny free will the scope to choose evil under the aspect of evil? Was it not preferable, in theology, to let God's goodness so dominate His choices as to make it metaphysically impossible for Him to command creatures to contradict their internal regulators?

This charge can be rebutted if we see Ockham first and foremost as a Franciscan. Those who fear that God cannot be trusted to be good to His creatures may well shudder at the extensive power and freedom Ockham assigns Him. By contrast, Ockham never anticipates Geach in warning his readers that "the fear of God for his power irresistible is at least the *beginning* of wisdom."[170] Rather, true Franciscan that he is, Ockham begins with a vivid sense of God's enormous generosity, in creating us in His image, in redeeming us, and in preserving us forever. He lets reason join the creator's praise by giving rational articulation to this reaction and joins Scotus' search for measures of divine liberality. The contrast between divine infinity and created finitude provides a metaphysical yardstick. Moral theory affords another. In the category of ethics, revelation leads the best of Aristotelian rational self-government to offer itself in love to its Creator; while in the sphere of merit, the obligation-free God gives created choices eternal significance by tying them to supernatural rewards. Others may now look with fear on the dark side of Ockham's modified right reason ethics, down the chasm of the potential breakdown of nonpositive morality. I submit that the More than Subtle Doctor looked on the bright side and saw in it an advertisement of God's grace in so aligning His commands with the dictates of right reason that the morally virtuous life is eternally consummated by a face-to-face vision of God Himself.

NOTES

1. Paul Helm, "Introduction," in *Divine Commands and Morality,* NY: Oxford University Press, 1981, 3.

2. Maurice de Wulf, *History of Medieval Philosophy,* translated by P. Coffey, London: Longmans, Green, and Co. 1909, 425.

3. Armand Maurer, *A History of Philosophy: Medieval Philosophy,* NY: Random House, 1962.

4. Maurer 287.

5. David Knowles, *The Evolution of Medieval Thought,* NY: Random House, 1962, 324.

6. De Wulf 425.

7. Gordon Leff, *Medieval Thought: St. Augustine to Ockham,* NY: Penguin Books, 1958, chap. 9, 289.

8. Knowles 324.

9. Helm 3.

10. Etienne Gilson, *The History of Christian Philosophy in the Middle Ages,* NY: Random House, 1955, Part XI, chap. 1, 497.

11. Armand Maurer 287. Interestingly, Peter Geach, otherwise no fan of William Ockham, defends roughly the position outlined by Maurer on

Ockham's behalf. Geach denies the inference from "Divine commands are the norm of morality" to "all knowledge of moral law comes through revelation," and takes the following position: "The rational recognition that a practice is generally undesirable and that it is best for people on the whole not even to think of resorting to it is thus *in fact* a promulgation to a man of the Divine law forbidding the practice, even if he does not realize that this is a promulgation of the Divine law, even if he does not believe there is a God" ("The Moral Law and the Law of God," reprinted in *Divine Commands and Morality*, edited by Paul Helm, NY: Oxford University Press, 1981, 165–174 [esp. 170].

12. Frederick Copleston, *A History of Philosophy, vol. 3: Late Medieval and Renaissance Philosophy, Pt. I: Ockham to the Speculative Mystics*, Garden City: NY: Doubleday-Image, 1963, 118–119.

13. Copleston 118–119.

14. Copleston 119–121.

15. Copleston 122.

16. Lucan Freppert, *The Basis of Morality According to William Ockham* (Chicago: Franciscan Herald Press, 1988) vii + 191pp.

17. *Ordinatio* II, d. 40; AW 225, 227. (AW = Duns Scotus on the *Will and Morality*. Edited and Translated by Allan B. Wolter. Washington, D.C.: The Catholic University Press, 1986).

18. Scotus, *Ordinatio* II, d. 17, nn. 28–39; AW 219.

19. Scotus, *Ordinatio* lib. I, d. 2, p. 1, qq. 1–2 (ed. Vatic., II 145–173).

20. Ockham, *Quodl.* II, q. 13 (OTh IX, 168).

21. Ockham, *Quaest. in II Sent.*, q. 20 (OTh V, 442).

22. Ockham, *Scriptum in I Sent.*, d. 17, q. 1 (OTh III, 450, 451).

23. Ockham, *Quodl. II*, q. 13 (OTh IX, 168).

24. Ockham, *Quodl.* I, q. 1 (OTh IX, 3); *Quodl.* VII, q. 15 (OTh IX, 761).

25. Ockham, *Scriptum in I Sent.*, prol., q. 12 (OTh I, 365).

26. Ockham, *Scriptum in I Sent.*, d. 38, q. un. (OTh IV, 578–582); *Tractatus de Praedestinatione et de Praescientia Dei et de Futuris Contingentibus*, q. 3; OPh I, 533–535.

27. Ockham seems to assume that while the really existing divine act of thought and will (which is identical with its act of will and understanding) is necessarily and immutably as it is, the intentionality of divine mental acts regarding future contingents is indeterminate, so long as the state of affairs is contingent. Thus, "God wills that Peter will be saved" is just as indeterminate and determinable as Peter's free choice to persevere to the end is. Thus, Ockham does not see divine choices about creation as atemporal the way Scotus does. See my book, *William Ockham*, (Notre Dame: Univ. of N.D. Press, 1987) chapter 31.

28. Ockham, *Tractatus de Praedestinatione et de Praescientia Dei et de Futuris Contingtibus*, q. 3 (OPh I, 536).

29. Ockham, *Quaest. in II Sent.*, q. 20 (OTh V, 435).

30. Ockham, *Quaest, in IV Sent.*, q. 16 (OTh VII, 358); *DCV* (DCV = *De connexione virtutem in Quaest. variae*, q. 7), a. 4 (OTh VIII, 393).

31. Ockham, *Quaest. in IV Sent.*, q. 16 (OTh VII, 353).

32. Ockham, e.g., *DCV*, a. 3 (OTh VIII, 363); *DCV*, q. 2, a. 2 (OTh VIII, 447).

33. Ockham, *Scriptum in I Sent.*, d. 1, q. 6 (OTh I, 490).

34. Ockham, *DCV*, a. 1 (OTh VIII, 333).

35. Ockham, *Scriptum in I Sent.*, d. 1, q. 6 (OTh I, 491–6).

36. Ockham, *DCV* , a. 3 (OTh VIII, 353).

37. Ockham, *Quaest. Variae*, q. 6, a. 10 (OTh VIII, 277).

38. Ockham, *Quaest. in III Sent.*, q. 7 (OTh VI, 211).

39. Ockham, *Quaest. in II Sent.*, q. 15 (OTh V, 350).

40. Ockham, *Quaest. in II Sent.*, q. 15 (OTh V, 341); *Quaest. in II Sent.*, q. 20 (OTh V, 443); *Scriptum in I Sent.*, d. 1, q. 2 (OTh I, 397, 399).

41. Ockham, *Quaest. in II Sent.*, q. 15 (OTh V, 341); *Scriptum in I Sent.*, d. 1, q. 2 (OTh I, 399).

42. Ockham, *Quaest. in II Sent.*, q. 15 (OTh V, 344).

43. Ockham, *Quaest. in II Sent.*, q. 15 (OTh V, 351).

44. Ockham, *Quaest. in II Sent.*, q. 15 (OTh V, 351); *Quaest. in IV Sent.*, q. 16 (OTh VII, 353); *Scriptum in I Sent.*, d. 1, q. 3 (OTh I, 410).

45. Ockham, *Quaest. in II Sent.*, q. 15 (OTh V, 351, 355). Cf. Aquinas, *Summa Theologica I*, q. 82, a. 1 c., who defines "coercion" the same way.

46. Ockham, *Quaest. Variae*, q. 8 (OTh VIII, 447).

47. Ockham, *DCV*, a. 2 (OTh VIII, 336–7).

48. Ockham, *Scriptum in I Sent.*, d. 1, q. 6 (OTh I, 502).

49. Ockham, *Scriptum in I Sent.*, d. 1, q. 2 (OTh I, 399); *Scriptum in I Sent.*, d. 1, q. 6 (OTh I, 502).

50. Ockham, *Scriptum in I Sent.*, d. 1, q.6 (OTh I, 503); *Quaest. in IV Sent.*, q. 16 (OTh VII, 350–1); *Quodl. I*, q. 16 (OTh IX, 88).

51. Ockham, *Quaest. in IV Sent.*, q. 16 (OTh VII, 352).

52. Ockham, *Scriptum in I Sent.*, d. 1, q. 6 (OTh I, 505).

53. Ockham, *Quaest. in IV Sent.*, q. 16 (OTh VII, 351–2).

54. Ockham, *Scriptum in I Sent.*, d. 1, q. 6 (OTh I, 503); *Quaest. in IV Sent.*, q. 16 (OTh VII, 350).

55. Ockham, *Quaest. in IV Sent.*, q. 16 (OTh VII, 350).

56. Ockham, *Quaest. in IV Sent.*, q. 16 (OTh VII, 351).

57. Ockham, *DCV*, q. 7, a. 3 (OTh VIII, 367); *Quaest. Variae*, q. 6, a. 10 (OTh VIII, 285).

58. Ockham, *Quaest. in IV Sent.*, q. 16 (OTh VII, 357–8).

59. Ockham, *Quaest. Variae*, q. 8 (OTh VIII, 444–5).

60. Scotus, *Ordinatio IV*, suppl. d. 49, nn. 9–10; AW 161.

61. Scotus, *Ordinatio III*, suppl. d. 33; AW 275.

62. Ockham, *Quaest. in III Sent.*, q. 9 (OTh VI, 282); *Quaest. in II Sent.*, q. 15 (OTh V, 340).

63. Ockham, *DCV*, a. 1 (OTh VIII, 323).

64. Ockham, *DCV*, a. 3 (OTh VIII, 348).

65. Ockham, *Quaest. in III Sent.*, q. 9 (OTh VI, 311).

66. Ochkam, *Scriptum in I Sent.*, prol. q. 12 (OTh I, 360).

67. Ockham, *Scriptum in I Sent.*, prol. q. 12 (OTh I, 360).

68. Ockham, *Quodl. II*, q. 14 (OTh IX, 177).

69. Ockham, *Quodl. II*, q. 14 (OTh IX, 177); CF. *Quaest. Variae*, q. 6, a. 10 (OTh VIII, 281–2).

70. Ockham, *Quaest. Variae*, q. 6, a. 10 (OTh VIII, 281–2).

71. Ockham, *Quodl. II*, q. 14 (OTh IX, 177).

72. Ockham, *Quodl. II*, q. 14 (OTh IX, 177).

73. Ockham, *Quodl. II*, q. 14 (OTh IX, 177).

74. Ockham, *DCV*, a. 3 (OTh VIII, 362).

75. Ockham, *Quaest. Variae*, q. 8 (OTh VIII, 409).

76. Ockham, *Quaest. Variae*, q. 8 (OTh VIII, 411).

77. Ockham, *DCV*, q. 7, a. 3 (OTh VIII, 358, 363); *Quaest. Variae*, q. 8 (OTh VIII, 414–16).

78. Ockham, *Quaest. Variae*, q. 8 (OTh VIII, 416, 418).

79. Ockham, *Quaest. Variae*, q. 8 (OTh VIII, 429).

80. Ockham, *Quaest, Variae*, q. 8 (OTh VIII, 429–430).

81. Ockham, *DCV*, a. 3 (OTh VIII, 363).

82. Ockham, *Quaest. Variae*, q. 8 (OTh VIII, 411).

83. Ockham, *DCV*, q. 7, a. 2 (OTh VIII, 335).

84. Ockham, *DCV*, q. 7, a. 2 (OTh VIII, 335).

85. Ockham, *DCV*, q. 7, a. 2 (OTh VIII, 335).

86. Ockham, *DCV*, q. 7, a. 2 (OTh VIII, 335).

87. Ockham, *DCV*, q. 7, a. 2 (OTh VIII, 335).

88. Ockham, *DCV*, q. 7, a. 2 (OTh VIII, 336–7).

89. Ockham, *DCV*, q. 7, a. 2 (OTh VIII, 336–7; cf. 354–5, 357).

90. Ockham, *Quaest. in IV Sent.*, qq. 10–11 (OTh VII, 195–7, 223).

91. Ockham, *Scriptum in I Sent.*, d. 17, q. 2 (OTh III, 473–4). Again, the possibility of merit depends upon the creature's freedom and hence his ability to elicit acts that are imputable, whether for praise or for blame: *Quodl. III*, q. 19 (OTh IX, 275); cf. *Quodl.* VI, q. 1 (OTh IX, 588); cf. *Scriptum in I Sent.*, d. 1, q. 2 (OTh I, 452). Likewise, the possibility of merit depends on the agent's ability to use reason [*Quaest. Variae*, q. 8 (OTh VIII, 437–441)]: to be meritous, an act must be done with knowledge and freely, although a demeritous act may be done with culpable ignorance, *Quodl.* II, q. 6 (OTh IX, 140). And Ockham argues that infused habits cannot, by their very nature, make a creature worthy of eternal life, because they are not within the power of the agent; cf. *Scriptum in I Sent.*, d. 17, q. 1 (OTh III, 462); *Quodl.* VI, q. 1 (OTh IX, 588).

92. *Ockham, Quodl.* II, q. 14 (OTh IX, 177).

93. For a full discussion of Ockham's claim that some acts must be intrinsically imputable (virtuous/vicious), and only acts of will can be such, see Rega Wood and Marilyn McCord Adams, "Is to Will It as Bad as to Do It? The Fourteenth Century Debate," *Franciscan Studies* 41 (XIX), 5–60.

94. Regarding acceptance or worthiness of eternal life, see Ockham, *Scriptum in I Sent.*, d. 17, q. 1 (OTh III, 446, 449, 452, 454–5); d. 17, q. 2 (OTh III, 471–2); *Quaest. in IV Sent.*, q. 3–5 (OTh VII, 55). Regarding God's hatred of creatures, *Scriptum in I Sent.*, d. 17, q. 1 (OTh III, 447, 449). Regarding a deed or person worthy of eternal punishment, *Quaest. in IV Sent.*, q. 3–5 (OTh VII, 47).

95. Ockham, *Scriptum in I Sent.*, d. 17, q. 1 (OTh III, 445).

96. Ockham, *Scriptum in I Sent.*, d. 17, q. 1 (OTh III, 452, 455); *Quaest. Variae*, q. 1 (OTh. VIII, 17–19, 21).

97. Ockham, *Scriptum in I Sent.*, d. 17, q. 1 (OTh III, 453–4); *Quaest. Variae*, q. 1 (OTh VIII, 19); *Quaest. in IV Sent.*, qq. 9–10 (OTh VII, 209); *Quodl. VI*, q. 2 (OTh IX, 591).

98. Ockham, *Quaest. Variae V*, q. 1 (OTh VIII, 21, 23–27); *Quaest. in IV Sent.*, qq. 9–10 (OTh VII, 198, 224–6); *Quaest. in IV Sent.*, q. 3–5 (OTh V, 55); *DCV*, q. 7, a. 4 (OTh VIII, 389); *Quaest. Variae*, q. 8 (OTh VIII, 435); *Quaest. in II Sent.*, q. 15 (OTh V, 353).

99. Ockham, *Scriptum in I Sent.*, d. 14, q. 2 (OTh III, 432).

100. And hence apart from merit and demerit, cf. *Quaest. in IV Sent.*, qq. 3–5 (OTh VII, 45); *Quaest. in III Sent.*, q. 9 (OTh VI, 281). Indeed, there are Biblical examples of this in God's giving a vision of Himself to Paul apart from any preceding merit [*cf. Quod. VI*, q. 1 (OTh IX, 587)]. Likewise, Ockham toys with the idea that God may predestine the Blessed Virgin Mary apart from any merit [*Scriptum in I Sent.*, d. 41, q. un. (OTh IV, 606–7); *Quaest. in III Sent.*, q. 2 (OTh VI, 154–6)].

101. Ockham, *Quaest. Variae*, q. 6, a. 11 (OTh VIII, 319).

102. Ockham, *Scriptum in I Sent.*, d. 17, q. 1 (OTh III, 449, 462); *Quodl. VI*, q. 1 (OTh IX, 588); *Scriptum in I Sent.*, d. 1, q. 2 (OTh I, 402).

103. Ockham, *Quaest. Variae*, q. 1 (OTh VIII, 14).

104. Ockham, *Quaest. Variae*, q. 1 (OTh VIII, 26).

105. Ockham, *Quaest. in IV Sent.*, q. 3–5 (OTh VII, 55).

106. Scotus, *Ordinatio IV*, d. 17; AW 239.

107. Scotus, *Ordinatio IV*, d. 17; AW 238–9.

108. Scotus, *Ordinatio IV*, d. 17; AW 233, 237.

109. Scotus, *Ordinatio III*, suppl. d. 27; AW 355, 363, 365. Right reason dictates that the best should be loved the most, and in its original condition the will can perform this act unaided by grace, according to Scotus.

110. Ockham, *Quaest. in II Sent.*, q. 15 (OTh V, 352).

111. Ockham, *DCV*, a. 4 (OTh VII, 391).

112. Ockham, *Quaest. in IV Sent.*, q. 16 (OTh VII, 352).

113. Ockham, *Quaest. in IV Sent.*, qq. 10–11 (OTh VII, 203–216).

114. Ockham, *Quaest. in III Sent.*, q. 9 (OTh VI, 279).

115. Ockham, *Scriptum in I Sent.*, d. 17, q. 1 (OTh III, 463–4).

116. Ockham, *Scriptum in I Sent.*, d. 17, q. 1 (OTh III, 455).

117. Ockham, *Quaest. in IV Sent.*, qq. 3–5 (OTh VII, 55).

118. Ockham, *Quaest. Variae*, q. 6, a. 11 (OTh VIII, 318).

119. Ockham, *Quaest. in III Sent.*, q. 9 (OTh VI, 281).

120. Ockham, *Quaest. Variae*, q. 1 (OTh VII, 16–17, 23–24).

121. Ockham, *Scriptum in I Sent.*, d. 17, q. 3 (OTh III, 477–8).

122. Ockham, *Quodl. VI*, q. 4 (OTh IX, 598).

123. Ockham, *Scriptum in I Sent.*, d. 17, q. 1 (OTh III, 456).

124. Ockham, *DCV*, a. 4 (OTh VIII, 384).

125. Ockham, *Quodl. I*, q. 1 (OTh IX, 3); cf. *Quodl. VII*, q. 15 (OTh IX, 761); *Scriptum in I Sent.*, d. 1, q. 5 (OTh I, 464). See section 1 above.

126. Ockham, *Scriptum in I Sent.*, d. 1, q. 4 (OTh I, 447); *DCV*, q. 7, a. 2 (OTh VIII, 335–6); *DCV*, q. 7, a. 3 (OTh VIII, 358).

127. Ockham, *Quaest. Variae*, q. 6, a. 11 (OTh VIII, 314).

128. Ockham, *DCV*, q. 7, a. 3 (OTh VIII, 366). Scotus makes a big distinction between the negative precept, which doesn't entail that God exists or has commanded anything, but only that the conjunction "*x* has a God who issues precepts and *x* does not conform to those precepts" ought to be false, or the conditional "if God exists, He alone must be loved as God" and the positive precept "Love the Lord your God with all your heart. . . ." He contends that the former pertain to natural law, strictly speaking, but the latter does not (*Ordinatio IV,* d. 17; AW 233, 237, 238–9).

129. Ockham, *DCV,* q. 7, a. 3 (OTh VIII, 365).

130. Ockham, *Scriptum in I Sent.,* d. 41, q. un. (OTh IV, 610).

131. Ockham, *DCV,* q. 7, a. 3 (OTh VIII, 359).

132. Ockham, *DCV,* q. 7, a. 4 (OTh VIII, 399).

133. Ockham, *DCV,* q. 7, a. 2 (OTh VIII, 338).

134. Ockham, *Quaest. in III Sent.,* q. 11 (OTh VI, 387).

135. Ockham, *DCV,* q. 7, a. 4 (OTh VIII, 386).

136. Ockham, *DCV,* q. 7, a. 2 (OTh VIII, 335); *DCV,* q. 7, a. 3 (OTh VIII, 348); cf. *DCV,* q. 7, a. 4 (OTh VIII, 399); cf. *Quaest. in IV Sent.,* qq. 10–11 (OTh VII, 230–1).

137. Ockham, *DCV,* q. 7, a. 4 (OTh VIII, 402–3).

138. Ockham, *DCV,* q. 7, a. 2 (OTh VIII, 336–7).

139. Ockham, *DCV,* q. 7, a. 4 (OTh VIII, 402–3); *Quaest. in IV Sent.,* qq. 10–11 (OTh VII, 231).

140. Ockham, *Quaest. in III Sent.,* q. 11 (OTh VI, 386).

141. Ockham, *Quaest. Variae,* q. 6, a. 10 (OTh VIII, 280).

142. E.g., Ockham, *Quaest. Variae,* q. 6, a. 11 (OTh VIII, 314).

143. Ockham, *Quodl. II,* q. 19 (OTh IX, 154–5).

144. Ockham, *Quaest. Variae,* q. 8 (OTh VIII, 436).

145. Ockham, *Quaest. Variae,* q. 8 (OTh VIII, 411).

146. Ockham, *Quaest. Variae,* q. 8 (OTh VIII, 428–9, 435).

147. Ockham, *DCV,* q. 7, a. 4 (OTh VIII, 387).

148. Ockham, *DCV,* q. 7, a. 4 (OTh VIII, 390).

149. Ockham, *Quaest. in IV Sent.,* q. 16 (OTh VII, 352).

150. Ockham, *DCV,* q. 7, a. 4 (OTh VIII, 391).

151. Ockham, *Quaest. in II Sent.,* q. 15 (OTh V, 352).

152. Ockham, *Scriptum in I Sent,* d. 1, q. 4 (OTh I, 447); *DCV,* q. 7, a. 2 (OTh VIII, 355–6); *DCV,* q. 7, a. 3 (OTh VIII, 358).

153. Ockham, *DCV,* q. 7, a. 3 (OTh VIII, 359).

154. Ockham, *DCV,* q. 7, a. 3 (OTh VIII, 365).

155. Ockham, *Scriptum in I Sent.,* d. 1, q. 1 (OTh I, 385).

156. Ockham, *Quaest. Variae,* q. 7, a. 4 (OTh VIII, 381).

157. Ockham, *Quaest. in II Sent.,* q. 15 (OTh V, 352).

158. Ockham, *Quaest. in II Sent.,* q. 15 (OTh V,352).

159. Ockham, *Quaest. in II Sent.,* q. 15 (OTh V,352).

160. Ockham, *Quaest. in II Sent.,* q. 15 (OTh V,352).

161. Ockham, *Scriptum in I Sent.,* d. 42, q. un. (OTh IV, 621). The question arises in this context because of Ockham's contention that God can be the total efficient cause of any created thing and hence of any created quality, which includes created volitions. The difficulty then arises if God could even cause an act of hating Himself. Ockham's unequivocal answer is "yes." But he maintains that in that case, neither God nor creature would sin—God because He has no obligations to violate, and the creature because the act would not be within his power—nor would the creature act meritoriously for the same reason [*Quaest. in II Sent.*, q. 15 (OTh V, 352); *Quaest. in IV Sent*, q. 16 (OTh VII, 355)].

162. Ockham, *Quaest. in IV Sent.*, q. 16 (OTh VII, 352).

163. Ockham, *Quaest. in IV Sent.*, q. 16 (OTh VII, 352).

164. Ockham, *DCV*, q. 7, a. 4 (OTh VIII, 386–390); *Quaest. Variae*, q. 8 (OTh VIII, 428–9, 435–6, 439–40); *Quaest. in II Sent.*, q. 15 (OTh V, 353).

165. Ockham, *Quodl. II*, q. 14 (OTh IX, 177). See section 4 above.

166. Ockham, *Quodl. VI*, q. 1 (OTh IX, 586).

167. Ascribed to Ockham by Helm 3. See also Baruch A. Brody, "Morality and Religion Reconsidered," reprinted in Helm 141–153.

168. As does Peter Geach, "The Moral Law and the Law of God," in Helm 165–174 (esp. 171–174).

169. Such a theory has been expounded in two versions by Robert Merrihew Adams, "A Modified Divine Command Theory of Ethical Wrongness" and "Divine Command Metaethics as Necessary A Posteriori," in Helm 83–119.

170. Geach 174.

Part Two

PRECURSORS OF CASUISTRY: Preaching and Teaching Cases

"To Persuade Is a Victory": Rhetoric and Moral Reasoning in the Sermons of Bernardino of Siena

FRANCO MORMANDO, S.J.

Therefore a certain eloquent man said, and said truly, that he who is eloquent should speak in such a way that he teaches, delights and moves. Then he added: "To teach is a necessity, to please is a sweetness, to persuade is a victory."

—Augustine, *On Christian Doctrine*, IV, XII, 27.[1]

PREACHING AND MORAL INSTRUCTION IN LATE MEDIEVAL SOCIETY

In the late summer of 1427, the popular preacher Bernardino of Siena arrived in the town whose name he now bears to deliver yet another eagerly awaited course of daily sermons to the people of both town and countryside.[2] Each day, for forty-five days, people numbering in the thousands gathered just before the break of dawn in the candle-lit arena of the town's main square, the Piazza del Campo. There, for three or more hours they sat listening to the "soft, clear, sonorous, distinct, explicit, solid, penetrating, full, rounded, elevated, and efficacious" voice of Friar Bernardino.[3] The world in 1427 was a confusing, frightening place: the devil was omnipresent and frequently had the upper hand; humankind was still largely at the mercy of the mysterious and capricious forces of Mother Nature; and, to add insult to injury, death by famine, plague, war, marauders, unjust lords, or absurd accident threatened to carry one off at any moment. Life was, above all, a constant moral test: who will pass, who will fail? Most decisions in daily life seemed to represent a choice between good and evil, salvation and damnation, heaven and hell. The possibility of mortal sin lurked at every corner. How would they know how to choose? The preacher would help them:

> Oh! How many will there be here today who will say: "I didn't know what I was really doing. I thought I was doing good and instead I was doing evil." And then, remembering this sermon, they will say to themselves: "Oh! Now my mind is clear about what I have to do. . . ." And when you go to draw up a contract, you will first do some thinking and say to yourself: "Now what did Friar Bernardino say? He said such and such: this is evil and mustn't be done; this is good; this is what I'm going to choose." And this takes place inside you only through the word which you hear in the sermon. But, tell me: what would happen to the world, that is, to the Christian faith, if there were no preaching? In a little while, our faith would disappear, because we wouldn't believe in anything of what we believe. That's why Holy Church has ordered us to preach every Sunday, a little or a lot, as long as we preach. And to you she has given the command to go and hear Mass.

Highlighting the unique importance of preaching, the friar then adds this piece of extreme advice:

> And if, between these two things—either to hear Mass or hear a sermon—you can only do one, you must miss Mass rather than the sermon; the reason for this is that there is less danger to your soul in not hearing Mass than there is in not hearing the sermon. . . . Tell me: how would you believe in the Blessed Sacrament on the altar if it weren't for the sermon which you heard? Your faith in the Mass comes to you only through preaching. Also: what would you know about sin if it weren't for preaching? What would you know about hell if it weren't for preaching? How would you know about any good act, and how you must go about it, if you didn't learn it through sermons? (R.149)

What occurred in Siena in the summer of 1427 took place in nearly every season in all of the greater and lesser towns of Christian Europe for centuries following the rise of the major preaching orders, the Franciscans and the Dominicans. The phenomenon lasted well into modern times. "The important role preaching played in the life of these eras . . .," John O'Malley has stated, "needs no proving to anybody who has studied them even superficially."[4] In that age before the triumph of printing, preaching was simply the most important means of mass communication, and Bernardino and company represented, in effect, the most important moral instructors of the people. Thus, the early history of moral theology is to be traced not only in canon law and in the confessional manuals, but in popular preaching as well. More people in premodern and early modern times derived their notions of God, the world, and the difference between good and evil from the sermons of the popular preachers than from the lectures and treatises of the university scholars.

RHETORIC AND MORAL REASONING: THE INTIMATE CONNECTION

The decisive influence of rhetoric in the historical development of moral reasoning has been brought to the fore by Albert Jonsen and Stephen Toulmin's new look at the origin and shape of high casuistry, *The Abuse of Casuistry: A History of Moral Reasoning*. Jonsen and Toulmin argue and demonstrate persuasively that, far from representing the abstract, atemporal, "geometric," simplistic application of universal principles to local cases, the ethical reasoning of high casuistry entailed a more sophisticated experience-based, concrete, temporal, "taxonomic" approach to moral decision making. This "taxonomic" method and "practical reasoning" mind-set, the authors point out, were the direct bequest of classical rhetoric, most notably Aristotle and Cicero. To these men Catholic moral theology traces some of its principal roots. In sum, the authors tell us: "Rhetoric and casuistry were mutual allies. It is not surprising to find the Jesuits, who were dedicated to teaching classical rhetoric in their colleges, become the leading proponents of casuistry."[5]

It is a long way, however, from the ancients to the Jesuits in the history of rhetoric and moral reasoning. In between those two rhetorical moments—the classical and the neoclassical—comes another major epoch, that of medieval rhetoric. The medieval rhetorical tradition, embodied most tangibly in the numerous *artes praedicandi* which flooded European libraries beginning with the thirteenth century, was as self-aware, as articulate, and as vigorous as that of its classical predecessors or its neoclassical successors. Its methods, mind-set, and moral theology ruled the European pulpit for at least 300 years: "From the thirteenth to at least the end of the fifteenth century, the continuity in the mainstream of preaching is striking."[6] In this mainstream, Bernardino of Siena towers above the preaching multitudes. In the forty years of his preaching career, thousands of Christians attended his public sermons. Popes, prelates, and more worldly princes sought out his advice; penal codes were reformed explicitly in his name and, after his death, his works were cited as *auctoritates* in such standard reference works as the *Summa angelica*.[7]

The attention which Jonsen and Toulmin have drawn to the significant link between rhetoric and moral reasoning in the age of high casuistry (1550 to 1650) motivates us to put the same question to the previous age and its rhetoric: What relationship was there between the two orbits of concern, preaching theory and moral instruction, in the century before the rise of casuistry? That is, what was the *forma mentis* of medieval rhetoric in its most mature stage, and how did this influence the moral reasoning of the preacher–moral theologians formed by and operating within that mind-set? Moreover, what contribution does an examination of medieval rhetoric add to our understanding of the history of moral reasoning?

In this essay, we will focus exclusively on the example of Bernardino of Siena, one of the last voices of the Italian Middle Ages. Though the friar was celebrated in his own age as a "reformer" of ecclesiastical oratory, the essential form and spirit of Bernardino's preaching are nothing new under the sun. Indeed, Bernardino embodies all that is characteristic of medieval rhetoric during the reign of the *artes praedicandi*—characteristic in everything except, of course, caliber, phenomenal success, and influence. The friar's preaching has the further advantage of being the most accessible of medieval sermonizing in terms of both extant printed texts and other contemporary documentation attesting to its form, content, and influence. What follows, however, cannot claim to be an exhaustive treatment of either Bernardino's theory and practice of preaching or his moral theology; our selective survey has been guided by the questions this essay seeks to answer.

There is, furthermore, an additional question we would like to raise, and since, unlike the others we have just announced, it is of easy answer, let us do so immediately. In Bernardino do we find any anticipation of the practical "taxonomic" approach described above that was to become a defining feature of the moral discourse of the succeeding age? The reply is no. When we enter the world of Bernardino's preaching and, thus, his moral theology, we enter a world painted typically in extremes of black and white and constructed upon an ample foundation of absolute moral principles drawn from Scripture and the patristic and canon law authorities, meant seemingly to cover the entire ground of human activity and possible moral decision making. Accordingly, when resolving cases of conscience, he proves to be, above all, a moral "geometrician," rather than "taxonomist." Completely revelatory of the friar's fundamental attitude toward the moral universe is his sermon on the unity, *firmitas*, and omniscience of the Christian faith, *"Quod fides sola est una et determinata, ad quam de necessitate quilibet obligatur."* What Bernardino says, in effect, in this sermon is that the church has no real doubts and has left no issue of real significance undecided:

> . . . there are some writings which the Church holds doubtful or indeterminate, for example, certain opinions of various doctors, even among the approved doctors, which contradict each other in certain matters which are not necessary for salvation: such as in the case of Solomon, whom Augustine thinks is damned while Ambrose believes him saved. (OOQ.I.35)

Bernardino does go on to add: "But according to Scotus and Hostiensis, whenever there is a disagreement of laws or of opinions which, however, are not against God and good mores, all other things being equal, the more humane (*humaniora*) is to be preferred." A consoling theoretical principle indeed; yet, in actual practice, what turns out to be the "more humane" in the friar's eyes may strike some as the very opposite. Consider, for example, the solution he proposes for the problem of feminine fashions, which are bankrupting the fathers and husbands of Tuscany:

> Do you know what needs to be done? First of all, we should burn at the stake the woman who dresses in this way, then her mother who allows her to do so, and then afterwards, the dressmaker who provides her with the clothes. (R.1088)

These hyperbolic outbursts are not infrequent in the sermons, though at times he is indeed capable of "more humane" solutions. An example of this is his advice to an adulterous wife who, the friar says, should not tell her husband that he is not the real father of their son: "for the heartache that [such a revelation] would give him; every time he looks at [the boy] he will suffer great pain and everyone would be staring at his head to see if the cuckold's horns had sprouted yet" (A.323).

A student of canon law for three years before entering religious life, Bernardino constantly raises *dubia* and *quaestiones* and examines *casus conscientiae*, making due logical and "typological" distinctions in scholastic–legal disputational fashion. However, as far as I have been able to detect, there is not one case which he does not solve by an utterly self-confident, mechanistic application of syllogistic logic and universal principles derived from his *auctoritates,* rather than by a taxonomic comparison of cases. In fact, Bernardino at times can come across as a Procrustes of moral theology. In general, his *modus operandi* typifies what Jonsen and Toulmin have censured as "a more principled but grossly simplistic approach to moral issues" which has done "humanity a disservice" and, in his day as in our own, "has produced bitter fruit."[8] Yet the picture is not entirely bleak; there are other elements in Bernardino's method which can speak to the modern mind and contribute in positive fashion to today's debate surrounding the foundations and contours of moral reasoning. These shall be summarized at the end of our study.

BERNARDINO'S PREACHING: MEDIEVAL, POPULAR, FRANCISCAN

Bernardino's approach to moral reasoning is determined to a great degree by its context, namely, the medieval, popular, Franciscan sermon.[9] Each of those adjectives is significant and implies a different set of attributes.

Bernardino, medieval preacher

Though his lifetime coincided with the beginnings and affirmation of the Renaissance in Italy, Bernardino the rhetorician is decidedly a personality of the Middle Ages. The spirit and form of the friar's oratory derive not from the humanists' discussions of classical eloquence, which were becoming the new fashion of his day, but rather from the medieval preaching manuals, the *artes praedicandi.* In both their organic structure and characteristic content, Bernardino's sermons are clearly the product of a mind trained according to the rhetorical principles of the Middle Ages.[10] In their very construction, the friar's sermons faithfully reproduce the form of the medieval sermon, also called the "thematic" sermon, from the *thema,* the Scriptural verse which opens the sermon and upon which, according to John of Wales's *De arte praedicatoria,* "the entire edifice of the sermon is built."[11] In the typical medieval and, thus, Bernardinian sermon, the "theme" is announced and, having invoked divine assistance (the *prothema,* in Bernardino usually a "Hail Mary"), the preacher, in the *corpus sermonis,* divides and subdivides the verse into smaller propositions of a theological, spiritual, or (as most often in Bernardino's case) moral or catechetical nature. Each of these is then meticulously explained and proven (the *dilatatio*) by multiple means of demonstration, usually involving linguistic analysis (definition and etymology), syllogistic or other forms of logical argumentation, *auctoritates concordantes,* and concrete examples drawn from nature and the everyday world of human affairs.

The initial metaproposition of the *thema* having been amply and methodically, if at times laboriously, dismantled and demonstrated, the preacher then brings his discourse to an end, this *conclusio* being a clear, neat summary of the various parts of the sermon. All along, the object of the preacher is to teach (hence, the use of explicit mnemonic devices), to delight (hence, the recourse to the theatrical and the narrative), and to persuade (hence, a major appeal to the emotions). This is not the place to illustrate how the Bernardinian sermon exemplifies each of these steps prescribed by the manuals. Our interest is Bernardino's *dilatatio,* wherein is revealed his characteristic approach to moral reasoning and persuasion.

In the past the thematic sermon was often called the "scholastic sermon." Although its origins are no longer believed to have been the university *disputatio,* this *forma praedicandi* nonetheless has much in common with the dialectic of the medieval schools, with its love for meticulous exactitude and finely articulated order. Whatever its precise origins, the thematic sermon and the body of theory that produced it were essentially a new creation in the world of the rhetorical arts.

From the time of ancient Rome until the thirteenth century, no real innovations had been seen or heard in Europe by way of oratorical theory. The fathers of the church, in supplying all other needs of the new institution, had not concerned themselves with matters of form and method of preaching. The two patristic texts most consulted by preachers, Augustine's *De doctrina christiana* and Gregory's *Cura pastoralis,* contained influential, enduring, but limited instruction on the preaching task.

This may seem curious to us but not to the medieval theoreticians: the orators of the church in its first centuries preached under the direct inspiration of the Holy Spirit and thus paid no attention to and had no need of "a method."[12] But the Spirit was "quenched" over time, so the widespread belief goes, and the preachers found themselves struggling for words. Hence, after 1200 years of virtual silence came the birth of the *ars praedicandi,* in which rhetoric once again is treated as a serious, elaborate, highly formal theoretical science. With individual extant treatises numbering more than 300, the *ars praedicand* is so distinct, so self-conscious, and so thorough a body of literature that it has rightly been called "the medieval analogue to the oratory of ancient pagan Rome."[13]

To be sure, the medieval sermon had its defects and proves an easy target of ridicule—for instance, in the allegorical acrobatics it performs with Scriptural texts, the naiveté and farfetchedness of its "true" stories of the supernatural, and its obsessive–compulsive hair-splitting dividing of texts. Bernardino himself frequently falls into such excess: to cite just one of many instances, in a 1425 sermon (D.92–107) analyzing "the *fifth* type of ignorance" (namely, to believe oneself in the state of grace when actually in mortal sin), he distinguishes and discourses on *three* separate "states" therein, each of which is then further segmented into respectively *seven* distinct "grades"!

Even so, as Gilson reminds us, "no period of history was more aware than the Middle Ages of the goals it pursued and of the means required for reaching them."[14] The medieval rhetoricians had clearly identified their task and accomplished that task with deliberateness, efficiency, and in harmony with the esthetic tastes and cognitive capacities of their audiences. The "scholastic" preaching method eventually was to collapse of its own dead weight, but in better days it succeeded in producing "an artistic, well-worked, grammatically and stylistically finished sermon . . . treating a definite subject with logical unity and to its fullest extent."[15] Even more importantly, it succeeded in "moving the will to do the good," the prime objective of the art of rhetoric. Even the Ciceronian humanist anticlerics of Renaissance Florence were obliged to acknowledge the effectiveness of this product, as effective as anything ever emanating from the forums of classical Rome.[16]

The principles of classical oratory were by no means unknown in the Middle Ages. The theoretical treatises and the orations of the ancients had survived and were studied as part of the *trivium*, the foundation of the medieval curriculum. Bernardino studied rhetoric both as an adolescent and again as an adult for four months in 1443 at the school of famed humanist educator, Guarino Veronese. Yet, despite these studies, Bernardino's oratory shows little trace of the classical. In a comparison, for example, of the Paduan *quaresimale* of 1423 with any of later sermon cycles (Florence 1424 and 1425, Siena 1425 and 1427)—that is, his production before and after the "sabbatical" at Guarino's school—the friar's preaching is unchanged in its fundamental (that is, medieval) character. The choice was deliberate: pagan oratory may have been appropriate for its task, in its world; Christianity, by contrast, represents a new dispensation, a new, fuller truth, and hence the adoption of a new rhetoric:

> And here you see how this warmth [of the word of the Lord] is life-giving, it gives life to both soul and body. And mind you, this is a different kind of teaching and knowledge, it is not the rhetoric of Tullio [*i.e., Cicero*]. This rhetoric of the word of God is better. What does it say? It says: "*Qui sitit veniat ad me et bibat.* Whoever is thirsty, come to me and drink." And in order that this word be spoken to the peoples, that the doctrine be preached, Isaiah tells us in chapter 58: "*Clama, ne cesses, quasi tuba exalta vocem tuam, et annuntia populo meo scelera eorum.* Call out and shout, and never silence your voice, and just like a trumpet . . . you too, shout high and low, and announce to my people their wickedness and their sins." (R.161)

Again, Bernardino is neither ignorant of nor opposed to classical models of eloquence. Classical eloquence, however, is for use in secular affairs—for instance, in the world of diplomacy—as is implied in Bernardino's complaint to the Sienese:

> And these young people who study Cicero do well in learning how to become public speakers, but I don't hear that there are many of them. It's a great shame for this city that there isn't a band of talented young men who would know how to put two decent sentences together when the need arises. (F.54)

We might observe that in such remarks Bernardino does not seem to distinguish form from content; it never occurs to him that perhaps the "pagan" form of classical rhetoric could possibly be adopted by Christians to transmit a Christian message and to teach Christian values with as much success as he was experiencing with his own "Christian" brand of rhetoric. Little did he know that within a couple of generations after his own death, precisely this transformation was to occur in sacred oratory, even among his fellow Franciscans, such as in the example of Friar Lorenzo Traversagni (1425–1505).[17] Though no opponent of reviving antiquity, Bernardino saw a moral abyss between the two civilizations, the "pagans" wallowed in a shadowy moral world of at best only partially glimpsed truth. With Christ, the new and full revelation of the clear, distinct, and salvation-gaining truth had finally been bestowed upon humanity. Repeating this *locus communis* of Christian apology in his comment on Psalm 119:130 ("The proclamation of your words illuminates and gives understanding to the simple"), Bernardino declares to the Sienese:

> It doesn't say the proclamation of Plato, or of Aristotle, or of Galen, or of Hippocrates, or of many other philosophers—not that I am condemning this either, not at all—however, I do not want to praise the latter as much as one should do of the former. Just as one can draw water either through a channel made of hard, clean stone or through one of soft clay which, unlike the first, will cause the water to become muddy, I am saying that there are some teachings which speak of the health of the soul and those which speak of the body. The latter speak of the earthly goods, the former speak of the spiritual, and here you can see why the *eloquia Domini,* the proclamations of the Lord, are better than any other kind of speech. (R.153–154)

Unlike the Christians, who believed their Scripture to be of divine dictation and hence the repository of absolute moral proof, the "pagans" had no sacred text they could use apodictically in their moral arguments. Hence, as James Murphy reminds us, all the classical rhetorician–moralist could, in effect, hope to achieve in his own moral reasoning and persuasion were probabilities: "No ancient pagan rhetorician ever conceived of any single mode of proof as being conclusive or binding."[18]

Instead, the Christian preacher–moralist could quote Scripture with confidence, knowing that its veracity was guaranteed by the all-knowing, all-powerful, wise, truthful God. (Of course, the human task was to penetrate the at times inscrutable, allegorical surface of the text, but Bernardino was confident that the *dottori* had mastered this challenge for all of Christian posterity.) To think that Scripture was anything less than a reliable, apodictic moral authority would, therefore, be to suggest that God is inadequate, deceitful, and unloving. This Bernardino openly asserts in the last of his already-cited *firmitates fidei,* entitled "That God would appear callous and unjust, if the Christian faith were not true":

> The . . . last proof of the truth of the Christian faith is the justice and fidelity of divine providence. If our Lord Jesus Christ had been in error, then . . . the providence of God would be callous

> and unfair since, through His own example, He would have given and would have permitted to be given the highest occasion of absolute error. Moreover, in no way is it believable that God has not provided humankind with a trustworthy way to salvation. . . . (OOQ.I.19)

The certainty of the Scriptures, then, provides the foundation for a moral logic in preaching that begins with absolute, unchanging premises.

Bernardino, popular preacher

By the adjective "popular," I mean to say that Bernardino's preaching was primarily intended not for small, restricted audiences of fellow preachers, theologians, and other university masters but for the general marketplace public of minimally lettered laypeople. Since his words were most likely to fall upon the ears of the rudimentarily catechized and the philosophically unsophisticated, one of Bernardino's foremost concerns was simply to be understood. This meant, of course, tailoring his subject matter and vocabulary to the level of his audience's understanding. With respect to the needs of the audience and the responsibilities of the preacher, Bernardino was an entirely self-conscious professional. He makes this abundantly clear in his third sermon to the Sienese populace in 1427 entitled "This sermon treats of the roles of the preacher and his listeners," where he underscores comprehensibility and utility as among the primary qualities of a good sermon.

Aiming for these qualities, Bernardino is obliged to reduce the complexity of issues and cases to a linguistic and conceptual form that can be more readily absorbed by his listeners. Though we should not exaggerate the extent of this process of reduction and simplification (many of his sermons are still remarkably intricate in the treatment of their respective subjects), it is, nonetheless, a constant reality of his popular preaching. For example, Bernardino shows himself ever eager to furnish his audience with clear, concrete rules that they can take home with them and apply directly to the moral decisions of their everyday lives. Thus, expressions such as "And take this as a general rule" (A.295) abound in the friar's vernacular sermons (those, unlike the Latin works, actually preached to the people), as Bernardino reduces yet another whole complicated moral discourse to a single, easy-to-remember sentence.

The friar does, on occasion, exhort his audience to seek out and shop around for a good, holy, and, above all, wise confessor ("even if you have to travel many miles to find one") with whom to discuss the specifics of one's moral actions (OOQ.I.174, A.44). However, Bernardino was well aware that confessors of this type were sadly and scandalously few and far between; this he bluntly laments on several occasions (for example, OOQ.I.171; IV.10, OOH.III.207b). Hence, his own effort to fill the void with as precise and tangible a form of moral instruction as possible, even if this meant leaving audiences with the impression that moral decision making was simply a technique of applying general rules to particular cases. Therefore, it may be that what has been said of the state of moral theology of a much later period (that is, after the rise of high casuistry) was true even in the early fifteenth century:

> [I]n some historical periods formal casuistry was replaced by more structured, abbreviated expressions of moral reasoning. Dependency on the wise personnel evolved into a dependency on formulated methods and rules. On those occasions, a shortage of teachers led to the formulation of such rules to guide the judgments of the less skilled and the less experienced.[19]

Bernardino, Franciscan preacher

Bernardino is thoroughly a product and perhaps the greatest exemplar of the Franciscan preaching tradition. "[O]ur apostolic life," Bernardino reminds his listeners, quoting chapter nine of the *Regula bullata,* "we have taken under the seraphic Francis who commands us in his Rule among other things: 'preach to the people of vice and virtue and of reward and punishment' and I have promised to observe it" (B.1). The "Franciscanism" of Bernardino's sermons colors and conditions his approach to moral reasoning and persuasion in two ways.

First, Franciscan preaching was meant to be, above all, penitential. Much of the friars' preaching, Bernardino's included, occurred during Lent and was intended to be propaedeutic to the annual reception of the sacrament of confession required of the faithful at Eastertime. Though Francis commands the preacher to speak of *both* virtue *and* vice, of *both* reward *and* punishment, in reality, it was the latter terms of those two couplets that received far more attention, at least in the sermonizing of Bernardino. Bernardino sees sin literally everywhere, with the possibility of damnation due to unrecognized or unconfessed mortal sins lurking in all corners. "Our entire life is a spider's web of sins spun by the devil," he warns his listeners in 1424, while elsewhere reminding them that ignorance of the law does not excuse a sinner before God and that omitting to confess even one sin invalidates the entire sacrament (A.134, OOQ.I.178, 206). Hence, we are left with the distressing impression that hardly a day goes by in which one has not committed grave sin. ("You have sent us all to damnation," Florentine humanist Giannozzo Manetti protested to Bernardino after one of his sermons.)[20] The task of moral discernment seems rarely that of deciding whether or not sin was committed; rather, it is usually that of judging the degree of its culpability and identifying the means for reparation.

A second feature of Franciscan popular oratory is its thorough predilection for the emotional and the theatrical. From Francis onward, Franciscan piety was, above all, affective. Accordingly, the Friars Minor were intent on moving people to repentance and conversion as much (if not more) by a "deliberate and skillful appeal to crude emotion"[21] than by any of the more subtle tools and techniques of rational persuasion. This is, indeed, the hallmark of the "pervasive and durable 'Franciscan' style" which transformed European Catholicism in the late Middle Ages. Through the written or spoken word, theater, and the plastic arts, it permeated Europe with, for example, those "large and gripping pathetic images, painted with the panchromatic variety of rouged bruises and carmined blood."[22]

No friend of the clergy, even humanist Poggio Bracciolini admitted (in his antimendicant treatise, *De avaritia*): "In one thing [Bernardino] greatly excels: by persuading and exciting the emotions, he manipulates the people and leads them wherever he desires, moving them to tears and, when the subject matter allows it, to laughter."[23] The realm of the affective plays as important a role as the cognitive in the friar's moral persuasion. Persuading his audience of the evil of a particular act or simply to hate sin and love virtue, Bernardino never fails to paint for them an appropriately emotion-laden, heart-touching picture or fantasy-stirring story. Bernardino's Good Friday sermons on the Passion of Christ are a good example of the friar's Franciscan–affective approach to moral persuasion, the underlying message of such sermons being "Look how much your sins have caused this innocent victim to suffer!"

Another excellent example are the friar's vernacular sermons (the *prediche volgari*) on usury, transcribed during their live performance by various tachygraphers. There, before his audience of merchants, housewives, and youth, Bernardino devotes most of his energy to evoking horror-inspiring images of the restless, tortured life; the gruesome, painful death; and the eternal punishment of the usurer.

This is not so in the friar's so-called *sermones latini* on the same topic, intended for a different audience. In these formal Latin treatises composed as reference works for fellow preachers, most of the friar's treatment of usury consists of explanations of the rational whys and wherefores of that sin as contained in Scripture and canon law. On the opposite side of the emotional spectrum are examples of Bernardino's appeal to a more positive, uplifting affect, such as in his Latin work, *De gloria Paradisi* (OOQ.2.309ff), where he delights and encourages his audience with visions of heavenly bliss. But such moments are rare.

MORAL ARGUMENTATION: "RATIO, AUCTORITAS, EXEMPLUM"

Since much of his preaching is concerned with moral instruction and persuasion, Bernardino has the task of proving to his audience the validity of the moral precept he has announced and persuading them to behave according to its dictates. How does he go about this task? The answer, in most cases, is a formulaic appeal to "ratio–auctoritas–exemplum."[24] Introductory (or concluding) announcements such as "Twelve propositions we will touch upon this morning concerning these factions, and for each proposition we will see the evidence of reason, authority and example" (R.463) are frequent in Bernardino. Recognizing the importance of these three components, the scribe who recorded Bernardino's Siena 1427 preaching cycle notes that the topic in question is treated with *"bellissimi esempi"* or *"bellissime ragioni"* or *"bellissime autorità."*

To demonstrate the sound truth of his proposition, Bernardino first makes an appeal to reason, *ratio*. He carries his listeners through a rational explanation of the proposition's meaning and implications, employing whatever tools and forms of logic seem most appropriate to him at the moment. It is impossible to summarize or illustrate all of the various ways the friar goes about this step; the important point here is his emphasis on rational analysis, logic, and, frequently, utilitarian common sense. One of his favorite techniques, however, is to engage one of his listeners in an imaginary dialogue, leading him or her through a step-by-step, question-and-answer process of logical demonstration. For instance, in arguing against those who say that the planetary influence abolishes our free will and hence moral responsibility, he says:

> But, you there, I want to debate this point with you. Answer me like a reasonable man. Do you believe in the goodness of God? Yes, you say. Okay, now tell me: do you believe that these constellations have more power than your own free will? If you consent and do what they make you do, you're saying that you are forced to do so and couldn't resist. Okay, answer me then, who is worse? You who does the evil or the planet which forces you to do the evil? If you answer that the planet is more evil because it forces you to do evil, then I say to you that God is even more evil than either you or that planet because He created that planet that is forcing you to do evil. Since God is the first cause, He is the worst of all. Look at this again step by step: if you do evil, you're evil; if you say "I was forced to do it," then the one who is forcing you is even more evil, and the one who created it [the thing that is forcing you to do evil] has to be the worst of all. (R.123–4)

Shortly thereafter in the same sermon, we find Bernardino involved in this "conversation" on the absolute authority of Church teaching:

> Who do you think is superior, God or an angel? God is worth more. Who is superior, an angel or the soul? An angel. What is superior, the soul or the constellations? The soul. What is superior, the constellations or the body? The body. What is superior, reason or the senses? Reason. What is superior, the Holy Church with her doctors or your own opinion? The Holy Church. Well, then, stick to what the Holy Church says and believes and holds and forget about your own opinion. (R.125)

This ratiocinative step is followed by a procession of corroborating *dicta* from the preacher's *auctoritates,* from Scripture, or from *un dottore,* "a doctor." The latter term means not only an official "doctor" or father of the church but also a canonist or some other ecclesiastically recognized *magister.* With little apparent interest for original speculation, Bernardino sees his pedagogical task primarily as that of summarizing and transmitting to the people in understandable terms the teachings of the "doctors": "The doctors teach us [preachers] and we make a bouquet of them and pass it on to you" (D.296). Accordingly, Bernardino's sermons are crowded with quotations from Scripture and citations from the friar's numerous "doctoral" sources.

Bernardino places great importance on his use of "the doctors" in preaching: "Do you know why [I had so much success in Lombardy]?

Because I was constantly armed with the sayings of the doctors" (H.216). Though the *dottori* may disagree—but only in matters irrelevant to salvation—they are, nonetheless, the revered, Spirit-inspired, seemingly infallible source of truth, equal in authority to Scripture itself. In other words, *auctoritas locuta, causa finita,* the friar often appears to suggest.

Bernardino's "arming himself" with the *auctoritas* of the doctors was not only a gesture of fidelity to the prescribed method of the medieval *ars praedicandi,* but also an act of self-protection against the dreaded and at times fatal charge of heresy. Bernardino's was an age of enormous ecclesiastical upheaval and at times violent challenges to the doctrinal authority of the church; the memory of the Great Western Schism and the Hussite and other heretical uprisings was yet fresh in everyone's mind. In such a climate, orthodoxy was, consequently, an item of prime concern for the church and certainly no less for Bernardino, who was denounced as an "heresiarch" for his propagation of the "novel" cult of the Holy Name of Jesus. In 1426, the friar was even brought to trial in Rome for these charges, but successfully acquitted himself (with the help of John of Capistrano).[25] Radical in his zeal and piety, Bernardino was, understandably, no radical in his theology.

After rehearsing the pronouncements of the "authorities," the friar then arrives at the *exempla,* the "examples," the third and final step of the typical Bernardinian *dilatatio:* "Hey! Take this nice big example . . . Listen now to the example . . . Here's a great example for you." These are the friar's constant exhortations, as he prods his audience to pay close attention to the story he is about to relate. On this single element, the masterfully executed, vivid, entertaining *exempla* recounted in an agile, vivacious, Tuscan vernacular, a great deal of the friar's enduring reputation in fact lies. The word *exemplum* was a term taken in its widest sense to describe any narrative, long or short, used to illustrate a moral or catechetical precept. Of historical, legendary, or fantastic provenance, these narratives range in length from rapid sketches in four or five lines all the way to well-developed short stories covering one, two, or even three printed pages of sermon text. Modern audiences familiar with the didactic tales of Aesop or Phaedrus would readily recognize the basic plots of many of these preacher's *exempla,* since they often are the very same tales refit in medieval wardrobe. The *exemplum* played a most useful role within the economy of the thematic sermon since it both "translated" into concrete, familiar, vivid imagery the preacher's abstract notions and provided a refreshing pause from an often lengthy and perhaps monotonous discourse. With its direct roots in the New Testament parable, the *exemplum* was widely recognized throughout the Middle Ages for its value as a pedagogical tool. Therefore, for centuries it received widespread attention from the theorists and anthologizers responsible for the numerous *artes praedicandi.*

Endowed with a natural gift for story telling himself, Bernardino states that the preacher, in teaching his flock about "the lofty matters of the heavens and the stars and sacred theology," must make these abstract notions concrete and readily comprehensible; he must work

> to make [his audience] able to touch them with their hands, that is to say, to speak of them in such a fashion and with complete clarity for our understanding so that [those who hear] can almost touch them and stroke them. (C.263)

These anecdotes, fables, and vignettes are the means through which abstract concepts acquire an immediately intelligible—and pleasing—tangibility. Therefore, Bernardino concludes:

> You should not criticize those speakers [*dicitori*] who, in order to show you the lofty things that exist above us, do so by means of big, palpable examples because that is what the art of good clear speaking is about. Jesus, font of eloquence, always used parables and concrete things in order to explain the kingdom of heaven; that is to say, through these human things we come to understand clearly divine things. (C.263–264)

Bernardino may himself have been one of those "speakers" whom he has just defended, so often does he feel the need to justify his use of such material:

> These big examples are captured more easily by the mind than rational explanations or the other things. Jesus Christ himself spoke through the analogies of examples. . . . Since there are a lot of people here today, I will give you examples so clear that I will be understood and my talk will be useful to all of you. (A.371, G.327)

Clear, useful, and entertaining, Bernardino's *exempla* have indeed proven to be the element of most enduring interest in all of his oratory.

CASUS CONSCIENTIAE, DUBIA, AND QUAESTIONES

The recourse to concrete circumstance and lived experience that we find in both the moral anecdote of medieval preaching and the paradigmatic case of high casuistry might tempt us to see in the former a precursor of the latter. The two phenomena, instead, are quite dissimilar. To repeat, unlike the paradigmatic case, the *exemplum,* a parable illustrating a single, often simplistic point in attention-getting fashion, was yet another element in the uncomplicated and undoubting geometry of the preacher's moral reasoning and persuasion. Bernardino never offers an analysis of the specific content of his didactic tales—fine distinction, nuance, and complexity are alien to the world of the *exempla*—nor does he ever apply them as a tool for the resolution of other, perhaps perplexing, moral cases.

Truly perplexing cases, however, are rare in the sermons of this popular preacher. To be sure, the friar is constantly raising for analysis and discussion *casus conscientiae, dubia,* and *quaestiones,* which do sufficient justice to the intricacy of detail and diversity of circumstances in the moral reality. (Though Bernardino uses three separate terms for discussing these concrete examples—*casus, dubia,* and *quaestiones*—in reality, by and large they seem to refer to the same circumstance: a specific moral situation drawn from "real life" in which it is not immediately clear how the general precept just enunciated is applicable.) Yet, at least in the eyes of the friar, the great majority of these cases are in fact easily resolvable. Bernardino's standard procedure is first to present and "prove," in the threefold fashion described, whatever general moral precept he has chosen for his sermon's focus and then to raise for discussion one or more cases or queries involving concrete situations in which the relevance or application of the just-announced general rule is not immediately obvious. (In one sermon on restitution to the Florentines in 1424, Bernardino describes and resolves in summary fashion twenty-seven specific cases!)

Doubts and queries usually find ready solution in some further rational explanation and distinction making or, more typically (in those cases of doctoral unanimity), in the ecclesiastical "doctors" who come to the rescue with what Bernardino communicates as a made-to-order, infallible opinion. However, every so often Bernardino is obliged to admit that the "doctors" are in disagreement over a particular case or question. How, then, is one to decide in such a situation? Bernardino, first of all, has reassured us that disagreement among the "doctors" only concerns issues that are not strictly necessary for salvation (OOQ.I.35); hence, our souls are not placed in jeopardy by the church's lack of a clear teaching on these matters.

For instance, consider the case of a usurer who at his death leaves an estate of ten thousand ill-gotten florins. Three thousand of these florins remain after restitution has been made to all identifiable parties; to whom does this sum of money belong? "There are various opinions among the doctors," the friar responds. Bernardino goes on to dutifully report these conflicting opinions: some say the bishop should get the money, others would give it to the dead man's confessor, and still others believe it is the property of his heirs. He then ends with his own advice: give the money to the bishop as the person of greatest "dignity of office and authority" (A.347–349).

On certain occasions, however, the friar reports the conflicting judgments of the "doctors" but surprises us by not giving his own opinion, and thus leaving the question unresolved. It is of interest to note that these (rare) unresolved cases are all found not in Bernardino's vernacular sermons (copied down "live" as they were preached to the people) but rather in his so-called *sermones latini.* The latter "sermons," to repeat, are doctrinal treatises of "preachable" material composed by the friar himself as reference manuals for his colleagues in the preaching trade, not for the general public. One instance of an unresolved case arises in his Latin treatise, *"De horrendo peccato contra naturam,"* and concerns sodomy or masturbation as grounds for separation:

> *Quaestio.* But can a wife dismiss her husband because of this crime?—The *Gloss* responds, XXXII, quest. 7, in the canon *Omnes* on the word "sodomite," saying: "It seems that a husband can be dismissed because of sodomitic activity; XXXII, quest. 7, *Adulterii;* there it is said that that crime is greater than adultery.—Likewise: What do you say if he pollutes his own wife outside of the cloister of shame, or if he pollutes himself with his own hand? Can he be dismissed because of this? It seems so because the word adultery refers to all illicit intercourse and all illicit use of the members, as per XXXII, quest. 4, *Meretrices,* and the following canon, which Laurentius concedes. I hardly believe that a husband can be dismissed because of any of these [crimes], as per XXXV, quest. 3, *Ordinaria."* End of quote from the *Gloss.* The first opinion is held by Huguccio and Raymundus in his *Summa* under the article concerning the number of witnesses. Innocentius is opposed, Extra, *De divortiis,* chap. 1.[26]

To cite just one further example: the friar's treatment of the question, "May interest be given to or exacted from one's enemies?" After a dutiful review of the opinions, pro and con, he offers no final resolution (OOQ.IV.364–366).

As far as I can tell, in the vernacular sermons Bernardino will leave no moral question hanging in suspense, whereas in the "privacy" of his Latin treatises destined only for the eyes of other clerical professionals, he is able to be somewhat more honest in admitting limits to the church's ability to adjudicate moral cases. Similarly, in his *sermoni latini*, Bernardino will bring forth cases which he then cautions his reader not to discuss in public, out of fear, one assumes, of misinterpretation, scandal, or confusion among "weak" Christians. For instance, he concludes his discussion of an exception to the rule regarding the obligation of restitution with the remark: "But such a case is not to be preached to the peoples but it is often necessary in giving advice, and is to be put into practice with much discretion" (OOQ.I.493).

In yet another Latin treatise, Bernardino addresses the question of what to do when faced with disagreement among the moral experts on a given matter. As he so often does in his sermons, Bernardino simply takes his answer *verbatim* from one of the scholastic masters, Henry of Ghent. The specific question Bernardino raises is: Is it a mortal sin to follow the more doubtful of the opinions in a question on which the doctors are in disagreement? A long quote from Henry's *Quolibeta* (V, q. 33) offers the following advice:

> . . . First, the status of the doctors must be taken into consideration, that is to say, how they reveal themselves in their determinations, whether they are truthful or false, or doubtful, which more, which less, of what kind of life they are, if they love the truth in deed or word, how learned they are on the matters which they are determining, or what kind of advice they gave to their friends or relatives in a similar case. Secondly, one must look at the foundations of their argument and the reasoning they give in arriving at their conclusions in such a case, [one must also consider] whose authorities are more persuasive and more expressive. (OOQ.IV.355–356)

Henry's advice goes on to distinguish, with respect to the person making the decision, between the learned and the unlearned (*literati* and *simplices*). The former type of person has the intellectual resources to carry out the just described process of rational and spiritual discernment and hence sins mortally (*mortaliter peccat*) if he rejects the opinion of the "doctor" who is the more intelligent, more thorough, more consistent, more virtuous, and hence more persuasive. The *simplices,* instead, should listen to the advice of others (presumably, wise, holy counselors) in choosing their part but, in any case, would not incur mortal sin, even if what they ended up doing were in itself mortally sinful. Their "simplicity" excuses them, "unless it is such a matter that concerns natural law or the rule of faith which they are obliged to know since in such cases 'simplicity' or ignorance which is not invincible does not excuse them" (OOQ.IV.356).

Bernardino never does answer the original question which occasioned the above advice (i.e., can one follow a more doubtful opinion). He (and Henry) also neglects to inform his audience about what is to be done when the process of discernment therein described fails in the end to shed further clarity upon the doubtful situation and the moral agent is "back to square one." The answer is, instead, supplied by another of the friar's Latin treatises boldly entitled, "With manifest reasons it is demonstrated that no one can be saved outside the one Catholic faith; and why there will be so great a multitude of the damned and so small a number of the saved." Chapter three of this "sermon" (largely taken from William of Auvergne's *De legibus*) in turn bears a title that summarizes in one sentence Bernardino's advice to the doubtful: "That when a person in great doubt and human reason does not make clear what is to be chosen, he must implore divine assistance" (OOQ.III.383). Quoting Scripture and Augustine, Bernardino (through William) assures his reader that God will never fail to supply the necessary illumination to all those who beseech him with "faithful and devout entreaty" "as long," however, "as negligence or some other manifest or hidden sin does not place an obstacle in the way." By "negligence," Bernardino means "negligence in seeking the truth;" in other words, one still has to do much homework in informing one's conscience. This requires

> not being negligent in foresight, in avoiding dangers and errors, in being attentive, in investigating the truth for oneself or in seeking it from others; and in devout entreaty, in imploring the assistance of God. (OOQ.III.384)

In certain situations of complete doubt, the human mind cannot be expected to have the answers: "Everything which is then to be done is in the hands of God . . . it is the responsibility of God alone to protect humankind nor is there left to humanity any other resource than to implore divine assistance" (OOQ.III.384). Bernardino declares that incessant prayer is "an excellent remedy when many and great doctors are found to be in opposition to each other in their opinions" even, he specifies, in such large public moral issues as the possibly usurious-forced, interest-bearing loans imposed on its citizens by the governments of Venice, Genoa, and Florence to finance the public debt.[27] Yet, in later discussing these loans, the friar simply relies on the usual scholastic procedure of *ratio–auctoritas–exemplum*, prefacing and concluding his analysis with a plea for divine correction should his judgments in so controverted a moral issue prove erroneous (OOQ.IV.307, 346).

Bernardino addresses the issue of the discernment of spirits several times in his preaching and, in fact, his Latin treatise on the topic, *De inspirationibus*, represents the most thorough, the most methodical treatment of the subject—complete with twelve specific rules of conduct—to appear in the church in any of the centuries before Ignatius of Loyola. The majority of the friar's rules are based upon a pleasure/pain criterion and would be difficult, in truth, to apply to moral cases. That is to say, Bernardino classifies "inspirations" according to those whose execution will bring pain, those which will bring pleasure, and those which will bring a combination of both. (For instance, Rule number five: *"The 'inspiration' must be accepted, if, in its execution, without mortal sin, the natural pleasure is less than the spiritual pleasure,"* [OOQ.VI.258].) However, his final rule is indeed pertinent: *"In doubtful and arduous actions, before proceeding, one must investigate as to the certainty of the will of God"* (OOQ.VI.288). For this, Bernardino directs the reader to seek the advice of worthy, "illuminated" spiritual superiors; to pray assiduously; and, finally, to simply let pass a certain amount of time. The third element (simply to wait patiently and let "time tell") is new and surprising, given the friar's usual commerce in quick, well-defined, close-ended solutions:

> Time indeed achieves many things which cannot be achieved either through the will or the industry or the power of men. Time calms the agitated sea, brings fruit to ripeness; the animals, the fish, the birds receive through it their growth. On occasion, God desires to illuminate us as to a choice of action, not through an angel or in some other way, but through the means of time, most especially if we persevere in prayer; time changes and along with it, many things change as well, and in all things it is God who

> sheds light on one's deliberations and doubts. . . . (OOQ.VI.290, cfr. R.819–820)

Elsewhere, in a vernacular sermon, "What course of action the soul must take when it is in doubt and does not know what to do," Bernardino again offers specific "remedies" for situations of doubt. He here reminds us once more to "obtain the advice of a person of good conscience, learning, and experience." But adds: "First, turn to God [in prayer], then go to one who is of good conscience" (C.165). The friar specifically recommends the power of the Holy Name of Jesus. Nothing is as powerful as the name of Jesus, the friar teaches, and accordingly, in cases of moral doubt:

> The first remedy is to stay close to the name of Jesus. If you have firm faith in him, he will give you the light so that you will no longer fear the dark of night and you will come to know what is the better road to take. (C.164)

Another remedy is to read Holy Scripture and other sacred writings. Bernardino says one should "delight oneself" (*dilettarti*) in this literature, that is, to immerse oneself in it and love it thoroughly. "Holy Scripture," he adds, "solidifies the mind more than reason; reason is more refined and subtle but is also more dangerous." However, praying is still "more perfect" than reading, as long as it is done "with humility, fidelity, love, and perseverance" (C.164). The final remedy is "to strip oneself of the disordered emotions of this world. Wherever emotion reigns, good judgment can never prevail" (C.166).

Surprisingly, when we turn to the Siena 1427 version of Bernardino's same instruction on discernment of spirits (R.761–821), we find no mention of the need for external moral authority (i.e., a confessor or other spiritual director) in the formation of conscience. Read by themselves, the 1427 sermons (#37 and #38 of the cycle) would thus appear to concede a great deal of moral initiative and autonomy to the individual conscience. I believe, however, the omission is purely an oversight on the friar's part, an understandable one in this case since in the 1427 sermons Bernardino seems largely (though not exclusively) concerned with decisions about fasting, pilgrimage, and other penitential and devotional practices. Given the age in which he wrote and given what he elsewhere says in his other (pre- and post-1427) sermons on discernment and confession, it is inconceivable that the granting of real moral autonomy to the laity was the friar's intention.

Lest more moral–doctrinal turmoil, more heresy, and more schism be inflicted upon the still-troubled, post-Avignon, and postschism church (see the prologue to *De inspirationibus*), Bernardino, I am convinced, would require that all moral decisions born of private prayer and discernment be measured against official church teaching through the mediation of a wise, holy confessor. This wise, holy confessor, in turn, could make use of the same Bernardinian rules and "remedies" in his own deliberations on the matter in question. "Discernment" rule number eight of the twelve given in *De inspirationibus,* in fact, reminds us that an *inspiratio* can be accepted only if "the soul is illuminated and strengthened in the truths of faith and mores" (OOQ.VI.271). All our beliefs and all our actions, the friar explains in his commentary upon this rule, must conform to the authentic teaching of the church. Furthermore, we have already heard Bernardino's blunt imperative: "Stick to what the holy church says . . . and forget about your own opinion" (R.125). The friar certainly allows for some field of moral autonomy to the lay Catholic but its dimensions, in the end, prove miniscule indeed. There may have been many forerunners of the Protestant Reformation in the fifteenth century but, given his usual deep suspicion of individual (especially lay) initiative, Bernardino was decidedly not among their number.

BERNARDINO AND THE MORAL ACT: A LACK OF METHOD

In the midst of his discussion of various and specific sins; of conscience; and of the form, function, and fruits of confession, Bernardino incidentally enunciates general principles by which one can evaluate morally any given human act. However, Bernardino—a popular eclectic teacher of the masses, not a careful systematic theologian—never sat down to compose a formal, theoretical treatise on the moral act. Consequently, when we juxtapose these disparate statements of moral principle, we find, in reality, serious contradictions and ambiguity among them, rendering them incapable of being blended into one coherent system. The two issues which Bernardino examines (and in doing so reveals his own lack of moral method) are, first, whether greater priority belongs to the intention or to the acts "in themselves vicious" and, second, whether evil can be done for good.

To begin with, Bernardino states categorically at least five times (OOQ.I.382, 433; OOQ.IV.270,343,433) that "Intention judges all human actions," repeating the common Latin proverb, "*Quidquid agant homines, intentio iudicat omnes.*" As a corollary to this, the friar even states that if you engage in an act which you firmly though erroneously believe to be a mortal sin, then it indeed becomes a mortal sin in your case (F.19). Yet, at the beginning of one of his antiusury sermons, the element of intention is completely ignored and certain acts are declared "vicious in themselves." He therefore announces as another general precept: "No condition or circumstance can excuse an act vicious in itself" (*actus ex natura sua vitiosus*, OOQ.IV.266). It would be important to know how Bernardino defines the "nature" of the acts in question (i.e., is the element of intention already incorporated into it?) but such further definition is never given.

Bernardino does qualify this precept by conceding that the evil, the *vitiositas*, of some acts can at times be removed. In the two examples he gives, however, it is only the command of God which removes the evil, as when in *Exodus* the enslaved Hebrews are permitted by God to steal from the Egyptians. But the important point here is that the friar does accept the category of "acts vicious in themselves." As a matter of fact, Bernardino seems to have an extensive list of these acts. Thus, while the circumstances of the act ("*quis, quibus, quid, quantum, quomodo, quare, quando*") are relevant to its moral evaluation, they can only aggravate moral culpability for these acts, and never diminish or eliminate it.[28] Nowhere, in fact, does the friar ever speak of circumstances as extenuating factors in the moral landscape.

Similar ambiguity and inconsistency appear in Bernardino's remarks on the question of using evil in order to do good. In two cases of conscience raised in his Latin treatises—"should a wife consent to unnatural intercourse with her husband in order to keep him from fornication with another woman?" (OOQ.I.213) and "is a man obliged to make temporal restitution even if that will expose him to some evident danger?" (OOQ.I.492)—the friar reminds his audience with the words of St. Paul (Romans 3:8) of the general precept that "evil must never be done in order to bring about the good." (In the second case, he adds "even less should good be done that will bring about evil.") Yet, in another passage from a second Latin treatise also on the topic of restitution, he teaches the principle of "using evil for the sake of the good" ("*bene uti malo*"). The paragraph in question reads:

> For, as Augustine [*De peccat. meritis et remiss.*, I, c.29, n. 57] bears witness, it is one thing to use evil for the sake of the good, and another to use the good for the sake of evil. And so, to use evil for the sake of the good is not a sin, but a good, since even God does this when he permits evil things to be committed and thereby

> brings forth the good of justice; but to use the good for the sake of evil is a sin. Therefore, to use the evil of usury for the sake of the good is a good; for a man uses that evil for the sake of the good when he seeks a loan out of need and is not able to obtain one without interest, [and goes ahead and accepts the loan at interest], not because he is in favor of that vice but only because he was forced to do so by his need. (OOQ.I.428)

Elsewhere, again in a Latin treatise and again with respect to usury, he re-states the same precept, quoting another source:

> . . . it is to be noted that, according to master Gerard of Siena of the Order of Hermits of St. Augustine, who, in turn, is quoting Johannes Andrea, in his *Mercurialibus,* in the rule *Peccatum,* "that evil may be permitted for two reasons: first for the good that may thereby come forth; secondly, for the greater evil that thereby may be avoided. In order to avoid a greater evil, evil is permitted in three ways: in order to avoid a spiritual evil in one's soul which is the greater evil, by permitting a corporal evil in one's body, which is the lesser evil; secondly, in order to avoid a greater spiritual evil by permitting a lesser spiritual evil, just as a lesser sin is often permitted in order to avoid a greater one; thirdly, in order to avoid a greater corporal evil by permitting another corporal evil which is lesser. (OOQ.IV.258–259)

Thus, the friar contradicts himself on the important question of whether one may use evil to effect the good; on two occasions he flatly rejects the possibility, while twice elsewhere he indeed allows for it under certain conditions. To conclude, therefore, a thorough, intellectually coherent, practical guide to the solution of moral cases is not to be extracted from the sermons of Bernardino.

CONCLUSION: BERNARDINO AND MORAL THEOLOGY TODAY

The popular preaching of Bernardino and of the countless other itinerant friars of the same stamp before and after him represents a significant chapter in the history of moral theology. But if his oratory does not offer a reliable, coherent guide to moral theology and is not an anticipation of the taxonomic moral reasoning of high casuistry, is there anything of enduring positive value in his work that can help us identify more effective approaches to moral reasoning and persuasion?

To begin with, the very fact of contradiction, inconsistency, ambiguity, and irresolution in the writings of the friar (by any reckoning, a person of above-average intelligence and methodical diligence) is a further humbling reminder to us that the complex realm of moral theology excludes the possibility of an infallible, all-encompassing map or black-and-white navigational chart. Despite Bernardino's claims to the contrary (in his public sermons to the people, that is), the "doctors" have not been able to provide ready-made resolutions to all possible moral issues and dilemmas—even significant ones such as that of usury—and certainly few that have proven of universal and enduring validity.

We have also pointed out a certain discrepancy between Bernardino's moral teaching of his public sermons and that of his "private" Latin treatises, the latter being more honest in its appraisal of the church's ability to provide answers for moral dilemmas. This he could not openly admit to the people in order to protect them, one supposes, from the shock and insecurity of realizing that in a frightening, perplexing, complex world the church did not have all the answers. Inevitably, those complexities broke forth in the casuistry of the next century.

Despite Bernardino's preoccupation with the preemptive moral *dicta* of ecclesiastical authority, in truth, the friar spends at least an equal amount of time forming the moral, spiritual *imagination* and appealing to the *affect* of his listeners. To repeat, Bernardino's Franciscan—and Mediterranean—piety is, above all, affective; in turn, affective piety is, above all, imagination-centered. Bernardino's constant working on the heart and the "right side of the brain" of his audience is everywhere evident: he does this through his expertly dramatic and vividly emotional narrative, the *exemplum;* through the many recreations (in intense emotional tones and glowing sensorial detail) of scenes from the lives of Jesus, Mary, and various saints and sinners; and through numerous other disparate forms which this unflagging appeal to the nonrational and nonconceptual took in the work of Bernardino which time and space do not here permit us to illustrate. Prominent among these, however, is his dissemination of devotion to the Name of Jesus through a novel, eye-catching artistic representation, the sunburst/IHS tablet that soon began appearing on the facades of public and private buildings all over Europe.

Bernardino, I chance to say, would have little trouble agreeing with the fundamental insight of the recent works of Philip Keane and William Spohn. Keane and Spohn remind us that the formation of truly

Christian value systems and, thus, the execution of truly Christian moral decisions are at least as much dependent upon the working of the imagination and the affect as they are on the precise, tangible weights and measures of legal "scientific" principles. "To the extent that it is an art, moral theology stands to be enriched by a stress on imaginative creativity," Keane has emphasized. Similarly, Spohn points out that moral "[d]iscernment focuses on emotions because they are the origins of action and its key guide."[29] Abstract and theoretical principles are necessarily limited in what they can bring to the "art" of moral theology. Even Bernardino came face-to-face with these limitations on a number of occasions in his moral discernment and had to counsel prayer and patient waiting as the final answer to certain doubts and dilemmas. But his constantly invoked exempla, those moral didactic tales drawn from "real life" on which so much of his fame first rested and still rests, are implicit acknowledgments of the fact that a moral discourse that is not fully grounded and realistically related to the actual, concrete, lived experience of men and women will never be victorious in its goal of persuading souls to recognize and choose the good.

NOTES

1. Trans. by D.W. Robertson, Jr. (New York: Library of Liberal Arts, 1959), 136.

2. All citations from Bernardino's sermons and treatises are to the following editions with their respective abbreviations:

OOH *Opera omnia.* 3 vols. Ed. J. De la Haye. Venice: Poletti, 1745.
OOQ *Opera omnia,* 9 vols. Florence: Quaracchi, 1950-65.
A, B *Le prediche volgari (Firenze 1424),* 2 vols. Ed. C. Cannarozzi. Pistoia: Pacinotti, 1934.
C, D, E *Le prediche volgari (Firenze 1425),* 3 vols. Ed. C. Cannarozzi. Florence: Libreria Editrice Fiorentina 1940.
F, G *Le prediche volgari (Siena 1425),* 2 vols. Ed. C. Cannarozzi. Florence: Rinaldi, 1958.
R *Le prediche volgari sul Campo di Siena 1427,* 2 vols. Ed. C. Delcorno. Milano: Rusconi, 1989.

All translations from the Italian and Latin are mine.

3. Maffeo Vegio (Bernardino's contemporary and early biographer), quoted by Eugene F. Policelli, "Humanism in the Life and Vernacular Sermons of Bernardino of Siena." (Ph.D. diss., University of Connecticut, 1973), 142-143.

4. John O'Malley, *Praise and Blame in Renaissance Rome: Rhetoric, Doctrine and Reform in the Sacred Orators of the Papal Court, ca. 1450-1520.* (Durham, N. Carolina: Duke University Press, 1979), 4.

5. Albert Jonsen and Stephen Toulmin, *The Abuse of Casuistry: A History of Moral Reasoning* (Berkeley: University of California Press, 1988), 88.

6. David D'Avray, *The Preaching of the Friars: Sermons Diffused from Paris before 1300* (Oxford: Clarendon Press, 1985), 255.

7. See Ernesto Bellone, "S. Bernardino come *auctoritas* nelle opere del Beato Angelo da Chiavasso (1410 c.-1495)." *Atti del simposio internazionale cateriniano-bernardiniano (17-20 aprile 1980)*. Domenico Maffei and Paolo Nardi, eds. (Siena: Accademia Senese degli Intronati, 1982), 333-357.

8. *Abuse of Casuistry*, 342.

9. For the sources, form, and content of Bernardino's oratory, see my "The Vernacular Sermons of San Bernardino da Siena, O.F.M. (1380-1444): A Literary Analysis." Ph.D. diss., Harvard University, 1983.

10. This is not to say that traces of what can be called a humanist temperament cannot be found in Bernardino's work. See my "The Humanists, the Pagan Classics and S. Bernardino da Siena." *Laurentianum* 27 (1986): 72-97.

11. Quoted by Etienne Gilson, "Michel Menot et la technique du sermon médiéval." *Les idées et les lettres*, 2nd ed. (Paris: Librairie Philosophique J. Vrin, 1955), 101, note 1.

12. Gilson, "Michel Menot," 108.

13. James J. Murphy, ed. *Three Medieval Rhetorical Arts* (Berkeley: University of California Press, 1971), 112.

14. Gilson, "Michel Menot,"95-96.

15. A. Zawart, *The History of Franciscan Preaching and of Franciscan Preachers (1209-1927): A Bio-biographical Study*. Franciscan Studies No. 7 (February 1928). (New York: Wagner, 1928), 280.

16. Cynthia L. Polecritti, "Preaching Peace in Renaissance Italy: San Bernardino of Siena and His Audience." (Ph.D. diss., University of California, Berkeley, 1988), 11.

17. See John W. O'Malley, "Form, Content and Influence of Works about Preaching before Trent: The Franciscan Contribution." In *I frati minori fra '400 e '500*, R. Rusconi ed. (Assisi: Università di Perugia, Centro di studi francescani, 1986).

18. James J. Murphy, *Rhetoric in the Middle Ages: A History of Rhetorical Theory from St. Augustine to the Renaissance*. (Berkeley: University of California Press, 1974), 276.

19. James F. Keenan, "The Function of the Principle of Double Effect," *Theological Studies* 54 (1993): 298.

20. Vespasiano da Bisticci, "Santo Bernardino da Massa," *Vite di uomini illustri del secolo XV* (Florence, 1938), 205.

21. Evelyn Underhill, *Jacopone da Todi* (London: Dent, 1919), 220.

22. J. V. Fleming, *An Introduction to the Franciscan Literature of the Middle Ages* (Chicago: Franciscan Herald Press, 1977), 186 -187.

23. Poggio Brocciolini, *De avaritia*, in *Opera omnia* (Turin: Bottega d'Erasmo, 1964), I:2.

24. See C. Delcorno, "L'*exemplum* nella predicazione di San Bernardino," in *Bernardino predicatore nella società del suo tempo*. (Todi: Centro di Studi sulla Spiritualità Medievale, 1976), 76-77.

25. See E. Longpré, "S. Bernardin de Sienne et le nom de Jésus." *Archivum Franciscanum Historicum* 28 (1935): 443-476; 29 (1936): 142-168, 443-477; 30 (1937): 170-192. It was at the Council of Basel that Bernardino was accused of being an "heresiarch:" see Gustav Beckmann, ed. "Tagebuchaufzeichnungen zur Geschichte des Basler Konzils 1431-1435 und 1438," in *Concilium Basiliense: Studien und Quellen Zur Geschichte des Concils Von Basel,* 8 vols. Ed. Gustav Beckman et. al. Nendeln/Liechtenstein: Kraus (1971 reprint of 1904 Basel edition), vol. 5, 149.

26. See the footnotes to OOQ.III.277 for a complete identification of the legal texts cited by Bernardino. Referring to this same passage, James Brundage states: "Either sodomy or masturbation, [Bernardino] declared, furnished more than adequate grounds for a divorce, a novel conclusion that several legal writers adopted" (*Law, Sex, and Christian Society in Medieval Europe* [Chicago: University of Chicago Press, 1987], 534). As we have just pointed out, the friar never really gives his opinion on the issue. Note that, in true scholastic manner, the *Gloss* begins (*Videtur quod,* "it would seem that") by appearing to accept the thesis which, however, in the end, it rejects (*Vix credo...,* "I hardly believe..."). Following the Gloss is Bernardino's summary statement about the lack of agreement among the "doctors" with respect to the issue and, on that note, Bernardino's *quaestio* comes to its inconclusive end. It can also be misleading to translate Bernardino's *dimettere* as "to divorce" without qualification, since today's meaning of that verb and its noun form differs from that of medieval canon law. Presumably Brundage is here using the word in its original sense, which he himself had defined on page 371 of his same work: "*Divortium* in canonistic language meant either a declaration of nullity (that a valid marriage had never existed) or else permission for a married couple to separate and establish independent households, but not to remarry."

27. Bernardino brings up the example of usury here because, in reality, despite his conviction that usury—i.e., any interest charged upon a loan—is a mortal sin and despite his many bold judgments on and condemnation of various kinds of interest-gaining business contracts and financial transactions, the friar was well aware through his study of the question that among his revered "doctors," as John Noonan tells us, "there is no agreement on the natural-law reasons why usury is a sin. Every juristic reason offered has been criticized by at least one prominent writer." (*The Scholastic Analysis of Usury* [Cambridge: Harvard University Press, 1957], 81. Cfr. OOQ.IV.307, 346.) (Hence, Bernardino contradicts himself: he has told us that no doctors disagree on issues pertaining to salvation, yet sees in the issue of usury ample occasion for falling into mortal sin and hence jeopardizing one's salvation.) Noonan also tells us that Bernardino has a place of distinction in the scholastic debate surrounding usury: at one point Bernardino is obliged to admit that "time" could be sold in the purchase of money. "Incredibly enough, St. Bernardine does not see that his fundamental admission here damages the whole usury doctrine. . . . There is, perhaps, nothing like Bernardino's blunder in the whole scholastic tradition of usury" (*Scholastic Analysis,* 76).

28. OOH.III.208a; OOQ.IV.36, 64, and 145; A.20-21; D.295; G.48.

29. P. S. Keane, *Christian Ethics and Imagination* (New York: Paulist Press, 1984), 46; W. C. Spohn, "Pragmatism and the Glory of God: An American Reading of Ignatian Discernment," in *The Labor of God: An Ignatian View of Church and Culture,* ed. W. J. O'Brien (Washington, D.C.: Georgetown University Press, 1991), 32.

The Casuistry of John Mair, Nominalist Professor of Paris

JAMES F. KEENAN, S.J.

Albert Jonsen and Stephen Toulmin's *The Abuse of Casuistry*[1] and John Mahoney's *The Making of Moral Theology*[2] invite us to reexamine the origins and merits of casuistry. Besides renewing in us an appreciation for casuistry, Jonsen and Toulmin, in particular, make the case that because the casuists were so authoritative, they were never self-conscious enough to articulate their method. Moreover, because Blaise Pascal's attacks on the Jesuits and their moral method were so swift, the casuists never had time to expound upon their craft. In light of that need, the authors of *The Abuse of Casuistry* provide the first methodological study of casuistry.

Rather than rehearse their contributions here, I examine a precursor of high casuistry, John Mair, and two cases concerning economics. In doing this, I am interested not in reconstructing sixteenth-century insights into usury, but rather in continuing what Jonsen and Toulmin began—that is, an examination of the casuistic method. To that end, after looking at Mair and the cases, I present ten fundamental presuppositions necessary for understanding casuistry's roots.

I add that though I am an advocate of casuistry, I believe the present enthusiasm for casuistry needs to be tempered. That belief becomes apparent, hopefully, in these pages. By the same token, some enthusiasm for this method ought to be sustained, precisely because the historical context out of which casuistry evolved is not unlike our present situation.

JOHN MAIR

The Scotsman John Mair (sometimes, John Major) (1467–1550) was arguably the most popular professor at Paris (1506–1518, 1521–22, 1526–31) on the eve of the Reformation. James Farge remarks that "His courses were probably the most popular in the University, as his name abounds in the certificates of study issued to arts graduates for these years. . . . Mair's teaching made him and the Collège de Montaigu the center of nominalist teaching in Paris for over a decade." His students included Antonio and Luis Coronel, David Cranston, George Buchanan, and Jacques Almain. His teaching influenced John Calvin and Ignatius of Loyola and his early companions, all of whom began studies at the Collège de Montaigu around 1528. Still, his popularity was not universal. Rabelais dismissed him as the author of *How to Make Puddings* and a student (George Buchanan) remarked that his teacher was "major in name only."[3]

Mair was embroiled in controversies. Erasmus's love for flourish met its nemesis in Mair's spartan influence on the Collège de Montaigu. The differences were not only stylistic preferences: Erasmus's appreciation for the fable and the Greek classics stood against Mair's love for the concrete and the contemporary. In Luther, too, Mair found a formidable challenger, whose sophisticated contentions merited profound refutation. Yet Mair was more than an ardent opponent of Erasmus and Luther and, therein, he was more complex. He was, for instance, first on the list of Paris theologians favoring Catherine of Aragon's case against her husband Henry VIII; that same year, however, he dedicated his commentary on Aristotle's *Ethics* to Cardinal Wolsey. Similarly, his constant critique of Thomism did not undo his close friendship with Peter Crockaert, the founder of the new Paris school of Thomists.[4] Finally, despite the fact that his most significant theological contribution was probably conciliarism, he remained within the Roman Church. In brief, his loyalties were often at odds with his thinking. One commentator writes, "Like many Catholic reformers before the Counter Reformation, Mair lacked the partisan qualities demanded by an age of controversy."[5] His biographer is briefer, "Mair was not a man of action."[6] Another concludes his study on Mair's economic thought by arguing that by being so faithful to the tradition, Mair's contribution to the field was limited.[7] According to many, then, the popular Scottish professor at Paris was a man unable to move.

That assessment is too facile. Another noted writer remarks, "It is the figure of John Mair which has attracted most attention on the part of Calvin scholars in recent decades."[8] The debate on Mair's influence on Calvin's thought is as interesting as the questions about the long-term effects of his political theory. Besides his extraordinarily strong conciliarist position,[9] Mair quite clearly shaped Buchanan's and, through him, Knox's political theory on the limits of papal and regal power.[10] Likewise, Francisco de Vitoria and Domingo de Soto cited Mair extensively in developing their theories on international law. On an ignominious note, in the famous debate between de las Casas and Sepulveda, the latter used Mair more extensively than anyone in legitimating the Spanish conquest of the people of the Americas.[11]

Where does one place Mair? John Durkan writes, "If we think of scholasticism as the old learning, then Mair is its last distinguished representative. . . . Yet Mair cannot be written off as a representative of the old learning, because circumstances forced him to gradually come to terms with the new situation in the world of learning."[12] The great historian Louis Vereecke proposes, "John Mair seems to have been the last scholastic."[13] Is Mair the end of the old order or the beginning of the new? A turn to his sexual ethics suggests the latter. John Noonan writes, "Between Alexander of Hales and Richard Middleton in the thirteenth century and some American theologians today, Mair is one of the rare English-speaking theologians to make a substantial contribution to the theological discussion of marriage." Mair argued that the legitimacy of intercourse is limited neither to the purpose of procreation nor to the avoidance of fornication and that pleasure in sexual activity is hardly sinful. Against Augustine and Huguccio, Mair invoked the "experience" of married couples.[14] Attributing greater authority to "experience" than to Augustine seems, then, to convey a modern more than a medieval bias.

My research suggests that Mair was a transitional figure and that his nominalism afforded him some footing in a world no longer comfortable with older systems. When his scholastic nominalism engaged new practical concerns, the result resembled what later became mature casuistry. Three further insights substantiate that claim. First, while the Thomists examined the theological tradition and the humanists the Greeks, Mair looked at the present and anticipated the future. In his *Commentary on the Fourth Book of the Sentences,* he asked, "Has not Amerigo Vespucci discovered lands unknown to Ptolemy, Pliny and other geographers up to the present? Why cannot the same happen in other spheres?"[15] The new questions raised by the maritime expeditions, for instance, prompted Mair to reexamine old ways of thinking. Second, as a result, the concept of authority, so significant in the scholastic method, was radically changed. Mair's new insights required, to some degree, a rejection, albeit nuanced, of the sanctioned views of Huguccio, Gregory the Great, Thomas Aquinas, and even Augustine. As the world expanded, local cultures and practices demanded newer directives, and tradition, failing to provide sufficient insight, had less influence. Moreover, in a world of competing authorities, Mair and his disciples offered no longer certain but only probable argument. Third, in this probable world, Mair employed the scholastic dialectic, but instead of using it to examine moral and immoral "objects" as the Thomists did, he drew analogies through a comparison of situations, experiences, and cases.

Though there has been recent research on Mair's speculative logic[16] and his theology[17] and on his specific teachings on politics,[18] ecclesiology,[19] sex,[20] and economics,[21] there remains outstanding a study of the moral logic he employed. That study is more urgent today when casuistry is being restored to ethical investigations. For instance, Jonsen and Toulmin describe members of a national committee on ethics unable to assume any particular ethical system but still capable of collectively resolving concrete dilemmas through casuistry.[22] Like Mair, they belong to a world where philosophical and religious beliefs are extraordinarily contentious, where newer authorities are emerging, where political and economic interests are forging a new world order, and where the academic world is again descending into particulars. In that type of world, casuistry emerged. Mair's world and his quest for a newer moral theory was not unlike our present situation.

THE CASES

To examine his search, I propose studying two specific cases treated by Mair. The first concerns maritime insurance. In 1237, Pope Gregory IX issued the decretal, *Naviganti vel eunti ad nundinas.* Of this decretal, John Noonan writes: "By any standard it is the most important single papal decree on the usury question with the exception of those containing the basic prohibition itself." The issue at hand concerned the first of the three sentence decretal: "One lending a certain quantity of money to one sailing or going to a fair, in order to receive something beyond the capital for this, that he takes upon himself the peril, is to be thought a usurer."[23] Rather than examine the historical importance of this decretal,[24] I consider Mair's treatment of it.

In 1530, a group of Spanish merchants living in Flanders asked the University of Paris to address the moral liceity of certain commercial practices.[25] One question concerned whether one who assumes the risk that another runs may receive payment for assuming that risk. John Mair responded, using the solution from his already published *Commentary on the Fourth Book of the Sentences* (1509).[26] There he made two distinctions. The first was a "contract based on location": if the merchandise arrives at the port of destination, the insurer receives his fee. Of this contract, Mair argued, no prudent person doubts its legitimacy. But the second held that if one is paid a fee he will pay the owner the worth of the cargo, if the cargo of the ship is lost at sea. This is maritime insurance, and Mair established its legitimacy through a series of analogies.

Mair noted that in the transport of goods there is always the general duty to assure the safety of the goods: the captain of a ship does this in maritime commerce and a coachman does it in landed transport. But, Mair asked, can the captain hire out this task, or should the captain reserve to himself the task of guaranteeing the cargo's safety? Mair responded that soldiers are licitly hired to board boats and to protect the cargo from several dangers. If then marines, the coast guard, and other military figures can be contracted and paid for providing security, why not the insurance agent? In presenting these introductory points, he employed the scholastic method, by presenting two common objections: the insurance is both useless and prohibited.

The first contends that, unlike the soldier or the captain, the insurer does not prevent possible loss of cargo; a sinking ship will sink whether insured or not. Mair responded by addressing not the state of the cargo, but the psychological state of the shipping merchant: his worries and sadness are allayed that at least if the cargo is lost, the worth is not. Moreover, by providing the insurance, the agent really enters into a partnership in which the worries and the worth of the cargo are equally born by agent and owner alike.

Highlighting the utility of this insurance, Mair turned next to answer the second objection, examining three sets of laws. First from the Scriptures, he noted the law to eat our bread from the sweat of our brow (Gen 3:19) and the injunction that we humans were born to work, the bird to fly (Job 5:7). Since the agent only underwrites the cargo, he fails to heed the Scriptures. Mair countered first that the agent assumes the merchant's worry and fear of loss and thus enters into a partnership. Then Mair added a theme that he repeated elsewhere. The Scotsman whose family came from simple estate mused on the children of wealthy families who do not work, but rather play and recreate with the amassed riches of their parents. Why are the Scriptures used against the agents instead of the wealthy?

Second, he looked at positive law and noted that the law has no injunctions against maritime insurance, but outlines, instead, conditions for when it would be fraudulent.

Third, he examined *Naviganti* to provide his final response on maritime insurance. He wrote, there, that the Roman Pontiff did not prohibit maritime insurance per se, but rather usury, which involves receiving a fee for a loan. The insurance agent does not receive a fee for a loan, but rather for his share in the partnership and for the service he provides, by underwriting the cargo and sharing in the anxiety. A usurious contract is different, then, from a contract of maritime insurance.

The second case concerns *cambium bursae*,[27] a practice that is little more than a lending exchange. Rather than define financing as usury (that is, as a fee for granting a loan), financiers and theologians sought a morally legitimate form of financing. Behind *cambium bursae* is the premise that one can loan another a certain sum and receive back something more than the sum. This difference or fee is not for the loan itself, but because, having made the loan, the lender loses a potential profit that could otherwise have been made. The fee for the loss of this potential profit (in Latin *lucrum cessans*) received some limited support in the late fifteenth century.[28] In the sixteenth century the interest in the concept grew; its proponents asked not whether a fee can be received for a singular loan, but whether an entire business or way of life can be instituted based upon the premise of *lucrum cessans*. This gave rise to the *cambium bursae*, the institutional expression of *lucrum cessans*.

This shift concretely concerned the merchant, however. *Lucrum cessans* simply asked whether occasionally a merchant could loan money and expect a fee in return. *Cambium bursae* asked whether a merchant could give up her or his affairs and take up money-lending as a way of life. In giving his answer, Mair treated several subjects.

As in the first case, this answer also appeared in 1509 when the first edition of his *Commentary on the Fourth Book of the Sentences* was published. Later it was incorporated into a *consultatio* given in 1530 by eight doctors from the University of Paris; John Mair's name was first among those signing the document. The *consultatio* was a response to the questions raised by Spanish merchants living in Flanders. This is not the first time these merchants asked the theology faculty for resolution of moral matters in economic affairs. Another *consultatio*, from 1517, answered an earlier set of questions.

Before considering these responses, we need to appreciate more who these merchants were. Religious students from Paris traveled to different cities from England to Flanders searching for funds to continue their studies. The students received support from these merchants. In fact, in the 1509 edition of Mair's *Commentary* he referred to the question of *cambium bursae*, having learned of it from those students returning from their "Lenten appeals" for help. Their travels then brought him familiarity with a new practice, that more than twenty years later would be evaluated in the *consultatio*.

These "Lenten appeals" seem to have lasted for some time. During the Lenten seasons of 1528, 1529, and 1530, for instance, Ignatius of Loyola, a poor student living at the Collège de Montaigu, apparently became familiar with Mair's 1509 account of the students and went to Flanders and England for funds to support his own studies. In England in 1530, Loyola's reading of Mair finally paid off.[29]

These merchants, then, were not unethical Neanderthals seeking a lenient judgment to legitimate their money making. Rather, they were interlocutors with the Parisian faculty, as well as benefactors for many students attending the university. Noonan notes then that a significant reason for why the church revised its teaching on usury was precisely because conscientious Christians were involved in financing.[30] They sought legitimate forms of financing through a variety of devices that first met with social satisfaction and later were presented to Paris for its faculty's final determination.

Mair responded to the case by taking two preliminary steps. First, he legitimated *lucrum cessans* by offering the case of the blacksmith. Say I borrow, for some time, from a blacksmith his anvil, hammer, and other items. I have left him not only without his work items, but also at a disadvantage for making a profit which he would have made if he had his instruments. In returning to him his instruments, I must also pay him for the loss of profit he would have made otherwise.[31] Thus, Mair distinguished usury, a profit for the loan itself, from compensation for the profits that were lost by the lender.[32]

Second, he proposed the case of Socrates the Parisian restaurateur, who regularly travels to Burgundy to buy wine. By buying the wine, he passes on to his clients a 20 percent increase over costs for the wine because of the labors and perils of his travels to purchase the wine. His neighbor, Plato, begs him for a large loan for another business which Plato knows will bring both him and Socrates a 20 percent gain each. Which is better: that Socrates goes about his own affairs and thus makes a profit only for himself, or that he helps his neighbor so that both can make a gain? Does not mercy require the latter?

In this case, Mair furthered the claims of *lucrum cessans*. In the blacksmith case he used justice to legitimate the interest; in the Socrates case, he invoked charity to command the action. Not only was *lucrum cessans* now permitted, it could be morally superior. With these basic insights, Mair examined *cambium bursae* and used the scholastic method to engage possible objections.

The first objection concerned social utility: a king provides for the city's temporal well-being, a bishop for the spiritual well-being, the merchant for commerce, but the lender simply lives off of another's labors. Mair responded that as a matter of fact, without the loan, there would be no commerce.

The next objection was Scripture's injunction to work by the sweat of one's brow. Mair responded that the lender is, as a matter of fact, involved in many concerns both of supporting businesses and of taking care of his family as well. On the other hand, lords, who spend their days on hunts with nothing to do but play and whose life brings no benefit to anyone, seem to be exempt from the Scriptural law.

The final objection was, if *cambium bursae* is licit, then there will be less commerce because potential merchants will prefer to be lenders. Mair responded with another case: Socrates is planning on attending six fairs, one every two months, for the next year. But before he leaves for the first, Plato presents him with a plan, through which a loan will enable him to go to the first fair and Socrates can stay home for the first two months and make the same profit through the loan. Later Cicero comes with the same proposal for the next fair, and after him, John, and others. As a result, Socrates is no longer a merchant, but a lender, yet six others have become merchants because of Socrates's good turn. Thus the practice of *cambium bursae* leads to more, not fewer, merchants.

In light of Mair's responses to these standard objections, the reader is surprised by Mair's final verdict: "The case is illicit; such a state of life is dangerous and dishonest, and needs to be rejected by all prudent men."[33] Mair refused, in the name of prudence, to develop this occasional practice into an institutional one. His reasons focused on speculation. He was concerned, indeed, that Socrates will no longer be a merchant; and that, rather than receiving the occasional requests from Plato and Cicero, Socrates would have to seek out others and press them into businesses that they may not have intended.

Though Mair rejected the simple *cambium bursae*, later in his *Commentary on the Fourth Book of the Sentences* he upheld the liceity of the famous, complicated "triple" or "German" contract, which eventually became the paradigm for licit financial loans. The *cambium bursae* did not sufficiently distinguish a loan's profit from a loss's repayment nor underline the required partnership for legitimate financing. On the other hand, the triple contract, proposed by Conrad Summenhart and his student John Eck, embodied the necessary distinctions. When these German writers sought theological approbation from the University of Paris, only one from the faculty responded, John Mair, who assented.[34] But Mair added that prudence cautioned against preaching the change to the merchants.

FOUNDATIONAL INSIGHTS INTO CASUISTRY

In light of these cases, several insights about Mair and the dawn of modern casuistry are here offered. These insights do not directly emerge from the cases. Rather they emerge when we compare Mair's method with other issues (e.g., the natural law, nominalism, essentialism) that help highlight the distinctiveness of the former. These insights, then, should demonstrate how moral reasoning operated during the time prior to the period treated by Jonsen and Toulmin. They should also highlight the strengths and weaknesses that are historically connected with a method presently enjoying popular interest.

First, a comparison of the scholastic writings of earlier figures like Thomas Aquinas with John Mair demonstrates how much Mair invoked ordinary figures involved in ordinary affairs. While the thirteenth-century Aquinas wrote about the object of justice, for instance, Mair considered the congruity of activities among a ship's captain, the coast guard, and the insurance agent. Admittedly, both used the same scholastic method: they proposed a question, presented a series of objections, offered a determination in the corpus and finally concluded with specific responses to the objections. But in Mair's scholastic writings, the corpus and the answers to the objections were not about the essential notion of an object like usury, loaning, justice, chastity, fortitude, temperance, or the like. Rather, the answers were replete with images of licit or illicit, embodied ways of acting. These images of Socrates the restaurateur, fair-goer, or clever investor cannot be found in the high scholasticism of the thirteenth century.

Second, by examining Mair we find a claim from Jonsen and Toulmin confirmed. They rightly point out that high casuistry was not the simple geometric application of a principle to a case but rather a taxonomic comparison of the congruencies between one controlling insight and another. That insight was not primarily a particular rule or norm; it was more like a right versus a wrong way of acting. The insight served as a standard for comparison, but the standard was a form of acceptable behavior, not a precept.

Third, herein the importance of nominalism for the birth of modern casuistry becomes evident. Earlier we saw Farge's assessment that Mair was the most distinguished nominalist at Paris during the first thirty years of the sixteenth century. Though John Mahoney critiques nominalism in *The Making of Moral Theology*,[35] nominalism's premises actually prompted the need for casuistry.

The nominalists denied the existence of essential objects, specifically the objects of justice or any other virtue or activity. Likewise, the nominalists denied universals: since there are no essences, there are no underlying or over-arching common natures. Thus, the nominalists insisted on the priority of the individual and of the radical singularity of each existent.[36] If the nominalists, then, wanted to determine standards for right ways of acting, they could not refer to objects, but rather to recognizable forms of right acting. Nominalism's proponents, moreover, were forced to look not for the same or universal properties among ways of acting, but only for similar ones. In the absence of essences, the nominalists looked simply for congruencies. Nominalists, then, became forerunners of casuistry.[37]

Fourth, many consequences result from the priority of the individual in nominalism. Let me mention just one. In natural law, Mair rejected the possibility of determining licit moral activity from animal activity. Because humans are not animals (rational or otherwise), the natural law is not something that binds humans to laws that govern animals. In discussing the licitness of conjugal activity for pregnant women, for instance, Mair considered the objection that elephants and other animals do not engage in sexual activity during pregnancy and therefore women should not. He responded by underlining the distinctiveness of human activity. Animals have different appetites than humans. As a result, some animals are pregnant in spring; other animals, in other seasons. Women are found to be pregnant at any time of year; thus, human natural desires for conjugal activity are not limited to any particular season.[38]

Fifth, the lack of classical objects forced a newness into moral commentary. Moral standards were no longer rooted in essences and, therefore, many moral judgments were no longer valid. As a result, the grounds for declaring certain activity as "essentially" wrong were reexamined. Though usury as taking advantage of another's loss was still condemned, the suffering incurred by a lender now merited compensation. The latter became accepted because such activity was congruent with other morally right activity. But the reexamination occurred not simply because new opportunities for financing were arising. Rather, since the foundations of earlier judgments were now disavowed, old issues and new ones received fresh estimation. Thus, Mair asked whether the deprivation of reasoning that occurs in sexual activity is itself wrong. Against the position of many classical theologians before him, he responded in the negative: during sleep, while being under anaesthesia, after long hours of study, the brain also shuts down. That something causes a temporary shutting down of the brain is not, in itself, morally wrong activity.

Sixth, just as the method and the specific resolutions were new, so were the cases themselves. The cases were literally humorous, and clearly the writer tried to catch the reader off guard. For instance, again on his sexual ethics, whenever Mair asked questions about rendering the marital debt and sexual satisfaction, he invoked case after case of Socrates having to satisfy his wife's demands. She is never given a name, but Mair provided a variety of occasions to which Socrates must rightly respond.

Seventh, still, nominalism was not all good news. In taking away essences from the determination of the rightness or wrongness of activity, the nominalists had dubious grounds for moral determination. Thus, not surprisingly, without universals, the theologians of the early sixteenth century published commentary on the more specific and codified *Sentences* rather than attempt a synthesis like a *Summa Theologiae*. Codes, not worldviews, were being shaped at this time.

Without these foundations, then, the nominalists turned to law. Above all, the nominalists looked to the divine prerogatives. God was absolutely free, and the creature's right conduct was measured by her or his compliance with the divine will or law. Considerably different from the rationalism of Aquinas, this measure of rightness engaged, as John Mahoney notes in his book, voluntaristic and legalistic structures.

The nominalist's casuistry, as it emerges in the sixteenth century, became considerably juridical and perhaps more than Jonsen and Toulmin highlight. Their decision to treat casuistry from Azpilcueta's *Enchiridion* (1556) to Pascal's *The Provincial Letters* (1656) describes the amazingly tolerant period of casuistry called probabilism. But before probabilism, there were casuists who were not simply opining, but deciding. These casuists were above all scholastics who wanted, like all scholastics before them, a determination. Thus, though probabilistic casuists held that where there is doubt there is freedom, their predecessors saw little value in doubt.

The concrete cases of Mair and his contemporaries were designed specifically to resolve doubt by rendering decisions. In this sense, these figures were not simply clever yet benign caretakers of the tradition; rather, more likely they were judges. In fact, Jonsen and Toulmin note that casuistry as practiced in antiquity—whether among Greeks, Romans, or Hebrews—was practiced by judges. The authoritative, rather than tolerant, roots of casuistry were always there.

Eighth, prudence, then, in this context is considerably different than prudence in the writings of other, earlier scholastics. In Aquinas, for instance, prudence is the virtue that all persons engaged to perfect the moral virtues interior to the agent.[40] Thus the primary end of prudence was to set limited goals for the agent's own growth. But in the sixteenth century, prudence sought to perfect not one's own internal nature, but rather the external conduct of society. In a manner of speaking, just as for Aquinas prudence perfected the virtues in the lesser powers, so for Mair and his contemporaries prudence governed the masses, through the judgments of these theologians.[41]

The judge's superiority in making prudential determinations should not be missed here. For instance, prudence led Mair to dismiss the liceity of *cambium bursae* and also dictated that some decisions should not be taught. On the triple contract, Mair affirmed its liceity but argued against the advisability of preaching it. Similarly, in arguing that pleasure in licit sexual conduct is not at all sinful, he concluded by arguing that this judgment ought not to be preached; only edifying material should be preached.[42] This is an authoritative period, and therein prudence exercises more juridical influence.

Ninth, certainly we find casuistry attractive because it gave such attention to circumstances and to the uniqueness of the situation;[43] still, at its inception in the sixteenth century it is not as accessible a method as we may wish. Though some of the specific determinations themselves were less oppressive than previous scholastic judgments, the casuists themselves did not seem to make their decision making process any more an egalitarian affair than their predecessors did. Not only were there prudential decisions to not inform the masses, but there is no evidence that the casuists were interested in teaching people prudence in the first place. On the contrary, their habit of making new rulings with greater frequency suggests that, like other eras in the church, the sixteenth century was one of keeping the laity reliant on others for decisions of conscience. Among the periods of moral "dependency" is this period of the judges. Jonsen and Toulmin's thesis that the casuists did not articulate their method because, among other reasons, they lacked time, presumes that they had a will to instruct others in the method. I find no evidence for that presumption.

Unlike Aquinas, for instance, who emphasized the importance of one's growth in the moral virtues and, in particular, prudence,[44] there is no evidence of interest in personal growth in the casuists' writings. I think one could say, in light of the evangelism at the beginning of the thirteenth century by people like Claire, Francis, and Dominic, that that period had greater interest in personal growth than the years of 1500–1530.

Finally, the irony about the birth of modern casuistry is that this helpful system was born simply when it was most vulnerable. To make this point, let me refer us back to Jonsen and Toulmin's experience on the bioethics commission. They note that consensus was achieved when through taxonomies they attained practical conclusions. Disagreement only occurred whenever individual members "explained their individual *reasons*."[45] Thus they agreed to determine one form of conduct as licit, another as illicit, but were unable to argue coherently why. Though it seems attractive to pluralists that diverse biases can achieve consensus, we have to ask on what grounds do they achieve it?

Precisely because there was no underlying system, likewise, Mair with others began this taxonomic method to compare insurance agents with the coast guard and blacksmiths with money lenders. The validity of the recognized and accepted conduct was simply presumed. But why something is right or wrong seems more *displayed* than *explained* both in Mair's and in Jonsen and Toulmin's writings. Reasons are lacking.

It seems then that casuistry can simply avoid addressing the very challenges a society faces, that is, determining why certain forms of conduct are correct and others are not. If the challenge is not faced, then casuistry's determinations with their supposed consensus are illusory. If, however, a common vision is articulated, argued, and accepted, then out of that context, casuistry could provide illuminating resolutions. Among practitioners who have some common vision, casuistry could flourish.

CONCLUSION

Before offering two proposals for future directions in the engagement of casuistry, I highlight anew an earlier point. The previous section ought not to be interpreted as an exhaustive interpretation of the sources and context of high casuistry. Rather, as I stated at the outset, I only seek to further an investigation into this period. Certainly, besides understanding the importance of nominalism, we need further study of voluntarism and rhetoric, especially preaching, to see how these influenced casuistry's evolution.

Still, from the limited vantage point that we have achieved, I offer in conclusion two proposals in order to utilize casuistry while avoiding its recurring liabilities. First, while there is no reason to suspect that a principle-based ethics could not profitably accommodate the taxonomic method of casuistry, the present turn to virtue ethics suggests strong grounds for hope in the future of casuistry. If casuistry can better function with a common vision, then the fact that virtue ethics precisely seeks to articulate that common vision provides, I think, a happy foundation for casuistry.[46] Moreover, virtue ethics with its interest in people's ordinary lives, rather than in norms, seems to be disposed to casuistry's taxonomies of forms of life.[47] Finally, if Jonsen and Toulmin are right in their argument that one reason for casuistry's collapse was a lack of moral idealism, then virtue ethics with its teleology supplies a variety of ends or ideals attractive for any concerned casuist.

Second, I think we need to develop a particular form of virtue ethics that appreciates the uniqueness of the human personality. Owen Flanagan notes "the deep truth that persons find their good in many different ways."[48] If the possibilities for moral development must attend to the distinctiveness of the individual person, then the real challenge for moral theologians today is not found in our predecessors' proclivities to "determine" every new or old issue. In constructing an objective but personal ethics, we will need to teach others the virtue of prudence, rather than to render prudential judgments. That will not be a simple task, but with a casuistry of virtuous living, it could be, at least, interesting.

NOTES

1. Albert Jonsen and Stephen Toulmin, *The Abuse of Casuistry* (Berkeley: University of California, 1988).

2. John Mahoney, *The Making of Moral Theology* (Oxford: Clarendon Press, 1988).

3. James Farge, *Biographical Register of Paris Doctors of Theology 1500–1536* (Toronto: PIMS, 1980).

4. John Durkan, "John Major: After 400 Years" *The Innes Review* 1 (1950) 131–157.

5. J. H. Burns, "New Light on John Major," *The Innes Review* 5 (1954) 83–101, at 96.

6. Aeneas Mackay, *Memoir of John Major of Haddington*, (Edinburgh: University Press, 1892) 78.

7. Frans Vosman, *Giovanni Maior e la sua morale economica intorno al contratto di società* (Rome: Academia Alfonsiana, 1985).

8. Alister McGrath, *The Intellectual Origins of the European Reformation* (Oxford: Basil Blackwell, 1987) 99. See Alister McGrath, "John Calvin and Late Medieval Thought," *Archive for Reformation History* (1986) 58–78; Karl Reuter, *Das Gründverstandnis der Theologie Calvin* (Neukirchen: Neukirchener Verlag, 1963) 20–21; Thomas Torrance, "La philosophie et la théologie de Jean Mair ou Major (1469–1550)" *Archives de philosophie* 32 (1969) 531–47; ibid., *Theology in Reconstruction* (SCM Press, 1965) 81–83; François Wendel, *Calvin: Origins and Development of His Religious Thought* (Durham: Labyrinth, 1950) 18.

9. Francis Oakley, "Almain and Major: Conciliar Theory on the Eve of the Reformation," *The American Historical Review* 70 (1965) 673–690.

10. Francis Oakley, "On the Road from Constance to 1688: The Political Thought of John Major and George Buchanan," *Journal of British Studies* 2 (1962) 1–31. Duncan Shaw, *The General Assemblies of the Church of Scotland, 1560–1600* (Edinburgh: Saint Andrew, 1964) 27–29.

11. Juan Gines de Sepulveda and Fray Bartolomé de las Casas, *Apologia* ed. Angel Losada (Madrid: Editora Nacional, 1975). It needs to be noted that Sepulveda's use of Mair overshadowed Mair's real contribution to political thought. Mair argued that both Christian and non-Christian princes throughout the world had legitimate authority if that authority was both bestowed by a previously reigning prince and recognized by the people of the land. Two exceptions to this rule were first, that through war, Christian princes could retake any original Christian lands now under a non-Christian prince's rule. Second, non-Christian princes of lands that were never Christian are divided into two categories, those who permit the spread of the Gospel and those who oppose it. In the first case, if a people and their prince convert to the Gospel then the prince's authority remains intact. In the second, the prince may be overthrown. Despite these tragic exceptions, that las Casas rightly attacked, Mair established first the authority of any people to have their own leaders and second, that a Christian prince of any race or color enjoyed ruling authority by the will of the people of that land. Thus, though Mair perpetuates the intolerance of Christianity's domination, he made considerable inroads into European hegemonistic claims. See Oakley above and J. H. Burns, "*Politia Regalis et Optima*: The Political Ideas of John Mair," *History of Political Thought* 2 (1981) 31–61; Louis Vereecke, "Morale et pastorale aux origines de la colonisation espagnole en Amérique," *Mission sans frontière* (Paris: Cerf, 1960) 143–193.

12. John Durkan, "The Cultural Background in Sixteenth-Century Scotland," *Essays on the Scottish Reformation, 1513–1625* ed. David Roberts (Glasgow: Johns, Burns, and Sons, 1962) 281.

13. "Giovanni Major sembra l'ultimo scolastico." Louis Vereecke, *Storia della teologia morale dal XIV al XVI secolo* (Rome: Accademia Alfonsiana, 1979) 122.

14. John Noonan, *Contraception* (Cambridge: Harvard, 1965) 310–322.

15. From the *Commentary of the Fourth Book of the Sentences,* quoted in Durkan, "John Major," 135.

16. Alexander Broadie, *The Circle of John Mair: Logic and Logicians in Pre-Reformation Scotland* (Oxford: Clarendon Press, 1985).

17. Besides Torrance and other Calvin scholars, see Louis Vereecke, "Liberté humaine et grâce divine à la veille de la Reforme," *Studia Moralia* 15 (1977) 503–522.

18. Vladimir Grabar, *Le droit politique et le droit international dans les questions de Jean Mair* (Kiev: Academie des Sciences Oukranienne, 1927).

19. See the articles by Oakley cited above.

20. S. Concha, *La teología del matrimonio en Ioannes Maior* (Santiago de Chile: 1971); Louis Vereecke, "Mariage et plaisir sexuel chez les théologiens de l'époque moderne (1300–1789)," *Studia Moralia* 18 (1980) 245–266; ibid., "Mariage et sexualité au déclin du moyen âge," *La Vie Spirituelle, Supplement* 57 (1961) 199–225.

21. Besides the works by Vereecke and his student Vosman, see R. de Roover, "La pensée économique de Jean Mair," *Journal des Savants* 2 (1970) 65–81.

22. Jonsen and Toulmin, *The Abuse of Casuistry,* vii–viii, 17–20.

23. The translation is from John Noonan, Jr., *The Scholastic Analysis of Usury* (Cambridge: Harvard University, 1957) 137. The Latin reads: "Naviganti vel eunti ad nundinas certam mutuans pecuniae quantitatem pro eo, quod suscipit in se periculum, recepturus aliquid ultra sortem, usurarius est censendus." The statement is so surprising that Denzinger wonders whether the word non is omitted after "usurarius." Denzinger-Schoenmetzer, *Enchiridion Symbolorum Definitionum et Declarationum* (Rome: Herder, 1976) 269.

24. See Noonan, Usury 133–153.

25. See Johannes Goris, *Étude sur les colonies marchandes méridionales (Portugais, Espagnols, Italiens) à Anvers de 1488 à 1567* (Louvain: 1925) 506–13; Ricardo Villoslada, *La Universidad de Paris durante los estudios de Francisco de Vitoria, O.P.* (Rome: Gregorian University Press, 1938).

26. *Commentary on the Fourth Book of the Sentences,* distinction 15, question 31, case 15, folio CIII. This case and its analysis appears in Louis Vereecke, "L'assurance maritime chez les theologiens des XVe et XVIe siècles," *Studia Moralia* 8 (1970) 347–85.

27. *Commentary on the Fourth Book of the Sentences,* distinction 15, question 36, folio CVII. The case and its analysis appears in Louis Vereecke, "La licéité du *cambium bursae* chez Jean Mair (1469–1550)," *Revue Historique de Droit Français et Etranger* 30 (1952) 124–138.

28. See Noonan, *Usury,* 118–20, 126–128, 131–143, 250–59. The concept ought not to be confused with *damnum emergens* (loss occurring), which referred to an initial loss sustained by making the loan itself. This received theological approval before *lucrum cessans* (profit ceasing), which referred to a loss

of that which could have been otherwise gained. Thomas Aquinas, for instance, condemned usury, *Summa theologiae* II–II, 78, 1, but permitted certain instances of *damnum emergens*, 78, 2, ad1. Later, as Noonan notes, Saints Antoninus of Florence and Bernardino of Siena recognized the liceity of *lucrum cessans*, see ibid. 115–126.

29. Paul Imhof and Karl Rahner, *Ignatius of Loyola* (London: Collins, 1979) 55.

30. Noonan, *Usury*, for example, 171–192, 194–195, 199–201.

31. From *Commentary on the Fourth Book of the Sentences*, distinction 15, question 30, folio CI.

32. See *Commentary on the Fourth Book of the Sentences*, distinction 15, question 36, folio CVII.

33. Ibid.: "Respondetur quod casus est illicitus et modus sic vivendi est periculosus, inhonestus ab omni prudenti viro excutiendus."

34. See his *Commentary on the Fourth Book of the Sentences*, distinction 15, question 49. The argument is recounted in Noonan, *Usury*, 211.

35. Mahoney, 180–184, 225–6, 240.

36. On the shift from Aquinas to nominalism, see Servais Pinckaers, "Autonomie et hétéronomie en morale selon S. Thomas d'Aquin," in *Autonomie: Dimensions éthiques de la liberté*, ed. Carlos Josphat Pinto de Oliveira and Dietmar Mieth (Fribourg: University of Fribourg Press, 1978) 104–123; ibid., "La théologie morale à la période de la grande scholastique," *Nova et Vetera* 52 (1977) 118–131; ibid., "La théologie morale au déclin du Moyen -âge: Le nominalisme," *Nova et Vetera* 52 (1977) 209–221.

37. So argues Louis Vereecke, "Les éditions des oeuvres morales de Pierre de la Palu (+1342) à Paris au début du XVIe siècle," *Studia Moralia* 17 (1979) 267–282; Ricardo Villoslada, *La Universidad de Paris*, 127–164. See also H. Oberman, *The Harvest of Medieval Theology, Gabriel Biel and Late Medieval Nominalism*, (Cambridge: Harvard UP, 1967).

38. In his *Commentary on the Fourth Book of the Sentences* distinction 31, the only question, ad 2; see discussion in Louis Vereecke's, "Mariage et sexualité au déclin du moyen âge."

39. See Louis Vereecke, "Mariage et plaisir sexuel."

40. See my "Distinguishing Charity as Goodness and Prudence as Rightness" *The Thomist* 56 (1992) 407–426 and *Goodness and Rightness in Thomas Aquinas's Summa Theologiae* (Washington, D.C.: Georgetown, 1992). See also Daniel Nelson, *The Priority of Prudence* (University Park: Penn State, 1992).

41. See John Treloar, "Moral Virtue and the Demise of Prudence in the Thought of Francis Suarez," *American Catholic Philosophical Quarterly* 65 (1991) 387–405.

42. *Commentary on the Fourth Book of the Sentences*, distinction 31, article 1, folio 204.

43. Marcia Sichol, "Women and the New Casuistry," *Thought* 67 (1992) 148–157.

44. Leonard Boyle, *The Setting of the Summa Theologiae of Saint Thomas* (Toronto: Pontifical Institute of Medieval Studies, 1982).

45. Jonsen and Toulmin, emphasis in text, 18.

46. William Spohn, "The Return of Virtue Ethics," *Theological Studies* 53 (1992) 60–75.

47. I argue as much in "Virtue Ethics: Making a Case as It Comes of Age," *Thought* 67 (1992) 115–127 and in "Confidentiality, Disclosure and Fiduciary Responsibility," *Theological Studies* 54 (1993) 142–159. Moreover, Martha Nussbaum demonstrates how these ends can be explained beyond culturally relative boundaries: "Non-Relative Virtues," in *Midwest Studies in Philosophy, Volume XIII* eds. Peter French et al. (Notre Dame: University of Notre Dame Press, 1988) 12–31.

48. Owen Flanagan, *Varieties of Moral Personality* (Cambridge: Harvard UP, 1991) 158.

Part Three

BRITISH CASUISTS

William Perkins (1558–1602) and The Birth of British Casuistry

James F. Keenan, S.J.

INTRODUCTION: THE GENESIS OF CASUISTRY

In the beginning of *The Abuse of Casuistry,* Jonsen and Toulmin narrated their experience on a national health commission. The diversity of ethical beliefs among its members threatened to preclude the possibility of any consensus on ethical issues. The members quickly recognized that without agreement on foundational principles, there was nothing from which they could deduce moral solutions for the issues that they needed to address. In lieu of the principles, they decided to create hypothetical cases related to the topics they were considering. For each topic they worked with a case to which they later added a variety of circumstances. The introduction of these circumstances to the case helped to highlight what were and were not the morally salient features that needed to be addressed. Not surprisingly, after adding enough new circumstances, the original case became so significantly altered that effectively another case emerged. From these cases and circumstances, the members were able to draft recommendations for national policies.[1]

Without any agreement concerning foundational ethical beliefs (e.g., reasons for being moral), the hierarchy of universal principles (e.g., justice, autonomy, beneficence), or the interpretation of general rules (e.g., no direct killing, respect the patient's wishes), the members achieved consensus on specific moral matters. By abandoning speculative concerns and resorting exclusively to practical reason, they articulated new insights, resolutions, and even future guidelines.

In writing their study of high casuistry, Jonsen and Toulmin argued that from this experience they came to understand the genesis of sixteenth-century casuistry in which a case, and not a principle, is the standard for solving ethical issues. As we shall see, high casuistry was born precisely from an inability of existing principles to solve moral problems. Thus instead of deducing solutions from principles applied to situations, the case, they claimed, was juxtaposed against the situation to bring to relief the points of congruency and contrast.[2]

The authors described a case as a standard precisely when it enjoyed in the 16th century the internal and external certitude that a principle enjoyed in the nineteenth and twentieth centuries. A case had "internal certitude" when its solution was argued cogently and prompted the ethical community to recognize right moral insight *in the argument itself.* Those who were publicly acknowledged as competent to solve ethical problems gave the case their "external certitude" when they recommended the case's solution. Internal and external certitude emerged then as the truth guarantors of a paradigm case's solution.[3]

Despite the claims of these two authors in their landmark work, further study of high casuistry is needed to determine the extent to which high casuistry actually engaged inductive as opposed to deductive logic. Their claim is striking because under the influence of later casuistry, which appears in the manuals of the nineteenth and twentieth centuries, many believed that casuistry was a simple system of applying a principle deductively to a case.[4] In later casuistry, the principle, not the case, was the standard of moral measure; the case was not the measure, but rather measured.

Nonetheless Jonsen and Toulmin, having insisted that high casuistry is born without dependence on principles, contended that principles pertain to seventeenth-century casuistry not as measures or standards but rather as effects: new principles emerged from the study of cases.[5] This description squares again with their own experience on the commission wherein congruency among the cases, insights, and solutions led to the articulation of new guidelines.

Case reasoning, then, is a method that leads to the discovery of needed new moral insights, which include, among other expressions, the articulation of new principles.[6] The validity of any principle, then, is derived from the casuistry which precedes and prompts its articulation: "Principles are perspicuous descriptive summaries of good judgments, valid only to the extent to which they correctly describe such judgments."[7] Even though, under the influence of manualism, many ethicists have argued for the priority of principles over cases,[8] a growing number of ethicists are contradicting that claim.

Jonsen and Toulmin reawakened our interest in casuistry precisely by positing the priority of inductive logic in high casuistry, as opposed to the deductive logic of late casuistry. Their claims about high casuistry need extensive investigations, and toward that end this essay examines in one instance why there is a turn to case reasoning in the first place and what the method looks like in its incipient stage.

THE BIRTH OF BRITISH CASUISTRY

The birth and the distinctiveness of British casuistry is better appreciated by a brief examination of the high casuistry on the European continent from 1560 to 1660. That casuistry grew out of two contexts: public policy and private piety.

For that hundred years casuistry was used in the schools to entertain some of the new economic, political, and territorial developments occurring both in the East and in the New World. From Jonsen and Toulmin we learn how, faced with new social claims, sixteenth-century thinkers turned to casuistry.[9]

Like the commission's inability to rely on principles, the sixteenth-century thinkers turned to casuistry due to the inability of existing principles to cope with emerging "new" situations. These situations arose from the explorations of the new world and the trade with the East, which prompted economic, political, and religious questions concerning ownership, financial supports, rights to self-governance, and duties to evangelize. The existing principles were incapable of sorting out the array of data or social issues that evidently required urgent responses.

From recent studies concerning confession and personal piety, we learn much about the development of high casuistry in that context.[10] Evangelizing practices in the sixteenth century prompted a renewed appreciation and frequent reception of the sacrament of confession. In particular, the Jesuits summoned their listeners to an examination of their lives so as to encounter God's mercy and to hear the call of Christ to follow Him. Whether in the context of their public preaching or private retreats, the Jesuits spoke about the greatness of God's love in the face of human sinfulness. This emphasis on God's love altered previous notions of grounds for confessing.

Until this time the confessor was known as doubly competent: as judge able to determine the gravity of a sin and as physician capable of applying the correct penance as a remedy for the soul. But in light of the invitation to encounter God's mercy, the confessor was called to become comforter as well. In *The First Jesuits,* John O'Malley writes, "The role that emerged most explicitly with the Jesuits was that of consoler or comforter."

The added competency did not make the role easier. O'Malley notes, "[I]nsistence upon the consolatory aspects of the sacrament within the juridical framework developed in the Middle Ages characterized the Jesuits' approach to confession and marked it with its many ambivalences." These ambivalences, coupled with the increased frequency, made the administration of confession more complicated, since abuses in the sacrament already "were being subject to so much criticism and ridicule." Faced with these new and extraordinary demands, Jesuits examined the personal circumstances involved in human action, not under the light of existing principles, but rather through cases. This study of cases became so important that the "faithful interpreter of Ignatius and the Institute," Jerome Nadal, recommended that Jesuit confessors study cases an hour daily.[11]

When casuistry was used for the confessional, it was not designed to give the laity permission for morally questionable behavior nor to provide them with guidelines for self-governance. Rather, it was devised for confessors to judge, to heal, and to comfort. The cases then were not promulgated for the masses, but were written in Latin for clergy to administer in the discreet privacy of confession. Margaret Sampson writes that casuistry "was intended not for the spiritual improvement of the laity but for the pastoral use of the clergy; the criteria by which it should be judged were not those appropriate to exhortatory or devotional literature but rather those of jurisprudence." She adds that the private, Latin, juridic form of the Jesuits' directives made them inaccessible to the laity and, therefore, prevented them from becoming public, prescriptive, permissive norms. Ironically, Pascal's popular attacks on the Jesuits (in which he quoted out of context or reconstructed particular solutions from the Jesuit casuists) made accessible to everyone these judgments that were designed to grant not license to the immoral, but cautious comfort to the perplexed.[12]

The genesis of the sixteenth century turn to casuistry in both the public and private arenas was due to an epistemological vacuum prompted by the ineffectiveness of previously helpful principles and rules. Like the experience of the commission, this genesis was occasioned not by stability and insight, but rather by doubt and uncertainty.[13] Casuistry helped sixteenth-century Europeans rethink how they ought to proceed morally and piously.

The genesis of casuistry in continental Europe that rose from the new and urgent demands that existing principles were incapable of addressing in both social and personal contexts is not unlike the birth of British casuistry in the seventeenth century. During their Reformation, the British experience of doubt about how to proceed with regard to loyalties, education, economics, and even family life led to the need for a new way to entertain sufficiently the variety of concerns that they had to face. Likewise, concern over one's own assurance of salvation prompted an individual approach to moral reflection that general rules were just incapable of addressing.

In the British situation, the existing principles were not the only inadequacies; the clergy were inadequate as well. J. C. Aveling describes well the British Christian's perspective by the year 1600:

> On both sides the laity thought their clergy too preoccupied with status and incomes, and the "evangelistic" and "clericalist" minority of clergy dangerous fanatics. Added to this the canonical situation for Catholics must have been hair-raising to simple priests, with countless—especially marital—anomalies and scandals. The minority of devout laity on both sides (containing a significantly large number of women) were severely critical of the "dumb dogs" and sought teaching, confession and spiritual direction from the more learned and evangelistic minorities of the clergy, the great Puritan divines and the more able Jesuits.[14]

In light of the upheaval of the Reformation and its concurrent political turmoil, together with the failure of existing principles to answer these contemporary urgent demands, British Christians turned to Jesuits and Puritan divines for religious and moral guidance.[15] Surprisingly, their pedagogies were not terribly different.[16] Aveling notes, "Pamphleteers amongst moderate Catholics and Anglicans were agreed that Jesuits and Puritans were tarred with the same brush."[17]

Despite the fact that some British concerns were very distinctive (especially concerning loyalty, secrecy, and truth telling)[18] British Catholics relied on earlier Continental casuistry.[19] Surprisingly, British reformers did as well. Thomas Wood remarks, "The consequence was ironical in the extreme. While the authority of Rome was officially rejected, and while the Reformed theologians were immersed in controversy, the Roman casuistical divinity was freely drawn upon for the guidance of souls within the Reformed Churches themselves. For the time being it was either the Roman product or none at all."[20] Despite a general reliance on the Jesuits, however, both Puritans and many Catholics resented them considerably.[21]

The reformers began eventually to write their own works of casuistry, but they acknowledged an indebtedness to the Continental contributors. In his *De Conscientia,* William Ames (1576–1633), the famous student of William Perkins, acknowledged the divines' indebtedness to the Catholics ("The children of Israel should not need to goe downe to the Philistines"), as did Jeremy Taylor (1613–1667) in the preface to his *Doctor Dubitantium* ("But for any public provisions of books of casuistical theology, we were almost wholly unprovided, and like the children of Israel...we were forced to go down to the forges of the Philistines").[22] But the reformers were not terribly successful in English academic circles in replacing Continental Catholic casuistry. Writing of the books at the English universities up until 1642, Aveling notes, "It is odd that so few English Protestant manuals of divinity (usually only Perkins and Davenant) rubbed sides on the college bookshelves with such a mass of Continental manuals. Even in 'Cases' it seems unlikely that Ames, Davenant, Sanderson and Taylor succeeded in ousting from favour the Catholic (mainly Jesuit) manuals in use."[23]

Though those who were not casuists relied on Jesuit casuistry, though British universities were well-stocked with their works, and though reformed casuists recognized the Continental casuists as their predecessors, there is little evidence that these new casuists ever read the Continental works. Elliot Rose contends that William Perkins was only acquainted with one casuist, John Vermeulen or Molanus, a Belgian who wrote *Theologiae practicae compendium.*[24] The Jesuit writer James Broderick (admittedly not necessarily impartial) claimed in *The Economic Morals of the Jesuits* that since the middle of the seventeenth century the singular source for quoting reputedly Jesuit casuistic judgments was Blaise Pascal's *Provincial Letters.*[25] Broderick's claims are supported by no less than Thomas Wood, who believed that Jeremy Taylor relied substantially on reports from Port Royal and noted that Richard Baxter cited Pascal as authoritative in the former's *A Key for Catholics to Open the Juggling of the Jesuits* (1659).[26] Indeed, despite their attacks on the Jesuits' reputed positions, the reformers' own arguments suggest that they did not realize that their own positions were quite similar to those of the Jesuits.[27] There seems then little evidence that the British reformers actually referred to or read European texts.

Nonetheless, even if the reformers had read them and even if they had discovered incredible similarities, still by a central, overriding presupposition the reformed casuist would distinguish himself from the Jesuit. "The Jesuits are not attacked because they use equivocation but because, not having true religion, they used it solely for a secular end."[28] The centrality of faith remained the keystone for understanding British reformed casuistry.

Why, then, did casuistry have such an evidently important role in the British Reformation? There were four fundamental reasons. First, the reformers needed some account of right and wrong moral conduct. They recognized that through casuistry the ordinary Roman Catholic received direction on what was sin and what was not, and they criticized themselves ("The Papists cast in our teeth, that we have nothing set out for the certain and daily direction of a Christian") for lacking that direction.[29]

Second, Catholics charged that the Reformation's *sola fide* invited "moral collapse." The latter's rejection of merit coupled with the doctrine of predestination, it was argued, doubly undermined incentives for moral action. The absence of guidelines for moral action coupled with an absence of motivational grounds for moral action created at times a "moral vacuum."[30]

Third, the rapid economic changes brought on by both the development of the New World and the trade with the East continued to raise new questions about social and economic ethical policies. As casuistry on these social concerns developed among Continental Europeans, likewise British Protestants needed their own guidelines not only for personal conduct, but also for social policies, especially where there was doubt about existing moral laws on commerce.[31]

Finally, Protestant consciences suffered great anxiety. The degree of doubt and uncertainty that prompted British reformers to consider the need for moral incentives and guidelines for personal action and social policy was not as severe as the anxiety that their followers suffered. As the reformers declared that faith is the assurance of salvation, they ironically prompted a fear in their listeners that each of them may not have had exactly what they were assured to have. In underlining the centrality of the act of faith, they made that act the central moral issue in the life of each believer. Thus the first British casuist named the greatest case of conscience that ever was: "How a man may know whether he be a child of God, or no."[32]

Two key factors help explain how this doubt about faith became such a key element in early British casuistry. First, prior to the Reformation the Church held that no one could have absolute knowledge of one's own salvation; such knowledge was beyond our grasp. Never knowing that one was saved was complemented with the consoling news that one could never know that one was damned. But by the sacrament of confession Christians had the opportunity of knowing at least that their sins had been forgiven, an overriding condition for salvation. Thus in the midst of uncertainty of one's eternal life, the confessional provided some semblance of hope.

The reformers' insistence on an unconditioned assurance of salvation required them to attack the sacrament that kept salvation so conditional. Thus the reformers removed the very institution, the confession of sins, that was a source of consolation for many.[33]

Second, the reformers (long before the nineteenth century) made a turn to the subject. For Catholics, the confessor was considered judge, but for the reformers, the individual's conscience was judge. The latter's authority resulted from the abandonment of the confessional and from the recognition that it was in the conscience that one made an assent of faith. Ironically, while Catholics vested the priest with the role of consoler, reformers could not; the near-conflicting roles of judge and consoler (of others) that caused Catholic confessors such difficulties were absolutely irreconcilable in the conscience of the reformed believer. This inability was due to the fact that consoling another is different from consoling oneself, especially when facing "the psychological truth that a man (sic) is his own strictest judge."[34] Without having a confessor, the reformed believer turned to casuistry as a source of "consolation for troubled consciences."[35]

While the reformers developed casuistry as a ministry of consolation, they also contributed significantly to their members' anxiety. As Catholic priests instilled their congregations with fear about their sinfulness and subsequent damnation,[36] the reformers also frightened their congregations, precisely about the matter they most feared, despair.[37] While priests contributed to their community's dependency on the confessional, the reformers encouraged their community's need for casuistry.

THE DISTINCTIVENESS OF BRITISH REFORMATION CASUISTRY

The centrality of the assent of faith prompted British reformed casuistry to be distinctive for its audience, its notion of authority, and the breadth of its scope. First, while Continental and British Catholic casuists wrote for confessors only, the reformers wrote for everyone. Their central preoccupation was not the Catholic issue of sinfulness, but the Reformation's assurance of salvation. By turning to the individual's conscience, they marked the individual as arbiter of all subsequent moral decisions; if conscience was to be judge of self, it would have to also be master of all other decisions as well.[38]

It is not clear how much the reformers wanted to heal the "pathology of conscience" and how much they wanted to establish an anthropocentric ethics, but in addressing the former, they developed the latter.[39] As Margaret Sampson writes, "The metaphor of the penitent as patient was common to Protestant and Roman divines, but where the Jesuits had envisaged a doctor equipped with medicines and the Jansenists more brutally with a knife and a lance, English divines sought 'to instruct and comfort all afflicted consciences' in such a way that they might learn to cure themselves."[40] Their casuistry was a casuistry of "self-reliance,"[41] where each believer was called to become her or his own casuist. As Henry McAdoo remarks in *The Structures of Caroline Moral Theology,* "More so than any other period...[this] age gave theology to the layman."[42]

The turn to the individual's conscience is also a turn to that conscience's authority. In fact, though the early reformers read the early Church writers and the scholastics, they invoked only the Scriptures and the reader's "right reason."[43] Thus external certitude lost credibility in Reformation casuistry, and only the internal certitude or cogency of an argument mattered.[44] Likewise, the reformers rejected the notion of probable opinion to the extent that it relied on the external authority of a writer rather than on his argument; they urged the reader not to any probable, more probable, or even tutior position, but rather to whatever was the more reasonable.[45] As they rejected the confessor as arbiter of moral matters, so they basically rejected the ethicist as a source of external certitude.

The Reformation's turn to the subject prompted, then, a broader context for the new casuistry; the reformers attempted "to enlarge the scope of moral theology by no longer confining it to the confessional."[46] Not shackled by the singular task of judging sin, reformed casuistry embraced the whole of life and emphasized the positive development of character.[47] This emphasis on character prompted the reformers to consider ascetical as well as moral matters.

Catholic moral theology has always separated itself from ascetical theology. In his preface to *A Manual of Moral Theology,* Thomas Slater, for instance, separated ascetical from moral theology and argued that the latter's textbooks are "not intended for edification, nor do they hold up a high ideal of Christian perfection for the imitation of the faithful. They deal with what is of obligation under pain of sin; they are books of moral pathology."[48] Likewise, as opposed to the development of character, Henry Davis wrote: "It is precisely about the law that Moral Theology is concerned. It is not a mirror of perfection, showing man the way of perfection."[49] Finally, Herbert Jone introduced his *Moral Theology* by remarking that in contradistinction to moral theology, ascetical theology "is concerned with the attainment of Christian perfection."[50] Against the mentality that compartmentalized moral theology into matters of sin and law only, the reformers maintained that "the subject matter of moral theology is man."[51] Their cases dealt not only with the assurances of salvation, but subsequently with the ordinary life and the need for virtuous insight to lead that life. Seventeenth-century British reformed casuistry, more than other casuistries, relied often on the virtues.

THE CASUISTRY OF WILLIAM PERKINS

William Perkins, a Puritan who remained an Anglican,[52] is the father of British reformed casuistry.[53] His influence on the Puritans is paramount; as Perry Miller explains, "We may say that they derived their ideas from the Bible, from Augustine and Calvin, Petrus Ramus and William Perkins."[54] Though the claim that he was "the most popular preacher of the late sixteenth century" is certainly disputable,[55] his writings established his international fame. His forty-six works were repeatedly published and translated, and many were brought to the New World. Likewise, they were taken to the East: the "East India Company saw to it that ships were amply provided with edifying reading matter. The essentials were a Bible and a Book of Common Prayer, John Foxe's *Book of Martyrs,* and frequently the works of the famous Cambridge divine, William Perkins."[56]

Perkins' casuistry developed out of his piety, "the term that best expresses Puritan religiousness."[57] His type of Puritan piety upheld the sanctity of God's law that condemns the unregenerate, but served as a guide for the regenerate who obediently heed it.[58] A description of this law ran through *A Golden Chain* (1592), which contained "the order of the causes of salvation and damnation according to God's word."[59] In order to make the law accessible to his readers, Perkins appropriated the method of Petrus Ramus. This method held that theology as "the art of living well" descended from general issues into specifics through a series of dichotomies, where syllogisms were sparse but axioms were amply used.[60]

Since the education of preachers and the entire laity were probably his greatest concerns,[61] Perkins appropriated Ramus' method as a teaching device.[62] In *The Art of Prophesying*, the first manual of its kind for Anglican and Puritan preachers, he taught the importance of making plain and simple the word of God. In particular, he directed preachers to focus singularly on the Scriptures for their citations and not on "human testimonies, whether of the philosophers or of the fathers."[63] Still, he wanted his preacher to be educated:

> If any man think that by this means barbarism should be brought into pulpits, he must understand that the minister may, yea and must, privately use at his liberty the arts, philosophy and variety of reading while he is framing his sermon, but he ought in public to conceal all these from the people and not to make the least ostentation.[64]

Despite this call for broader education, Perkins' innumerable citations in his practical theology were nearly exclusively Scriptural. As W. Fraser Mitchell remarked, Perkins' "standpoint is that of extreme Calvinism, which, taking its stand on the Bible as the Word of God, could not tolerate that the Holy Text should be intermingled with profane utterances of men."[65]

Perkins' preaching was expository. In instructing the congregation, Perkins' Puritanical Anglican preaching emerged as an "exegetical ultraliteralism." His literal application of the Scriptures, his avoidance of human literature, and his strict practical demands marked equally his exegesis and his sermons.[66] His first biographer, Thomas Fuller, remarked in *Abel Redivivus*, "His sermons were not so plain but that the piously learned did admire them, nor so learned but that the plain did understand them. Perkins brought the schools into the pulpit, and unshelling their controversies out of their hard school terms, made thereof plain and wholesome meat for the people."[67]

Perkins' casuistry grew out of his preaching, which was clearly more instructional than motivational, more practical than speculative. "The genius of Perkins is to be found in his ability to apply with striking effect the theology of the Reformation to the exigencies of Elizabethan England in the language of the average man."[68] Like Ramus, his plain sermon is filled with practical theology, for theology "was the science of living blessedly for ever."[69]

The aim of his practical application of the scriptures was "preparation of the elect for the hereafter."[70] For Perkins, practical theology was always meant for an audience of believers aware of their own mortality. Perkins' *Salve for a Sick Man* (1595), translated into five languages, was probably the most influential "Art of Dying" manual in Puritan literature. Therein he portrayed death with human realism: fear is inseparable from death and the sorrow of separation is terribly painful. But dying can become an occasion of great benefit to oneself and to those present. This opportunity required, then, right preparation; because "eternal life begins not after death, but here and now."[71] Perkins wrote, "Men should everie day prepare themselves to death."[72]

Still, Perkins did not invest the moment of death with too much significance; this "consoler" knew "that not only wicked and loose persons despaire in death, but also repentant sinners." As for the "ravings and blasphemings, they are the effects of melancholy, and of frenzies which often happen at the end of burning feavers . . . We must judge a man not by his death but by his life."[73] Curiously, Perkins' confidence in the elect enabled him to uphold the "goodness" of the chosen even in the face of apparent wrong-doing, like despair on one's deathbed. His overriding belief in the goodness that comes from faith in one's salvation kept him from the commonplace error of deducing a person's badness from one's external actions.[74]

Perkins' confidence in the faith of his reader prompted an appeal to the reader's self-understanding. In the beginning of his *A Grain of Mustard Seed* (1597), he reminded the reader of the ease with which one can become a "very child of God." Even a measure of grace the size of a mustard seed, "the least measure of grace that can befall the true child of God," is sufficient for salvation. "The right understanding of this point is the very foundation of true comfort unto all troubled and touched consciences."[75] After comforting the reader with the Good News of the Scriptures, he invited the reader to consider that "the foresaid beginnings of grace are counterfeit unless they increase." So as to "quicken the seeds and beginnings of grace" he offered a series of "spiritual exercises."[76]

Reference to another seed metaphor helps us to understand Perkins' method. Perkins knew that he had to scatter seed on fertile soil. To that end, as he unfolded the meaning of the Scriptures, he concurrently appealed to the listener's own self-understanding. By tapping into the listener's fears and hopes, he tilled the soil of the listener's own self so as to make the listener want to receive the saving word. This dual exposition of the Scriptures and the self runs throughout his writings.

Perkins was quite aware of the incredible anxiety that his reader experienced (and that he occasionally promoted!).[77] But he always referred the reader back to her or himself, often through "intense, prolonged introspection,"[78] though always anchored on the certainty of the Scriptures. He trained the reader to find certainty about one's self in the Scriptures and in God's will.

The claim of finding within oneself (as one read the Scriptures) the expressed will of God led non-Puritans to describe the method as solipsistic.[79] But Perkins would have denied this charge; the search was not to find one's own will, but rather to find and understand God's will for the self in the reading of the Scriptures.[80]

The place wherein one examines oneself is the conscience, "where God and man bear mutual witness to an act."[81] He began *A Discourse of Conscience* (1596) with a definition of conscience: "Conscience is appointed of God to declare and put in execution his just judgment against sinners: and as God cannot possibly be overcome of man, so neither can the judgment of Conscience being the judgment of God be wholly extinguished."[82] Conscience then enjoyed greater than human authority, for it bore God's judgment and God's law. But conscience has a second property, "an infallible certenty of the pardon of sinne and life everlasting."[83]

After explaining that "certentie of faith is whereby anything is certenly beleeved," he distinguished three issues of certainty.

> Generall certentie, is to beleeve assuredly that the word of God is truth it selfe, and this both we and Papists allow. Speciall certentie, is by faith to apply the promise of salvation to ourselves, and to beleeve without doubt, that remission of sinnes by Christ and life everlasting belong unto us. This kind of certentie we hold and maintaine, and Papists with one consent deny it; acknowledging no assurance but by hope. Morall certentie, is that which proceeds from sanctification and good workes, as signes and tokens of true faith. This we both allow, yet with some difference. For they esteeme all certentie that comes by workes to be uncerten and often to deceive: but we doe otherwise, if the workes be done in uprightnesse of heart.[84]

These three definitions of certainty were key to Perkins' moral insight. God's Word was the exclusive source of all certainty, and each person found within the conscience God's specific judgment and therein the certainty of life everlasting. Thus one's moral goodness, as we saw in the *Salve for a Sick Man,* originated not with one's action, but with one's righteousness by God's Word and extended into all subsequent works done in faith.[85] But these works were not completely our own; rather, they were collaborative with God.

The intimacy that characterized a reader's self-understanding as immediately before God also described the kind of call that the reader received to respond and to collaborate with God.[86] The immediacy of God's involvement in the world is found then in the belief not only that eternal life has begun for the elect, but also that the world is God's stage: history is the unfolding of God's will. This Augustinian view of history is caught by the prominence two Scriptural dicta have in the practical theology and casuistry of Perkins. Thomas Merrill notes the first:

> The aim was to bring morality into a consistent relationship with Christian faith, to bring all of human activity under the immediate judgment of the will of God. St. Paul's dictum, "Whatsoever is not of faith, is sin," better than any other Scriptural quotation epitomizes the cardinal principle of seventeenth-century English casuistry. The phrase is ubiquitous in Perkins' works.[87]

After convincing the listener that from the first moment of faith, through which we are saved, all subsequent moments must belong to that faith, he then appealed to the second dictum: "A man's steps are directed by the Lord" (Ps. 37:23).[88] For Perkins, all moral matters were matters of faith. To this end, he invoked the authority of the reader's own conscience to consider the pertinence of the Scriptures, and he did this, in his practical writings, almost always by cases.

THE CASES OF WILLIAM PERKINS

Perkins' case method evolved from his expository style of preaching. In *A Grain of Mustard Seed*, for instance, each section is prefaced by a singular insight (which he oddly called "conclusions"), whose meaning he considered and then moved on to the next section with another insight. The first conclusion, was "A man that doth begin to be converted is even at that instant the very child of God, though inwardly he be more carnal than spiritual." His text addressed, of course, the assurance of salvation.

In like manner he began his *The Whole Treatise of Cases of Conscience* that appeared in three books posthumously in 1606. There Perkins reminded the reader that the casuist was a preacher and that both vocations were a call to bring "comfort": "The Lord God hath given me a tongue of the learned, that I should know to minister a word in due time, to him that is wearie" (Is. 50:4).[89] He turned immediately to the "troubles of conscience."[90]

In this work, Perkins presented 148 cases, often, though not always, prefaced with the word "case" or "question."[91] They were specific and ordinary and had none of the imaginary or pictorial qualities that were found in high Continental casuistry (for example, in Peter of Navarre's (d. 1594) classic case of the pregnant woman whose legitimate flight from a charging bull prompts a spontaneous abortion).[92] Rather they were pithy and, at times, almost resembled a scholastic "question."[93] They were dull. Nonetheless, they were thoroughly practical and concrete, without the least hint of being speculative or theoretical. Moreover, they lacked any inclination to prompt academic interest. And yet, they enjoyed immediacy: they were not questions that Socrates raised, but rather ones that ordinary people worried about.

The reader then was invited to consider the question and the response. The response, where Perkins probed the person's conscience to make it sensitive to the Gospel, had a meditative quality to it; the reader was invited more to consider the case rather than to read a stated answer in it. The case was then a "point" along the journey to self-understanding, certainty, and fear of the Lord. *The Whole Treatise of Cases of Conscience* reads like a self-help manual for simple, pietistic people who are offered developing "points" for consideration. Three examples are helpful.

In the first book, after four brief introductory chapters on conscience and sin, Perkins began the fifth chapter with the question, "What must a man doe that he may come into Gods favour and be saved?" He gave an answer in four stages: "humble himselfe before God...beleeve in Christ...repent of his sinnes...performe new obedience unto God." At each stage he presented several cases. In the first, humility, he offered four cases; the two briefest are here:

> II. *Case.* What must a man doe, that findes himselfe hard hearted, and of a dead spirit, so as he cannot humble himselfe as he would? *Ans.* Such persons, if they humble themselves, they must be content with that grace which they have received. For if thou be truely and unfainedly grieved for this, that thou canst not be grieved, thy humiliation shall be accepted. For that which Paul saith of almes, may be truly said in this case, that *if there be a readie mind, a man shal be accepted, according to that he hath, and not according to that he hath not.*

> IV. *Case.* Whether it be necessarie in Humiliation, that the heart should be smitten with a sensible sorrow? *Answ.* In sorow for sinne, there are two things: first, to be displeased for our sins: secondly, to have a bodily moving heart, which causeth crying and teares. The former of these is necessarie, namely, in the heart to be deepely displeased with our selves: the latter is not simply necessarie, though it be commendable in whomsoever it is, if it be in truth; for Lydia had the first, but not the second.[94]

In the next chapter, he asked "How a man may be in conscience assured of his owne salvation?" He referred the reader to Romans 8:16, "And the spirit of God testifieth togither with our spirits, that we are the sonnes of God." But he raised the case, "How Gods spirit gives witnesse, seeing now there are no revelations?" He answered that there is the testimony of the Holy Ghost found in the preaching of the Word. He then posited another case, what if we lack this testimony? He answered that "sanctification of the heart will suffice to assure us." This testimony of our adoption belonged to "our Spirit, that is, our conscience sanctified and renewed by the Holy Ghost." But what if we lacked this testimony too? "*Answer.* Men must not despaire, but use good meanes, and in time they shall be assured." He then provided some twenty points from the Scriptures to help in that assurance.[95]

Finally, he asked in the seventh chapter, "How a man beeing in distresse of minde, may be comforted and releeved?" Here Perkins, who had been awakening the readers' conscience to the double movements of hope and fear, with sufficiently slighter emphasis on the former, answered by first making clear that even if the "distressed partie...cannot repent nor beleeve" then we should ask "whether he desire to beleeve and repent?" If the reader did, then "Remission of sinnes and life everlasting is thine." Once the moment of assurance in faith was achieved, then Perkins led the reader to takes steps in following the Lord. Here the "comfort which is ministered" must "be allayed with some mixture of the law."[96]

The remaining two books concerned, then, those steps. The second book treated our relationship with God and entertained cases related to oaths, vows, perjury, fasts, Sabbath observance, and the reception of communion. Noteworthy were the many cases about oaths, especially circumstances surrounding their obligatoriness.[97] Here, the reader may have found difficulties in the writer's consistency. For instance, one case asked "if a man take an oath by feare and compulsion, is he to keepe it, yea or no?" Instead of providing any insight from Scripture, he reported that divines were divided; on his own position, he wrote, "I leave it in suspense."[98]

About communion he raised the case of one who "after often receiving, still doubteth, whether he hath faith or no?" He urged the person to "strive against doubting." But if the doubting prevailed, he pressed the person to "strive to beleeve." If the person later experienced feelings of hardness of heart, he stressed the difference between unfelt and felt hardness and called the latter a blessing.[99] Perkins never abandoned the reader.

In the third book, about the person's relationship with other people, he turned immediately to virtue. Perkins' virtues were analogous to Thomas' infused rather than acquired ones, more Augustinian than Aristotelian. Virtue, wrote Perkins, "is a gift of the Spirit of God, and a part of regeneration, whereby a man is made apt to live well."[100]

He divided this book into three parts: prudence, virtues that order us in ourselves (clemency, anger, and temperance), and virtues in relation to others (equity, justice, and fortitude).[101] The entire book was filled with sayings and stories from the Scriptures. Under clemency, interestingly, everything pointed to conflict; the first cases concerned lawsuits, which Perkins endorsed. He responded to possible Scriptural injunctions (Lk 6:29, Mt 5:40; 1 Cor 6:7) by constantly referring to Paul's use of the law (Acts 25:10). He then considered questions about self-defense and the use of force, and again his answers were based on Scriptural passages.[102] Later, treating the cases concerning temperance, he asked, "How farre a man may, with good conscience, proceede in the desiring and seeking of riches?"[103] He answered Scripturally, using standards like moderation and necessity as opposed to abundance. When he reflected on cases of eating and drinking he repeatedly referred to the Pauline response that in all things indifferent, Christian faith grants liberty,[104] but not to cause scandal.[105]

When Perkins did not invoke the Scriptures, he referred the reader to classic insights from virtue ethics. This switch seemed an easy one for him, inasmuch as he found virtuous insight compatible with the Scriptures. Thus, he endorsed the insight that each person has one's own rule: "one man's particular example, must not be a rule of direction to all"; "a man's owne appetite, is not to be made a rule of eating for others."[106]

Breward rightly claims that Perkins' casuistry emphasized prudence and moderation; for Perkins, in matters of liberty the prudential was the moderate.[107] In his *Epieikeia or a Treatise of Christian Equity and*

Moderation (1604), he gave the case of "a boy pinched with hunger" who steals. He argued against either extreme of a harsh punishment (death!) or none at all. Clearly, the boy needed a moderate form of punishment to reform him.[108] Later, he returned to the topic of lawsuits and remarked that "though a man forgive the injury and wrong done him, yet may he safely in some cases go to law for recompense of that law."[109] Perkins' moderation recognized the need to forgive with the right to recompense.

The virtuous moderation, like the prudential judgment itself, was for Perkins always personal. In the *Treatise of the Vocations or Callings of Men* (1603) he advised that "every man must be measured according to his own condition and degree."[110] Thus, he addressed the reader, above all, as an individual and in this treatise focused on the unique task of discerning one's vocation.[111]

Nonetheless, his attentiveness to an individual's uniqueness was always coupled with social responsibility. This complementarity appeared also in his *Christian Economy or a Short Survey of the Right Manner of Erecting and Ordering a Family, According to the Scriptures* (1609). While not casuistry per se, it was similar to *The Whole Treatise,* a practical immediate guide for family life, using the Scriptures, heeding the conscience, attending to individual roles and the particularities of personalities.[112]

CONCLUSION

What can we say then about Perkins' legacy? First, his casuistry was a development of his work in preaching, combining the Scriptural with the practical for the singular purpose of understanding the will of God at this moment. His cases were singularly dependent upon the Scriptures and took aim at the emotional dispositions of the reader, just as the sermon appealed to the affections of the listener.

Second, he engaged the reader as a person. Though Continental casuists sought to make the confessor sensitive to the needs of the penitent by entertaining hypothetical individual circumstances, Perkins addressed ordinary people directly in English, inviting them to consider themselves personally. This invitation was not only for self-understanding, but also for self-governance.

Third, he was confident in human reason to this extent: that only the believer thinks rightly, because only the believer is humble and obedient to God. Clearly, the conscience was a "part of the understanding."[113] While he urged the reader to seek God's will, that quest was an evidently rational one. Perkins always sought a rationally compelling casuistry, with prudence, not obedience, as guide. Indeed, his notion of reason was rich: affective, self-reflective, attentive to needs (one's own and one's family, as well as both state and church), decisive, and while obedient to God's will, singularly unique. Moreover, though his casuistry is Scripturally based, he conveyed it as always reasonable.

Fourth, while upholding the individual's capabilities, he depended on law.[114] Right law was always both moderate and expressive of God's will. He engaged law not only in fundamental matters like God's judgment and specific ones like lawsuits, but more in the very language he used. Above all, the case method itself was fundamentally a legal device, and concepts like conscience and epikeia were derived specifically from judiciary contexts.

Fifth, Perkins' triple confidence in the Scriptures, in one's conscience, and in the law allowed him to face existing doubt. For Perkins there was no denying the depth and breadth of the doubt that he encountered. But he met doubt never as general, but always as specific, concrete, and personal.

Sixth, there was, then, an immediacy here. The particularity of the person, the significance of the circumstance, and the priority of the reader's experience all pointed to the need to understand exactly the matter at hand. The logic (nominalistic?) was uncannily practical.

Seventh, if we consider Jonsen and Toulmin's distinction between high casuistry's taxonomies and manualist casuistry's geometries, then Perkins' method was unique. On the one hand, though he used a few syllogisms and within them had principles or general rules from which he deduced insights, the rarity of their use stands in contrast to their habitual appearance in nineteenth-century manuals. Certainly, like Ramus, Perkins loved Scriptural axioms, which he used to post parameters. But the axioms were not principles or rules and were intended to illustrate, rather than to deduce, solutions. On the other hand, there were also no clever inductive schemes as found in high Continental casuistry. Perkins never pitted one case against another, and though he engaged the affections of the reader, he rarely provided pictorially rich cases for the imagination.

The case was neither the measure that it was in inductive casuistry nor the measured that it was in deductive casuistry. It was rather the point of departure, almost like a scholastic (but practical) question. Like a passage from Scripture, he treated it in an expository fashion, engaging the sentiments of the reader while turning to the Scriptures.

The engagement was more important than the resolution, though with good expository style, it led the reader to deeper and deeper insights. Though the unique concreteness of the case kept it from any specific logical model, we find at the birth of British casuistry a rhetorical structure akin to the sermon.

Eighth, while the singular case was unique both in the specificity of the matter and in its appropriateness to the reader, Perkins by emphasizing the virtues kept the case from becoming atomistic or radically reductive. He insisted on the need for individual guidelines for each reader not for privatistic reasons, but rather because of the virtuous insight that right conduct was derived from the fitting and the mean. Likewise, one case led to the next, not only by the addition of circumstances, but also because Perkins presumed, as his favorite Psalm 37 expressed, that we progress in the Lord. Each case was then an invitation to step in the right direction. Thus, virtue's emphasis on measured advancement was thoroughly expressive of Perkins' agenda: the test of faith was that one flowered.

Finally, there was little reference to sin here and considerable reference to the future, especially everlasting life. By emphasizing the virtues, Perkins presented us with a strong teleological view of ethics, tempered only by his moderation and legal interests. But the bottom line was not the breaking of laws or customs, but the personal development of the reader and the reader's own ability to govern self. Small reason why this casuistry would be enormously influential in the New World.[115]

NOTES

1. Albert Jonsen and Stephen Toulmin, *The Abuse of Casuistry: A History of Moral Reasoning* (Berkeley: University of California Press, 1988) 18.

2. Ibid. 47–74.

3. Ibid. 250–266.

4. John Gallagher, *Time Past, Time Future: An Historical Study of Catholic Moral Theology* (New York, Paulist Press, 1990).

5. On moral epistemology, Thomas Kopfensteiner, "Globalization and the Autonomy of Moral Reasoning: An Essay in Fundamental Moral Theology," *Theological Studies* 54 (1993) 485–511; "Historical Epistemology and Moral Progress," *Heythrop Journal* 33 (1992) 45–60.

6. I have argued that principles enjoy certitude when they express the congruency of a set of cases that enjoy both internal and external certitude in "The Function of the Principle of Double Effect," *Theological Studies* 54 (1993) 294–315. See similar arguments in John Kekes, *The Examined Life* (Lewisburg:

Bucknell University Press, 1988) 50. See also my "Prophylactics, Toleration and Cooperation: Contemporary Problems and Traditional Principles," *International Philosophical Quarterly* 29 (1989) 205–220. Without denying that the validity of a moral principle is derived from the inductive casuistry that precedes it, I now recognize that casuistry attains greater certitude when it can articulate new principles. I have learned this from comments from Charles Curran and Stephen Pope and the writings of Kopfensteiner and Noonan.

7. Martha Nussbaum, *The Fragility of Goodness: Luck and Ethics in Greek Tragedy and Philosophy* (New York: Cambridge Univ. 1986) 299; see also her "Non-Relative Virtues: An Aristotelian Approach," *Midwest Studies in Philosophy. Vol. 13. Ethical Theory: Character and Virtue,* ed. P. French, T. Uehling, and H. Wettstein (Notre Dame: Univ. of Notre Dame, 1988) 44.

8. E. J. Mahoney tried to reawaken interest in casuistry, but argued that it always depends on the principles it applies in *The Theological Position of Gregory Sayrus, O.S.B. 1560–1602* (Ware: Jennings and Bewley, 1922) 136–138. See also the debate in Kenneth Kirk, *Conscience and Its Problems: An Introduction to Casuistry* (New York: Longmans, Green and Co., 1948) 381–383.

9. Besides Jonsen and Toulmin, see John Mahoney, *The Making of Moral Theology* (Oxford: Clarendon Press, 1987) 135–143.

10. On the evolution of casuistry and the institution of confession see the very important work, Thomas Tentler, *Sin and Confession on the Eve of the Reformation* (Princeton: Princeton University, 1977). See also his debate with Leonard Boyle: respectively, "The Summa for Confessors as an Instrument of Social Control," and "The Summa for Confessors as a Genre, and its Religious Intent," *The Pursuit of Holiness in Late Medieval and Renaissance Religion,* ed. Charles Trinkhaus and Heiko Oberman (Leiden: E. J. Brill, 1974) 103–125, 126–130.

11. John O'Malley, *The First Jesuits* (Cambridge: Harvard Univ., 1993) 136–152, at 141. On Nadal, see 147.

12. Margaret Sampson, "Laxity and liberty in seventeenth-century English political thought," *Conscience and Casuistry in Early Modern Europe,* ed. Edmund Leites (New York: Cambridge Univ., 1988) 72–118 at 76.

13. See Kenneth Kirk, *Some Principles of Moral Theology* (New York: Longmans, Green, and Co., 1934) 13–14, 191–201; *Conscience* 106–212; 255–377.

14. J. C. Aveling, "The English Clergy, Catholic and Protestant, in the 16th and 17th Centuries," *Rome and the Anglicans,* ed. Wolfgang Haase (New York: Walter de Gruyter, 1982) 55–142, at 106.

15. See D. M. Loades, "Relations between the Anglican and Roman Catholic Churches in the 16th and 17th Centuries," *Rome and the Anglicans* 1–53.

16. Jean Delumeau, "Prescription and reality," *Conscience and Casuistry* 134–158.

17. Aveling, "The English Clergy," 95.

18. Johann Sommerville, "The 'new art of lying': equivocation, mental reservation, and casuistry," *Conscience and Casuistry* 159–184.

19. Mahoney's work on Sayrus presents a distinctive alternative to the Jesuits' writing. On the Jesuit influence, see George Mosse, *The Holy Pretence*

(New York: Howard Fertig, 1968) 34–47; Peter Holmes, *Resistance and Compromise: The Political Thought of the Elizabethan Catholics* (New York: Cambridge Univ. 1982); ibid., "Elizabethan Casuistry," *Catholic Record Society* 67 (1982); Elliot Rose, *Cases of Conscience* (Cambridge Univ. 1975).

20. Thomas Wood, *English Casuistical Divinity* 38. *The Theological Position* and the Puritans in Wood, *English Casuistical Divinity During the Seventeenth Century* (London: SPCK, 1952).

21. On anti-Jesuit sentiment see the Catholics in Mahoney, *The Theological Position* and the Puritans in Wood, *English Casuistical Divinity During the Seventeenth Century* (London: SPCK, 1952) 59–63, 103–108; on Perkins' deep anti-Catholicism see William Perkins, *William Perkins 1558–1602 English Puritanist*, ed. Thomas Merrill (Nieuwkoop: B. De Graaf, 1966) xii–xiii, xvii.

22. Quoted in Wood, *English Casuistical Divinity* 39–40.

23. Aveling, "The English Clergy," 123.

24. Rose, *Cases of Consciences* 90–101.

25. James Broderick, *The Economic Morals of the Jesuits* (London: Oxford Univ., 1934).

26. Thomas Wood, *English Casuistical Divinity* 60–61; 106–107.

27. For instance, see Johann Sommerville's argument that the Protestant tradition on lying was either identical to or more relativistic than the Catholic position in "The 'new art of lying'," 159–184. On Perkins' own position on lying ("if any truth be to the hindrance of God's glory or the good of our neighbor it must be concealed" *Works* I, 450; *Works* II, 183) see George Mosse, *The Holy Pretence* 48–67, at 54.

28. Mosse, *The Holy Pretence* 46.

29. From Richard Rogers, *Seven Treatises* (London, 1603) preface, as quoted in Ian Breward, "William Perkins and the Origins of Reformed Casuistry," *Evangelical Quarterly* 40 (1968) 3–20, at 9.

30. Merrill ed., *William Perkins* xi.

31. Wood, *English Casuistical Divinity* 101. See also H. D. Kittsteiner, "Kant and casuistry," *Conscience and Casuistry* 185–213, esp. 209ff.

32. William Perkins, *Workes* (London: J. Legatt, 1612) 421, as quoted in Gordon Keddie, "Unfallible Certenty of the Pardon of Sinne and Life Everlasting: The Doctrine of Assurance in the Theology of William Perkins," *Evangelical Quarterly* 48 (1976) 230–244, at 230.

33. See Tentler's conclusion, *Sin and Confession* 363–370.

34. Merrill, *William Perkins* xiv.

35. Breward, "William Perkins and the Origins," 6.

36. Besides Tentler, see Delumeau, "Prescription and reality," 148ff; O'Malley notes that despite the overriding concern for consolation, Jesuits too preached a fair amount of fire and brimstone, *The First Jesuits* 81–83

37. Baird Tipson, "A Dark Side of Seventeenth-Century English Protestantism: The Sin Against the Holy Spirit," *Harvard Theological Review* 77 (1984) 301–330.

38. Ian Breward argues that it was not Perkins' views on begging or the neutrality of wealth that led to "the secularization of Christian social thought," but rather his appeal to individual judgment. Perkins' emphasis on the individual set the stage for all subsequent Reformation casuistry, William Perkins, *The Work of William Perkins,* ed. Ian Breward (Appleford: Sutton Courtenay, 1970) 77–79, see also 25, 31.

39. Breward, "William Perkins," 14.

40. Sampson, "Laxity and liberty," 99.

41. Wood, *English Casuistical Divinity* 65.

42. Henry McAdoo, *The Structure of Caroline Moral Theology* (New York: Longmans, Green, and Co., 1949) 15.

43. McAdoo, *The Structure* 79–82.

44. Wood, *English Casuistical Divinity* 49–51.

45. Kevin Kelly, *Conscience: Dictator or Guide?: A Study in Seventeenth-century English Protestant Theology* (London: Geoffrey Chapman, 1967) 163–175; Wood, *English Casuistical Divinity,* 72–79.

46. McAdoo, *The Structure* 122.

47. Ironically, British casuistry was rejected eventually at the end of the seventeenth century because it became overly specific and tried to influence judgment more than character. See Edmund Leites, "Casuistry and character," *Conscience and Casuistry* 119–133.

48. Thomas Slater, *A Manual of Moral Theology,* 2nd ed., 2 vols. (New York: Benziger Brothers, 1908), I:6. In his *Cases of Conscience* (I:36) he writes that the object of moral theology "is not to place high ideals of virtue before the people and train them in Christian perfection...its primary object is to teach the priest how to distinguish what is sinful from what is lawful . . . it is not intended for edification nor for the building up of character." As quoted in McAdoo, *The Structures* 10–11.

49. Henry Davis, *Moral and Pastoral Theology* (London: Sheed and Ward, 1941) I, 4.

50. Herbert Jone, *Moral Theology* (Westminster, MD: Newman Press, 1959) 1.

51. McAdoo, *The Structures* 16.

52. Despite his Puritanism, Perkins never questioned the legitimacy of the Church of England. Breward, "William Perkins," 10.

53. This assertion is undisputed. However, McAdoo's *The Structures of Caroline Moral Theology,* in an attempt to develop the distinctive legacy of Anglican casuistry, omits Perkins, Ames, and other Puritans. Wood's *English Casuistical Divinity* argues that Anglican and Puritan casuistries are virtually indistinguishable. Gordon Wakefield in *Puritan Devotion* affirms Wood's claim (London: The Epworth Press, 1957) 114.

54. Perry Miller, *The New England Mind, The Seventeenth Century* (Boston: Beacon Press, 1954) 7.

55. Mosse, *The Holy Pretence* 48.

56. Louis Wright, *Religion and Empire: The Alliance between Piety and Commerce in English Expansion 1558–1625* (Chapel Hill: Univ. of North Carolina Press, 1943).

57. Jerald Brauer, "Types of Puritan Piety," *Church History* 56 (1987) 39–58, at 39. Perkins clearly fits into the nomistic type, one of the five types advanced by Brauer. See also *The Work of William Perkins* 66–67, 108–109.

58. Donald McKim, "William Perkins and the Christian Life: The Place of the Moral Law and Sanctification in Perkins' Theology," *The Evangelical Quarterly* 59 (1987) 125–137.

59. William Perkins, "A Golden Chain or the Description of Theology," *The Work of William Perkins* 175–259.

60. See Walter Ong, *Ramus, Method and the Decay of Dialogue* (New York: Octagon Books, 1974); ibid, *Ramus and Talon Inventory* (Cambridge: Harvard Univ., 1958).

61. Ian Breward, "William Perkins and the Ideal of the Ministry in the Elizabethan Church," *The Reformed Theological Review* 24 (1965) 73–84; K. R. M. Short, "A Theory of Common Education in Elizabethan Puritanism," *Journal of Ecclesiastical History* 33 (1972) 31–48.

62. Donald McKim, "The Functions of Ramism in William Perkins' Theology," *The Sixteenth Century Journal* 16 (1985) 503–517; Ibid., *Ramism in William Perkins' Theology* (New York: Peter Lang, 1987).

63. William Perkins, "The Art of Prophesying," *The Work of William Perkins* 331–349, at 341. In this edition, the editor Ian Breward updates Perkins' spelling; in the other edition, which presents the "Discourse on Conscience" and "The Whole Treatise of Cases of Conscience," the editor Merrill retains the original spelling. Rather than update Merrill's edition I retain it, believing, in fact, that Merrill made the right choice.

64. Perkins, "The Art of Prophesying," 345.

65. W. Fraser Mitchell, *English Pulpit Oratory from Andrewes to Tillotson* (London: SPCK, 1932) 100.

66. Erwin Gane, "The Exegetical Methods of Some Sixteenth-Century Puritan Preachers: Hooper, Cartwright, and Perkins," *Andrews University Seminary Studies* 19 (1981) 21–36, 99–114, at 111. See Perkins, *William Perkins* ix, xvi.

67. As quoted in Jonathan Long, "William Perkins: 'Apostle of Practical Divinity'," *Churchman* 103 (1989) 53–59, at 55.

68. Long, "William Perkins," 57.

69. Donald McKim sees this as key for understanding the Ramist influence of Perkins, see his "The Functions of Ramism," 508 and *Ramism in William Perkins' Theology* 122. Similarly, Perkins, *The Work of William Perkins* 445.

70. Gane, "The Exegetical Methods," 113.

71. David Sceats, "Precious in the Sight of the Lord," *Churchman* 95 (1981) 326–339, at 336. See also Wakefield, *Puritan Devotion* 143–153.

72. William Perkins, "A Salve for a Sicke Man, or a Treatise of the Right Way to Die Well," *The Workes of that Famous and Worthie Diuine in the Vniuersity of Cambridge, M. W. Perkins*, ed. J. Legatt (Cambridge, 1608) 484–508, at 492. Quoted in Sceats, "Precious," 338.

73. Perkins, "A Salve," 488. Quoted in Sceats, "Precious," 335.

74. See my "The Problem with Thomas Aquinas's Concept of Sin," *Heythrop Journal*, 35 (1994) 401–420.

75. William Perkins, "A Grain of Mustard Seed," *The Work of William Perkins* 389–410, at 392.

76. Perkins, "A Grain of Mustard Seed," 404–405.

77. Barbara Donagan, "Godly Choice: Puritan Decision-Making in Seventeenth-Century England, *Harvard Theological Review* 76 (1983) 307–334.

Michael Malone, "The Doctrine of Predestination in the Thought of William Perkins and Richard Hooker," *Anglican Theological Review* 52 (1970) 103–117. See also Wakefield, *Puritan Devotion* 124–129.

78. Donagan, "Godly Choice," 312.

79. See Donagan, "Godly Choice," 307–308, 325–327.

80. Gordon Keddie, "Unfallible Certenty," 230–244.

81. Merrill, *William Perkins* xix.

82. William Perkins, "A Discourse of Conscience," *William Perkins* 1–78, at 3. See his "The Whole Treatise of Cases of Conscience," ibid., 87–240, esp. 99–101.

83. Perkins, "A Discourse," 49.

84. Perkins, "A Discourse," 49.

85. This is a clear appreciation of the distinction between goodness and rightness. See for instance, "The Whole Treatise," 90, 129; Josef Fuchs, "Morality: Person and Acts," *Christian Morality: The Word Becomes Flesh* (Washington, D. C.: Georgetown Univ., 1987) 103–117; James Keenan, "A New Distinction in Moral Theology: Being Good and Living Rightly," *Church* 5 (1989) 22–28.

86. See Michael McGiffert, "Grace and Works: The Rise and Division of Covenantal Divinity in Elizabethan Puritanism," *Harvard Theological Review* 75 (1982) 463–502; ibid., "From Moses to Adam: The Making of the Covenant of Works," *The Sixteenth Century Journal* 19 (1988) 129–155. In the latter work McGiffert shows how the Covenant of Works, being rooted eventually in Adam instead of Moses, enabled Perkins to make the claim that the judgment of the law was universal and not only for the elect.

87. Perkins, *William Perkins,* xv. See, for instance, its use in the case in "The Whole Treatise,": "How may a man doe a good worke, that may be accepted of God, and please him?" 109–111. Not surprisingly, Perkins' favorite grounds for attacking the Catholics is that their positions are not biblical; see Gane, "The Exegetical Methods," 108.

88. Donald McKim, "The Puritan View of History or Providence Without and Within," *Evangelical Quarterly* 52 (1980) 215–237, at 229.

89. Perkins, "The Whole Treatise of Cases of Conscience," 87.

90. Ibid., 89.

91. Donald McKim gives the number 148, in *Ramism in William Perkins' Theology,* 99. Most readers would have great difficulty in determining where a case begins and ends.

92. John Connery, *Abortion: The Development of the Roman Catholic Perspective* (Chicago: Loyola University Press, 1977) 124–129; Navarre makes the case in *De ablatorum restitutione,* b. 2, c. 3. (Brescia, 1605).

93. The reader finds in Perkins a profound reliance on the scholastics. See, for instance, his description of the seven principal circumstances surrounding sin, "The Whole Treatise," 96–98.

94. Perkins, "The Whole Treatise," 102–111, at 103–105.

95. Ibid. 111–118, at 111–113.

96. Ibid. 118–126, at 118, 124.

97. See George Mosse's discussion on Perkins in *Holy Pretence,* in which he argues that "underlying this casuistry was the need of the moment" 48–66, at 60.

98. Perkins, "The Whole Treatise," 145.

99. Ibid. 138–139.

100. Ibid. 163.

101. Ibid. 165.

102. Ibid. 173–180.

103. Ibid. 189.

104. Ibid. 198.

105. Ibid. 200, 203.

106. Ibid. 203–204.

107. Breward, "William Perkins and the Origins," 19. Other comments on Perkins and virtue see Woods, xii–xvi, 47, 138–139; Mosse, 41.

108. Perkins, "Epieikeia or a Treatise of Christian Equity and Moderation," *The Work of William Perkins* 477–510, at 487.

109. Ibid. 499.

110. Perkins, "Treatise of the Vocations or Callings of Men," *The Work of William Perkins* 441–476, at 466.

111. Ibid. 460. See McKim's discussion about parents' responsibilities for divining God's will for their children, Ramism 35.

112. Perkins, "Christian Economy or a Short Survey of the Right Manner of Erecting and Ordering a Family, According to the Scriptures," *The Work of William Perkins* 411–439.

113. Perkins, "Discourse on Conscience," 5.

114. See note 57 above.

115. I want to thank the Institute for the Advanced Study of the Humanities at the University of Edinburgh for providing me with a fellowship for the Spring of 1993 to study casuistry and the Association of Theological Schools for providing me with a grant to support that study.

Moral Sources, Ordinary Life, and Truth-telling in Jeremy Taylor's Casuistry

RICHARD B. MILLER

INTRODUCTION

It is often thought that casuistry in the early modern period was the sole possession (and liability) of Roman Catholicism. Renowned for its permissiveness, hair-splitting arguments, and excessive appeals to authority, Catholic casuistry was disparaged by critics like Blaise Pascal who sought a clear, unambiguous set of ethical directives.[1] But in the seventeenth century the Puritans and Anglicans developed an alternative tradition of casuistry, often mixing conceptual tools provided by their Catholic rivals with moral guidance drawn from Scripture. Like their Catholic counterparts, English Protestants in the early modern era found themselves confronted by new problems for which traditional sources provided uncertain answers. The expansion of finance and international trade, encounters with the New World, the rise of nation-states and national economies, and the emergence of a powerful mercantile class generated moral questions about prices and wages, usury, trade, dominion, and the rights of indigenous populations in the Americas. Within Britain itself, reformers found it necessary to clarify the terms of civil and ecclesiastical authority, owing to tensions between traditional Anglicans and those who favored Calvinist theology and ecclesiology.[2] With the abolition of the episcopacy in 1643, the executions of Bishop Laud and Charles I, the Irish uprising, the civil war, and the Puritan interregnum, the century was rife with cases concerning religious toleration, truth telling in situations of persecution, sedition and tyrannicide, and the terms of a just war, to name a few.

Among the most prodigious of the Anglicans was Jeremy Taylor, Bishop of Down, Connor, and Dromore in Ireland. Educated at Cambridge and Oxford, Taylor served as a chaplain to Laud and Charles I, was an ardent royalist during the civil war, and was a tireless Erastian. During much of his life he held no position of official importance, but he published widely and preached often. Although his writings led to imprisonment twice, in 1654–55 and 1657–58, he generally found protection from political repression by sequestering himself in the British countryside and by enlisting influential, liberal patrons. In 1660, after several delays, he published his monument to casuistry, *Ductor Dubitantium: Or the Rule of Conscience,* dedicated to the restored monarch.[3] That same year Charles II appointed him vice-chancellor of the University of Dublin, and Taylor immediately set out to reorganize the institution. He lived out his last years in Ireland; he died and was buried in Dromore in 1667.[4]

Written over a twenty-year period and reprinted three times before the end of the century, *Ductor Dubitantium* is an enormous work divided into four parts. Book I deals with the conscience—the formal cause of virtue—and matters of moral psychology: the relationship between conscience and reason; subjective certainty; the erroneous, thinking, doubtful, and scrupulous conscience; and different forms of probable arguments. The second and third books address the material causes of virtue, the laws of God and humanity. Book II focuses on the natural and divine law, the relationship between reason and revelation, positive and negative precepts, and the relationship between the Old and New Testaments. Book III, the longest, addresses civil and ecclesiastical laws, especially their respective areas of jurisdiction. Book IV is mercifully brief and deals with the final and efficient causes of virtue. It focuses on voluntary and involuntary actions, and conditions of moral accountability.

Yet this appearance of order is deceptive, for *Ductor Dubitantium* is an elephantine, labyrinthine miscellany of rules, cases, Latin and Greek citations, and digressions.[5] It constitutes over one-fifth of Taylor's published writing, and he fully expected it to establish his fame.[6] He was destined for disappointment. The *Ductor* was published soon after the Restoration; as a result, many of Taylor's cases, especially pertaining to civil and ecclesiastical power, ceased to have much relevance. But it was not merely that circumstances were untimely for Taylor. He was garrulous, providing lengthy discussions of arcane issues—e.g., the relationship between the first and second commandments, how to prove the truth of Christianity according to intrinsically probable reasoning, what to do with a guest who drinks too much, and (perhaps the biggest nonissue in the history of casuistry) whether it is permissible for a man to marry his mother-in-law. Although Taylor's devotional prose inspired the likes of John Wesley,[7] his casuistry is prosaic and redundant, leading John Henry Newman to marvel about the "array of quotations, anecdotes, similes, and good sayings strung upon how weak a thread of thoughts!"[8] For these reasons, as George Worley writes, "*Ductor Dubitantium* fell exceedingly flat on its generation; and . . . it now lies undisturbed in the dusty cemeteries of deceased literature."[9]

A greater problem is that Taylor fails to address several issues germane to his own concerns: the nature of law, the relationship of God to the world and human nature, the nature of the virtues, and the relationship between law and reason or between law and cosmos. Instead, the *Ductor* is a patchwork of erudition that reflects Taylor's many years of Renaissance learning, drawing freely from classical Greek, Roman, biblical, patristic, and medieval sources. The final product is a tome that is unwieldy, eclectic, and inconsistent in several respects.

Put simply, the *Ductor* is Janus-faced. Part of it echoes the thought world of medieval scholasticism, represented in many respects by the theology of Thomas Aquinas. Taylor shares with Aquinas a trust in reason and a corresponding suspicion of the will (and its potential arbitrariness) as an independent moral guide. The will must be guided by "right reason." In the Thomistic outlook, moreover, reason is substantive; it has the capacity, in principle at least, to ascertain the implications of the natural law, which reflects God's reason. The eternal law participates in rational creatures insofar as they ascertain the dictates of the natural law, some of which are self-evident and others of which can be inferred from essential human ends and inclinations.[10] Linked to this understanding is the idea that God's reason commands certain actions because they are good and prohibits other actions because they are evil. In this scheme the right is joined to the good insofar as persons who abide by the natural law contribute to their own flourishing as humans. Individuals who coordinate their intentions with natural human purposes participate more fully in their humanness and enjoy an increase in being. Moral motivation is thereby secured on humanist grounds; the life of a good person is also a good life for that person.

The other part—a more significant portion—of Taylor's casuistry pulls in the opposite direction, drawing from sources that rebelled against medieval scholasticism's confidence in reason, divine order, and essentialism. Trust in the ability of human reason to ascertain essences is replaced by a skepticism about the existence of universals. This *via moderna*, drawing from William of Ockham, holds to the nominalist notion that universals only name individual existents; universals are only a product of the mind and have no extramental existence as such.[11] At stake in this critique, among other things, is a theological point: Ockham argues that the theory of universals implies a limitation of divine omnipotence, as though divine creativity could be constrained by eternal ideas or essences.

One outcome of this nominalist theory is to underscore the absolute sovereignty of God's legislative will. Nominalists hold not that God commands an action because it is good, but that it is good because God commands it. The idea that God commands something because it is good appears to bind divine sovereignty to some "external" standard. Moral sources shift, in other words, from rationalist to voluntarist and juridical foundations, from God's eternal reason to the unlimited power of God's commanding will.

Ockham's nominalism does not produce an antirationalist moral theory, but his overall account of reason is modified by his understanding of God's freedom and goodness.[12] For those who are influenced by Ockham, practical reason has less to do with discovering ends and universals, and more with how to interpret and apply divine commands to situations that are not explicitly mentioned in the Bible.[13] Substantive reason is modified by a view of human rationality as chiefly interpretive and instrumental. Moreover, separating commands from an order of reason makes it more difficult to secure humanist grounds for moral motivation. Instead, motivation is linked to penalties and rewards that will come from God, as promised in revelation.[14]

Taylor did not see this tension between medieval theology and the *via moderna* as fatal. In his mind, whether our actions contribute to the conservation of the natural world is more important than whether we abide by right reason or God's will. Rationalist and voluntarist sources can be forced together (more or less) to underwrite an early modern concern: the affirmation of ordinary life.[15] For however free God may be to command or prohibit, in Taylor's mind God is not willing to undermine the goodness of creation. As a result, Taylor's understanding of divine sovereignty is qualified by his belief that God would never will to destroy the conditions for human well-being in everyday life.

Such an affirmation of everyday affairs allows Taylor to sidestep some of the tensions between the medieval and modern influences on his thought.[16] This consequence will become apparent when we examine his casuistry of truth telling: lying, mental reservation, and equivocation. Taylor's appreciation for the *via moderna* enables him to call attention to the prohibition of lying in the Bible. His appreciation for the medieval tradition allows him to strengthen this ban by echoing the traditional claim that lying violates the essence of speech. But because ethics should be attentive to practical matters, the prohibition of lying cannot subvert some basic practical exigencies of this-worldly existence. Taylor thus departs from the absolute prohibition of lying, allowing everyday, temporal goods to trump the mandate always to tell the truth.

To see how this is so, two sets of preparatory comments are in order. The first has to do with Taylor's view of conscience, reason, and law; the second pertains to his embrace of ordinary life.

MORAL SOURCES

Taylor understands conscience and reason to be closely connected. The conscience has an innate knowledge of laws, divinely implanted in our minds. It is measured by "the law of natural and essential equity and reason, . . . which is put into every man's nature." Those who lose their reason lose their conscience as well; the conscience is a monitor by which we accuse or excuse ourselves. As a practical faculty the conscience pertains to human behavior, and one of its tasks is to apply laws to conduct. It is "nothing other than right reason reduced to practice, and conducing moral actions."[17]

In this respect Taylor's understanding of conscience follows that of Aquinas. For Aquinas the conscience is a rational act, "a certain pronouncement of the mind."[18] In its broadest sense, the conscience has two dimensions. First, there is the law of the intellect, the intuitive or acquired knowledge of first principles. This knowledge, called *synderesis,* contains "the precepts of the natural law, which are the first principles of human action."[19] Second, there is *conscientia,* or conscience in a narrower sense, which is "nothing else but the application of knowledge to some action."[20]

Similarly, for Taylor the conscience has two components. First, it includes a "repository" of practical principles in the mind. Conscience contains "all the natural and reasonable principles of good actions, such as God is to be worshipped, do to others as they should do to you, the pledge is to be restored, by doing harm to others you must not procure your own good, and the like." These are "universal principles, consented to by all men without a teacher."[21] But knowledge of such principles is not sufficient for moral conduct. Also necessary is their application, the "conjunction of the universal practical law with the particular moral action."[22] This application is the work of conscience, narrowly understood.

This line of thought sets the *Ductor* apart from voluntarist and fideist approaches to conscience and practical affairs. Against the former, Taylor distinguishes between the dictates of reason and the inclinations of the will, stating that our self-examination is the "office of the knowing, not the choosing faculty."[23] The will is unable to accuse or excuse; it lacks a reflexive, discursive function. Left to the will alone, "we would all stand upright at doomsday."[24] One of the tasks of conscience, then, is to find a "fit motive for the will."[25] Without reason's guidance, the will is arbitrary, subject to contingency.

Against fideism, Taylor goes to great pains to show that Christianity is not unreasonable. God has one, not two wills, and thus would not produce contradictory directives in reason and revelation. Reason alone cannot generate all the truths of revelation, but it does provide a negative test: "Whatsoever is certain in reason, religion cannot contradict that."[26] Indeed, Taylor insists that reason itself is no rival to divine sovereignty: "Whatsoever right reason says cannot be done, we cannot pretend from Scripture, that it belongs to God's almightiness to do it."[27]

This emphasis on reason appears most clearly in Taylor's discussion of probabilism, the doctrine that, in cases of doubt, a probable opinion in favor of liberty may be followed even if the contrary opinion is stronger. Probabilism relies on the idea that a doubtful law does not apply and remains uncertain even when stronger opinions weigh in its favor. Following tradition, Taylor distinguishes between intrinsic probability, based on sound reasons, and extrinsic probability, based on the weight of expert opinion.[28] In most instances the former is to be preferred over the latter because it is relatively more certain and rests on our own deliberations. We are to subject the arguments of authority to reasonable inquiry unless we are strapped for time, tend toward self-justification, or are thoroughly perplexed.[29] What is central for Taylor is that reason, not the will, guides our behavior; relying on authorities is more often a matter of unreasoned choice than reflective deliberation. Extrinsic probability subjects the will to contingency, not reason, and leaves us open to chance.[30] Echoing the Greeks and Stoics, Taylor views rationality as the basis of our self-control.

Yet for Taylor we do not simply need reasons, but weighty ones. Thus it is not enough to adopt the doctrine of probabilism, which allows weak reasons to prevail over stronger ones. Taylor's view, known as *probabiliorism,* holds that a law ceases to apply only if countervailing reasons are stronger than those that support a rule.[31] Once again, voluntarism is the culprit; one who chooses the less probable opinion, "omitting that which is more, makes the determination by his will, not by his understanding, and therefore it is not an honest act or judgment of conscience, but a production of the will."[32]

At the same time Taylor does not endorse a hyperrationalistic account of conscience. He strongly discourages a "scrupulous conscience," and in this regard his understanding of right reason takes on distinctive contours. For Taylor, self-examination is a virtue, but with limits. Taken to extremes it becomes a sickness, "a trouble where the trouble is over, a doubt when doubts are resolved; it is a little party behind a hedge when the main army is broken and the field cleared."[33] Evaluating our conduct "by atoms and unnatural measures, and being over righteous, is the way not to govern, but to disorder our conscience."[34] If they become the source of ongoing self-doubt, the workings of conscience can be counterproductive, an obstacle to action in our everyday affairs.

What are the remedies for scrupulosity? For Taylor the answer lies in having a religion tied to ordinary life. "He that would cure his scrupulousness must take care that this religion be as near as he can to the measures and usages of common life," Taylor writes, urging us to avoid "excess in mortifications and corporal austerities," as well as legends of the saints.[35] "Let us take care," he urges,

> that our religion be like our life, not done like in pictures, taken when we are dressed curiously, but . . . dressed with the usual circumstances, imitating the examples, and following the usages of the best and the most prudent persons of his communion; striving in nothing to be singular, not doing violence to anything of nature.[36]

Our introspection should be moderated, in other words, by common sense. It should not render us unusual, or socially dysfunctional.

In this regard Taylor distances himself from the position of strict tutiorism, the doctrine that in matters of doubt one is to take the safer, stricter course of action. He argues that the safer course may be overly scrupulous if countervailing reasons obtain. To act as if safety obliges when a contrary opinion is more probable is "a prudent compliance, either with a timorous or with an ignorant conscience, . . . but very often an effect of a weak understanding, that is, such a one which is inclined to scruple, and dares not trust the truth of his [own] proposition, or God with his soul in the pursuance of it."[37] Tutiorism can be the product of unreflective rigorism, failing to recognize that good arguments can justify liberty. The moral ideal for Taylor is not moral purity, but an ability to function well in society. Thus he writes that charity asks us to act "carefully and wisely, and follow the best we can."[38] Religion should not be commended for severity or perfectionism; it should not produce martyrs. Rather, "that religion is best which is incorporated with the actions and common traverses of our life."[39]

Taylor's probabiliorist position, then, paves a middle way between a more permissive probabilist position, on the one hand, and a strict tutiorist position, on the other. He suggests that the latter is the dark side of the former, leading us to doubt ourselves for reasons that are less weighty than those that we can provide. Both extremes result from a deficiency of reason: probabilism because it derives from an "intervening will" and scrupulosity because it follows from a "weak understanding" of the just causes that can support liberty. The individual of right reason, then, must balance the demands of freedom and authority, heeding the demands of everyday life.

* * * * * *

Given this emphasis on right reason in matters of conscience, Taylor's comments about the law of nature are surprising. The natural law is not a substantive rational capacity according to which the eternal law participates in human beings, as it is for Aquinas. Taylor emphasizes the juridical quality of the natural law, not its rational dimensions. Thus he defines the law of nature as a "universal law of the world, or the law of mankind, concerning common necessities to which we are inclined by nature, invited by consent, prompted by reason, *but is bound to us only by the commands of God*."[40]

For Taylor the natural law must first be distinguished from natural right: *jus naturae* and *lex naturae* do not imply each other. The rights of nature are individual and presocial; they include "a perfect and universal liberty to do whatsoever can secure me or please me."[41] Natural rights, in other words, pertain to an individual's appetites and inclinations, and they pit one person against another. "Whatsoever we naturally desire," Taylor writes, "naturally we are permitted to." Thus, to save my life, I am permitted to "kill another, or twenty, or a hundred, or take from his hands to please my self, if it happens in my circumstances and power, and so for eating, and drinking, and pleasures."[42] These rights exist outside the law of nature, and they obtain unless and until such laws prohibit them. "Where the laws of nature cease, there the rights of nature return."[43]

Unlike the Thomistic theory of the natural law (and the duties it produces), this account of natural rights does not provide a vision of a common, shareable good. For a Thomist, a common good does not decrease in quantity because it is shared; sharing a common good does not mean that each person receives a diminished portion of the good in question. But for Taylor natural rights incline us toward common goods in a different sense. Goods are "common" only in the sense that they may be procured outside social or legal restraints. They are commonly *available*, but not shareable. Rights to common goods must be understood, then, as hedonistic and competitive, "as that by which the stones in the streets are mine or yours; . . . I may take them up and carry them to my bed or turf, where the natural, wild, or untutored man does fit." Natural rights are "*nullis in bonis*," and imply no positive duties toward—or enjoyment with—other individuals.[44]

In contrast to the *jus naturae*, the *lex naturae* denotes for Taylor a set of provisions God has made to meet basic necessities. The law of nature serves in part to protect us from each other as atomistic individuals, binding us to observe needs we possess in common—including our preservation as a race or society. We are unable to ascertain common necessities on our own; we lack the capacity to join ourselves (as individuals) to others in a social union. Without the natural law, Taylor suggests, our asocial, hedonistic impulses might overrun the need for collective survival. Thus, God gave the law of nature "to mankind for the conservation of his nature and the promotion of his perfective end."[45] It is a constraint upon our natural liberties, a fetter to our freedom. As a rival to our individual rights, it must be "superinduced," that is, declared by God.

This is not to suggest that the natural law for Taylor is wholly irrational or heteronomous. It is, as he writes, "a transcript of the wisdom and will of God written in the tables of our minds."[46] But Taylor adds that reason is generally unreliable, that "every man makes his own opinions to be laws of nature, if his persuasion be strong and violent."[47] It is better, he says, to see reason as "an instrument of the law of nature," that by which we interpret and apply the natural law to different circumstances.[48] Thus the most we can say is that the conscience provides only an indirect declaration of God, to be supplemented by the direct promulgation of revelation. Accordingly, the law of nature is not a law of our being, understood as a principle that structures moral reasoning or the inclination toward natural perfection and human community, as it is for Aquinas. Rather, "God first made or decreed it to be a law, and then placed it [in the conscience] for use, and promulgation."[49]

In this respect Taylor reveals his Ockhamist—not his Thomist—leanings concerning the origin and character of moral laws.[50] The first line of the *Ductor,* it is important to note, describes providence not as the eternal, unchanging mind of God, but as God's will, active in history: "The circles of divine providence turn themselves upon the affairs of the world so that every spondle of the wheels may mark out those virtues which we are then to exercise, and every new event in the economy of God is God's finger to point out to us by what instances he will be served."[51] Indeed, God governs the world not as eternal reason, but "by several attributes and emanations from himself."[52] This suggests that we are to look not to the order of creation for moral direction, but to the sovereign agency of God as recorded in the Bible.[53]

The effect of this theology is to alter the sources of moral authority. Justice lies not in universals that shape the order of being, but in divine legislative agency. Taylor thus writes, "God cannot do an unjust thing, because whatsoever he wills or does is therefore just because he wills and does it."[54] It is noteworthy, moreover, that in support of this statement he invokes the authority of Ockham:

> Upon the account of these premises it follows, that it is but a weak distinction to affirm some things to be forbidden by God because they are unlawful; and some to be unlawful, because they are forbidden. For this last part of the distinction takes in all that is unlawful in the world, and therefore the other is a dead member and may be lopped off. So Occam affirms against the more common sentence of the schools. . . : Everything is good or bad according as it is commanded or forbidden by God, and no otherwise. Nothing is unlawful antecedently to God's commandment.[55]

This means that the law of nature can be dispensed with by divine power, and the *Ductor* goes on to describe how, in the course of history, God recurrently changed his laws: "For when God commanded Abraham to kill his son, the Israelites to rob the Egyptians and to run away with their goods, he gave them a commandment to break an instance of the natural law, and he made it necessary that Cain should marry his sister."[56] The natural law is alterable, relative to necessities in different times and places. God has the power to annul nature as a whole; similarly, God can annul nature's laws, "which are consequent to nature and intended only for her preservation."[57]

This last point is important because in it Taylor is making two different claims. On the one hand he is articulating his Ockhamist view of God's freedom. Yet he is also saying that the intention of the natural law is to preserve the natural world. This second claim serves to mute the implication that God's will might be arbitrary or destructive. Taylor's key objective is that we understand (and apply) divine rules with the conservation of nature in mind. The idea that the natural law is alterable is meant not simply to ensure divine freedom, but to assure us that such alterations have a recognizable purpose, the well-being of nature and humanity. Accordingly, Taylor writes, "As [God] can take away the necessity from this person at this time to eat and can supply it otherwise, so he can also *conserve human society* in the mutation of cases and extraordinary contingencies as well as in the ordinary effects of justice."[58] Divine voluntarism, in other words, is not wholly capricious or unpredictable; it is constrained in part by God's prior commitment to creation.

Taylor's voluntarism grows out of practical, not speculative or theological, interests. Applications of the law of nature to human affairs must work within the opportunities and constraints of ordinary life. The idea is to make sure that the general well-being of humanity is not lost amidst a morass of moral rules. Our moral codes, in other words, ought to have as their basis humanistic, everyday needs. Taylor writes:

> Nothing less than the value of a man, or the concernment of a man is the subject of moral laws, and God having given to a man reason to live justly and usefully, soberly and religiously, having made these reasonable and matters of conscience by a prime inscription, has by such prime reasons related to God or man bound upon us all moral laws.[59]

Divine voluntarism provides Taylor with a theological basis for avoiding a morality of absolutes; it may be the case that, owing to human necessities, the rules must change or give way to other duties. In Cain's case, for example, incest was necessary for the preservation of the race and was only a temporary measure.[60] A conservative necessity was at stake; the ban on incest was therefore trumped by more fundamental exigencies of the time.

The effect of these Ockhamist notes in the *Ductor* is to create a theory of presumptive, but not absolute, rules. Human necessities are not meant to justify a utilitarian theory; we are not advised to ascertain the relative balance of pleasure over pain when deliberating about how to act. Rather, Taylor articulates a theory in which we are to abide by conventional codes to the extent that they preserve our everyday needs. They remain in force until we can determine that a rival divine mandate ought to prevail. Thus Taylor writes, "Until God changes his own establishments, and turns the order of things into new methods and dispositions, the natural obligations are sacred and inviolable."[61]

In this regard Taylor seems intent on crafting a morality of modest expectations. His concern with moral absolutes, like his worries about the scrupulous conscience, is that morality can be oppressive and counterproductive. Stern morality can be debilitating, and the *Ductor* by no means articulates an ethic for heroes. Instead we must relax some of our expectations: "If the strict and severer sense of the law be too great for the state and strength of the man, if it be apt to make him despair, to make him throw away his burden: to make him tire, to be weary of, and to hate religion, his infirmities are to be pitied, and the severest sense of the law is not to be exacted of him."[62] The idea, once again, is that we must do the best we can; what matters is how we live everyday life, not whether we have exceptional moral gifts. Taylor remarks, "The gentler sentence and sense of laws is to be applied to ease the weary and the afflicted, him that desires much and can do but little, to him that loves God and loves religion, to him that endeavors heartily, and inquires diligently, and means honestly, to him that has everything but strength, and wants nothing but growth and time, and good circumstances and prosperities of piety."[63]

ORDINARY LIFE

Although Taylor's Thomist and Ockhamist sources might seem to operate at cross-purposes, in his mind they were held together by an affirmation of ordinary life. Right reason and conscience must be informed by a religion that "is . . . incorporated with the actions and common traverses of our life";[64] similarly, the natural law must be understood in terms of God's will to conserve the natural world. We are now in a position to see what this affirmation of ordinary life implies for Taylor.

Simply put, it concerns those aspects of life pertaining to production and reproduction, what we need to do to continue and renew existence.[65] Following the Reformation's emphasis on the dignity of vocations and everyday work, this ethic asks that we reevaluate labor and the professions. In effect, the affirmation of ordinary life assigns an enhanced status to the profane. Sobriety and self-discipline are given a central place, and everyday affairs are understood as providing the arena in which God can be glorified. Calling for an innerworldly asceticism, it replaces the asceticism of monastic vocations.

The affirmation of ordinary life thereby breaks down the distinction, central to medieval Catholicism, between lower and higher forms of activities. Indeed, at the heart of this affirmation is a rebellion against an ethic of hierarchy, which ranks religious and monastic life above that of secular affairs. The traditional ethic, drawing from the Greeks and medieval Christianity, assigns production and reproduction an infrastructural role.[66] Practical activities, labor and family, provide only the external necessities for the worthier life of contemplation or religious asceticism. But the Reformation rejected this hierarchy, esteeming ordinary life as good in and of itself. What was important in work and marriage was not what one did, but how well, how devoutly, one carried out one's vocation.[67] The value of one's personal commitment replaces an ethic of religious austerity and performance. In particular, marital relations are esteemed above virginity, and special emphasis is placed on the ideal of loving, companionate marriage. A social leveling is thus inherent in the affirmation of ordinary life. As Charles Taylor writes, in the seventeenth century "the center of the good life lies now in something which everyone can have a part in, rather than in ranges of activity which only a leisured few can give justice to."[68] In effect, the mainline reformers aligned themselves with the productive artisan classes and against aristocratic groups, which prided themselves on leisure.[69]

Jeremy Taylor's casuistry falls squarely within this trend. Everyday practices, he remarks, are eligible for virtue: "To walk, to eat, to drink, to rest, to take physic for the procuring [of] health, or the ease of our labors, . . . to talk, to tell stories, . . . is good, not only naturally, but morally, and may also be spiritually so."[70] This endorsement is especially apparent when Taylor addresses the merits, and limits, of religious observance:

> If by the service of God is meant the virtue of religion expressed in external action, as saying our prayers, receiving the holy sacrament, visiting Churches, sitting at the memorials of martyrs, contemplation, fasting, silence, solitude, and the like, then

> it is as certain that the service of God in this sense is to be preferred before many things, but not before all things, not before many things of our ordinary life, not before many things of civil society.[71]

Keeping holy days is important, he observes, but such rites are "not to be preferred before bodily labor in our trade, if that labor be necessary for the feeding our family with daily bread."[72] Temporal needs are important, and may trump various spiritual goods. If, for example, a priest commands his congregation to worship and the prince commands some members of the flock to defend the city walls, those members are obliged to obey civil authority.[73] Spiritual goods generally rank above temporal goods, but not always: "Actions of high and precise religion may be the excellences and perfections of a human soul, but the offices of civil government, their keeping men in peace and justice, their affrighting them from vile impieties, may do much more good to mankind, more glory to God in the whole event of things."[74]

But it is not simply that Taylor complicates the traditional hierarchy between spiritual and temporal goods. He wishes to blur distinctions between various temporal callings as well. The main point is that *how* one carries out one's calling is more important than *what* that calling happens to be. The idea, echoing the Puritan Joseph Hall, is that "God loveth adverbs."[75] So Taylor writes, "Whatsoever the employment of a man's day or a man's life be, though never so mean, yet if it be done with a single eye, and with an intuition to Christ, is a holy employment."[76] A prince who refuses the offer of an empire because it does not belong to him is no better than a poor herdsman who "dwells upon his own acre, and feeds his little yokes and couples of sheep on highways and mountains, and looks not ambitiously on his neighbor's farm." Taylor continues: "For there is no virtue but may be loved and courted, delighted in and commended in every state and circumstance of life: and though it be not exercised in noble temptations, and trials proper to the most excellent and remarked persons; yet the very images and little records of trial may express a love and choice which may be equal to that which is prosperous by the greatest exercise and indication."[77]

This concern for the goods of production and reproduction impinges upon Taylor's casuistry in important ways. It means, among other things, that ethical expectations must be calibrated to everyday, practical considerations. There must be a realism in what should be demanded of people; a casuistry that exacts too much is unworkable and inhumane. Thus, religious laws should be charitable and easy, "fitted to the infirmities and capacities of all men."[78]

Yet Taylor's ethic of modest expectations should not be confused with laxism. It is not unfettered liberty that he is after, but an honest understanding of our many duties in everyday life. Our morality may generate conflicts, in other words, between legal codes and practical realities, and casuistry goes awry when it undermines the good of life itself. As we shall see when it comes to the duty of truth-telling, Taylor holds consistently to the idea that "nothing is fit to be put in balance to the life of man; and therefore when a man's life and a man's goods are compared abstractly, these are extremely outweighted by that."[79] The regard for ordinary life can generate a conflict of duties, and one task of the *Ductor* is to determine when standard moral codes are to remain in place and when they are to give way to practical necessities.

CASUISTRY AND TRUTH-TELLING

Taylor's casuistry about lying had to reckon with the overpowering influence of Augustine, whose rigorist, absolute ban (*On Lying, Against Lying*) established the standard doctrine throughout the medieval period.[80] Augustine's rationale is twofold: Lying violates the teaching of Scripture, and it contradicts the purposes of language itself. According to the first rationale, there is the Decalogue's prohibition in Dt 5:20 against bearing false witness, Jesus' command in Matt 5:37 ("Let what you say be simply 'Yes' or 'No'; anything more than this comes from the devil"), and Paul's admonition in Eph 4:25 ("Putting off falsehood, let everyone speak the truth with his neighbor").[81] According to the second rationale, we must consider the essence of speech itself. Augustine writes, "It is evident that speech was given to man, not that men might therewith deceive one another, but that one man might make known his thoughts to another. To use speech, then, for the purpose of deception, and not for its appointed end, is a sin."[82] Setting aside jokes, Augustine remarks that lying occurs when we have one thing in our minds and another in our speech, seeking to deceive. Lying involves duplicity, "a double thought: the one, of that thing which he either knows or thinks to be true and does not produce; the other, of that thing which he produces instead thereof, knowing or thinking it to be false."[83]

But it is also the case for Augustine that we might serve lesser goods—temporal goods—by lying. The duty to tell the truth is absolute, but not all lies are equally wrong. Depending on whether they satisfy another genuine need, some lies are more pardonable than others. Lying in order to convert another to believe in Christianity is worse than lying to protect an innocent person from an unjust arrest, which is worse than lying to protect oneself or others from sexual violation. The first lie is more grievous than the second because lying for the sake of spreading Christianity is a corruption of Truth itself. Such a lie can produce no temporal good.[84] And, while the second lie serves some temporal good, it is worse than the third lie because hindering authority is more heinous than failing to protect a private individual's body. Augustine prohibits utility from trumping duty, while conceding that considerations of utility allow for degrees of wrongdoing.

In this regard Augustine's theology, especially a theology of creation, shapes his ethics. His belief that creation—the result of God's graciousness—constitutes a realm of relative goodness prevents him from ignoring the tension between duty and utility in cases of truth-telling. For Augustine, the theological issue at stake is Manicheanism. If temporal goods were absent in his casuistry, he would find himself divorcing the order of redemption from the order of creation, leading to an endorsement of a Manichean worldview. The Manichees considered the created order to be worthless, if not evil. But by affirming the relative goodness of the created order, Augustine was able to endorse the value of temporal goods (like political authority) and the disvalue of temporal evils (like sexual violation) in his ethics of truth telling. Thus for Augustine all lies are unlawful and jeopardize one's chances of salvation, but they are not equally sinful because they are more or less useful. Lies on behalf of utility vary in gravity, depending on the type of temporal goods—real goods—that they serve.

Yet for Augustine these goods are infrastructural. They provide external aids for pilgrims exercising virtue on their way to the heavenly city. As such, temporal goods have a subordinate status in his ethic, providing an incomplete, earthly peace. The relative goods of bodily existence and political life furnish the material conditions for members of the city of God to pursue their lives of virtue.[85] These relative goods may be lost against our will, and they are incommensurable with goods that are necessary for final communion with God.[86] In Augustine's hierarchy, goods of our earthly existence must always remain subordinate to eternal goods, goods that are requisite for salvation. As a result, the pursuit or protection of goods like bodily integrity or political order may never trump the mandate to tell the truth. The loss of temporal goods in Augustine's scheme is incomparable with the loss of an eternal good, like the good of truth.

Taylor's casuistry of lying takes this tension between truth-telling and rival temporal goods one step further, producing a presumptive but not absolute prohibition of lying. He begins his discussion of lying by recalling the Scriptural ban, citing Pr 13:5 ("A righteous man hates lying") and Col 3:9 ("Lie not to one another").[87] A lie, he continues, is "something said or written to the hurt of our neighbor, which cannot be understood otherwise than to differ from the mind of him that speaks."[88] To the biblical ban on lying Taylor adds an important rationale: Lies are wrong insofar as they deny another the right to the truth. He writes: "For there is in mankind a universal contract implied in all . . . intercourses, and words being instituted to declare the mind, and for no other end, he that hears me speak has a right in justice to be done him, that as far as I can what I speak be true." To say one thing while thinking another "is a perverting [of] the very end and institution of words, and evacuates the purpose of laws, and the end of oaths."[89] To this Taylor attaches the weight of Augustine's opinion, noting that Augustine defends an absolutist position. But Taylor observes that Augustine also appears to leave the door open to alternative arguments. Augustine condemns all lying, Taylor writes, "unless peradventure (says he) you are able to give us rules when a man may lie, and when he may not."[90] *In Taylor's mind, the task of casuistry about truth-telling is to rise to Augustine's challenge.*[91]

Like Augustine's, Taylor's ban on lying is premised in part on the end of speech itself: Words are instituted to reveal the contents of the mind, "and for no other end." On the basis of the essence, or end, of speech, he derives the mandate to tell the truth. In this instance his logic is essentialist and teleological, focusing not on God's declared will but on the natural end of speech. On these grounds Taylor speaks about the right of truth, a natural right that is owed to others.

But for reasons we have seen, the rights that derive from nature are subject to qualification in Taylor's theory. They pertain to the *lex naturae* which, as I have said, is not always obligatory. Moreover, consequentialist considerations accompany the affirmation of ordinary life that may qualify the right to truth. A lie is not simply that which betrays the mind and intends to deceive; it is something said or written that hurts the neighbor. Such an injury stands *in addition* to the injustice of lying, and as a separate concern it provides Taylor with some latitude in settling difficult cases. A deliberate falsehood that is not injurious, by Taylor's lights, either is not a lie or a justified lie. In this way he constructs a general, presumptive prohibition against lying, but not an absolute ban. The right to receive the truth ordinarily belongs to everyone, but it may sometimes be withdrawn "by a superior right supervening, or it may be lost, or it may be hindered, or it may cease upon a greater reason."[92]

For example, a paternalistic lie is permissible. A statement that contradicts the mind but which may be charitable and useful to another is not sinful. Children and madmen, for example, have no right to the truth; nor do hypochondriacal patients, on whom physicians may use "little arts of wit and conzenage."[93] But such lies are permissible only if some good is involved; even persons who have no right to truth "are defended by the laws from injury."[94] In addition, we may lie in order to generate inquiry and truth; fictions may be told to "him that believes a false opinion, and cannot any other way so easily be confuted."[95] Such fictions should be aimed at another's improvement; they are "like the supposing a false proposition in disputation, that upon that false supposition a true conclusion may be erected."[96]

Similarly, it is permissible to tell a lie to save the life of an innocent person—something that Augustine would never concede.[97] In circumstances when lying would clearly save an innocent party from harm, the lie is the lesser of two evils, and lying is not only permissible, but commendable. "To save a man's life is better than a true story," Taylor writes, urging us to measure one set of goods against another.[98] Likewise, princes may not lie to their people, "unless there is in it no harm, but all good, as in order to persuade the people to a duty, or to their benefit, they in matters of public life being like children."[99]

Nor are lies in war evil, for war occurs outside the law of nature, where the enemy has no right to the truth. Rather, wars take place where the rights of nature—and the liberties therein—apply. Indeed, in war both parties make a tacit consent to relinquish the right to truth, and lying may help one's cause: "If you tell a false tale to him to deceive him, when you are fighting against him, he is a fool if he believes you, for then you intend to destroy him, but you are not unjust, you are in a state of war with him, and have no obligation upon you towards him."[100] Lying is an aid in strategy, "an engine of war," against which the enemy must stand guard.[101] Once again, we are to measure one set of goods against another. In war "you [are] no more obliged to tell him truth than to spare his life, for certainly of itself killing is as bad as lying."[102] Treaties and truces between the proper authorities move the opposing parties from the state of war into the law of nature, thereby binding them to keep their promises. But apart from promises made with consent and by proper authority, the rights of nature suspend the duty to tell the truth.

In all these cases a temporal good competes with the good of truth-telling, and Taylor is willing to grant that goods other than the truth ought sometimes to prevail. His concern for temporal goods requires him to make concessions to moral complexity and conflict, allowing practical concerns to override the duty always to tell the truth. Taylor adds that most persons are willing to accept trading off such temporal goods against their right to hear the truth. When a "man is willing to receive advantage, there is no harm done, if he be deceived that he may not be undone."[103] This is because suffering the loss of truth is proportionately less evil than losing one's life. Taylor poses the analogy: "He that is in danger of drowning is willing enough to be pulled out of the water, though by the ears, or the hair of the head"; similarly, reasonable persons will exchange the loss of truth for the benefit of remaining alive.[104] Not all temporal goods should be traded off; it is not acceptable, for example, to lie in order to protect fame or reputation. It is rather that the basic goods of life, the *sine qua non* of human existence, are eligible as rivals to the duty of truth-telling.[105] Physical life, victory in battle, childrearing, education, political life, medical care, and social intercourse provide Taylor with the kinds of reasons to meet Augustine's challenge to "give us rules when a man may lie."

Taylor describes circumstances surrounding lying so that it can sometimes fall outside the standard prohibitions. Just as taking another's property is occasionally pardonable, so too with taking away the truth. In both cases there are times when it is safe to presume that another person will take leave of her rights. Taylor remarks, "He that receives the good is willing to receive it with the loss of a useless or hurtful truth, and therefore there is no injustice done; as he that takes his neighbor's goods, for which he has reason to believe his neighbor willing, is no thief, nor the other the deceiver."[106] Although the Decalogue prohibits stealing and lying, circumstances can be more complicated, allowing for exceptions. An assumption of permission can surround rights that otherwise protect property and speech. In the case of truth-telling, we can generally presume the hearer's desire to receive charity at the expense of the truth.

A similar logic shapes the *Ductor*'s treatment of mental reservations, which represent a somewhat different problem. This case, which Augustine does not address, concerns the morality of hiding part of the truth from another. One expresses a half-truth and secretly reserves the remainder, hoping that one's interlocutor will not press for further details. The effect may be to deceive the listener. But for Taylor the paradigm provided by the case of lying shapes his casuistry of mental reservation: "In the same cases in which it is lawful to tell a lie, . . . it is lawful to use a mental reservation."[107]

This is not to say that Taylor sets out to produce a permissive position. Indeed, his interests may have been quite the opposite. In the sixteenth and seventeenth centuries Catholics had been sought out and executed in England, and the doctrine of mental reservation provided them with apparent moral justification for evading interrogation and prosecution. So as an example of an illegitimate mental reservation, Taylor cites the case of Edmund Campion, a Jesuit tried under the Act of Treason and executed in 1581. While under oath Campion allegedly gave his name to the magistrate as Butler, adding the reservation "It is the name that I have borrowed, or my name for this time." That is no different from a lie, Taylor writes, for what is central is whether Campion's speech intended to deceive someone to whom the truth was owed. No less than lying, mental reservation "is a perverting [of] the very end and institution of words."[108] The main consideration is whether the interlocutor has the right to hear the truth. (In Taylor's mind, Campion's case met this condition and his mental reservation was unwarranted. This is because, for Taylor, the authority of government is unimpeachable.)[109] When an interlocutor lacks the right to truth we have no need for mental reservations; we may be better off lying, so long as our aims are charitable and useful.

Equivocations are similar to mental reservations in that both conceal part of the truth from one's hearers. An equivocation takes advantage of the fact that we allow a word or phrase to have several legitimate meanings. Equivocations occur when a speaker avoids clarifying the meaning of her utterance, hoping that the interlocutor will interpret it differently than she intends.[110] The effect is to deceive, taking advantage of verbal ambiguities.

For Taylor such "amphibious" statements are to be understood within the general paradigm provided by his casuistry of lying: When it is lawful to lie, it is lawful to equivocate. The ban against lying and equivocation should be understood in presumptive terms, open to qualification by concerns that derive from the regard for ordinary life. In the case of equivocations, however, such qualifications are easier to produce. Since ambiguities are less controversial than lying, we have somewhat greater latitude when using them. A verbal ambiguity is morally neutral, strictly speaking: It "is true as well as false, and therefore it is in its own nature innocent; and it is only changed into a fault when it is against justice and charity, under which simplicity is to be placed."[111] Ambiguity is part of speech itself, not a violation of its essence. Thus, necessity permits equivocations more readily. They are acceptable "in arts and sciences, in jest and intercourses of wit, in trial of understandings and mystical teachings, in prudent concealments and arts of secrecy."[112]

In more difficult cases, the paradigm of lying still applies. So long as we use words in their natural or common senses, we may prevaricate when it seems necessary to charity and when we are under no obligation to speak the complete truth. For example, it is lawful to equivocate if a wicked person may draw a false conclusion and thereby be prevented from injuring another person. In speaking truly we are not responsible for the wicked person's error, and ministering to a wicked person's deception for another's benefit is no sin. "An equivocation is like a dark lantern," Taylor writes. "If I have just reason to hold the dark side to you, you are to look to it, not I."[113] In effect, the wicked person denies herself the full rights of social intercourse, including rights to the truth.

CONCLUSION

Taylor's casuistry of truth-telling takes Augustine's endorsement of the relative importance of temporal goods one step further, thereby producing a presumptive but not absolute duty to tell the truth. What was, in Augustine's casuistry, the basis for determining the relative severity of different lies assumes greater positive weight in Taylor's discussion. In other words, the basis for creating a hierarchy of wrongdoing for Augustine becomes, for Taylor, the grounds for weakening the prohibition of lying and generating competing obligations. Saving a life, political duty, success in war, medical care, family needs—practices in which we continue or renew life—all place pressure on the duty to tell the truth. Taylor's embrace of ordinary life as more than an infrastructural good—as a good in itself—allows him to qualify Augustine's ban and strengthen the merits of rival duties.

Unfortunately, Taylor does little to specify which temporal goods may trump the duty of truth-telling. There is little in the *Ductor* to indicate when "the value of a man, or the concernment of a man" might provide a basis for witholding truth from another. Taylor rather suggests that we consider such a possibility on a case-by-case basis. Duties to third parties, political obligations, military victory, medical care, and domestic relations all provide spheres in which the duty to renew or continue life might conflict with the duty to tell the truth. But Taylor eschews any attempt to organize or systematize how the goods of ordinary life might be ranked in relation to truth-telling. Either he thought that the meaning and weight of basic goods of ordinary life were obvious, or he feared that developing such specifics might lead to legalism and scrupulosity.

In any event, Taylor's shift from the Augustinian position is clear, and he is aware of the stakes involved. He represents the contest between truth-telling and other temporal goods as a tension between love and fairness. The problem with the absolute ban against lying is that it privileges justice at the expense of charity, thereby overlooking other goods that we might produce if we weakened Augustine's prohibition. "Truth is justice when it does good, when it serves the end of wisdom, or advantage, or real pleasure, or something that ought or may be desired; and every truth is not more justice, than every restitution of a straw to the right owner is a duty."[114] A "real service" may be done to others by lying, Taylor writes, "in which case only I say that it may seem allowable."[115]

The result is an ethic that is not only more permissive than Augustine's position, but also more complex. The second of these concerns drives Taylor's casuistry of truth-telling. He is not interested in generating liberties that are unavailable in the traditional ban; rather, he is concerned with alerting us to other responsibilities that complicate the moral life. For him, unlike Augustine, cases of lying can produce real conflicts of duty, generating situations of moral perplexity. Augustine might retort that, in situations of perplexity, Taylor's own advice should be to follow the safer course, which would favor the (stricter) teaching of tradition. But Taylor's response is that following tutiorism may be overly scrupulous, that a rigorist morality can be a sign of weakness.

Taylor's casuistry finds more general, theoretical sanction in his account of the natural law, which (owing to its Ockhamist undercurrents) fails to produce a morality of essential acts and absolute prohibitions. It is also qualified by a concern for the neighbor's more general well-being and an appreciation for the genuine goodness of ordinary life. To the modern mind, with its secular orientation, Taylor's casuistry doubtless has some appeal. But in the end, his complaint is not merely that Augustine's ban is too stern or otherworldly. It is also too simple.[116]

NOTES

1. See Blaise Pascal, *The Provincial Letters*, trans. with an introduction by A. J. Krailsheimer (New York: Penguin Books, 1967).

2. Albert R. Jonsen and Stephen Toulmin, *The Abuse of Casuistry: A History of Moral Reasoning* (Berkeley: University of California Press, 1988), 158. For a study of British casuistry, see Edmund Leites, ed., *Conscience and Casuistry in Early Modern Europe* (Cambridge: Cambridge University Press, 1988); H. R. McAdoo, *The Structure of Caroline Theology* (London: Longmans, Green and Co., 1949); Thomas Wood, *English Casuistical Divinity During the Seventeenth Century, with Special Reference to Jeremy Taylor* (London: S.P.C.K., 1952); Camille Wells Slights, *The Casuistical Tradition in Shakespeare, Donne, Herbert, and Milton* (Princeton, N.J.: Princeton University Press, 1981), chaps. 1, 2, and passim.

3. Jeremy Taylor, *Ductor Dubitantium: Or the Rule of Conscience* (London: Royston at the Angel in Ivy Lane, 1660) [hereafter *DD*].

4. Edmund Grosse, *Jeremy Taylor* (New York: Greenwood Press, 1968).

5. In this regard I take exception with the claim that Taylor was a systematic casuist in Edmund Leites, "Conscience, Casuistry, and Moral Decision: Some Historical Perspectives," *Journal of Chinese Philosophy* 2 (1974): 55.

6. Margaret Gest, *The House of Understanding* (Philadelphia: University of Pennsylvania Press, 1954), 23.

7. C. J. Stranks, *The Life and Writings of Jeremy Taylor* (London: S.P.C.K., 1952), 115.

8. Cited in Lindsay Dewar, *An Outline of Anglican Moral Theology* (London: A.R. Mowbray and Co., Ltd., 1968), 44.

9. George Worley, *Jeremy Taylor: A Sketch of His Life and Times, with a Popular Exposition of His Works* (London: Longmans, Green, and Co., 1904), 193.

10. Thomas Aquinas, *Summa Theologiae,* I–II, Q. 91, art. 2; Q. 94 art. 2.

11. Relevant texts can be found in Arthur Hyman and James J. Walsh, *Philosophy in the Middle Ages: The Christian, Islamic, and Jewish Traditions* (Indianapolis: Hackett Publishing Co., 1973), 609–52.

12. For helpful discussions of Ockham on this point, see David W. Clark, "Voluntarism and Rationalism in the Ethics of Ockham," *Franciscan Studies* 31 (1971): 72–87; Linwood Urban, "William of Ockham's Theological Ethics," *Franciscan Studies* 33 (1973): 310–50; Kevin McDonnell, "Does William of Ockham Have a Theory of Natural Law?" *Franciscan Studies* 34 (1974): 383–92; Marilyn McCord Adams, "The Stucture of Ockham's Moral Theory," in this volume.

13. For an instructive account of this influence in Luther's thought, see B. A. Gerrish, *Grace and Reason: A Study in the Theology of Luther* (Chicago: University of Chicago Press, 1979).

14. As Adams shows, Ockham coordinated a rationalist account of right reason with a more voluntarist approach to moral motivation by distinguishing between the nonpositivist elements in moral theory from the category of merit/demerit.

15. Charles Taylor, *Sources of the Self: The Making of Modern Identity* (Cambridge: Harvard University Press, 1989), part III.

16. For an instructive discussion of these tensions, see Robert Hoopes, "Voluntarism in Jeremy Taylor and the Platonic Tradition," *Huntington Library Quarterly* (August 1950): 341–354. Although Hoopes correctly calls attention to the nominalist currents in Taylor's casuistry, he may overstate the extent to which Taylor's moral sources are at odds with each other. Or so I hope to show in this chapter.

17. DD, Bk. I, 38.

18. Thomas Aquinas, *Summa Theologiae,* I, Q. 79, art. 13, ad 1.

19. Ibid., I–II, Q. 94, art. 1, ad 1.

20. Ibid., I, Q. 79, art. 13. For an instructive historical overview of conscience in the Roman Catholic tradition, see Charles E. Curran, *Themes in Fundamental Moral Theology* (Notre Dame, Ind.: University of Notre Dame Press, 1977), 191–203.

21. DD, Bk. I, 31.

22. Ibid., 9.

23. Ibid., 6.

24. Ibid., 6.

25. Ibid., 154.

26. Ibid., 61.

27. Ibid., 53.

28. Ibid., 120. For a discussion, see Jonsen and Toulmin, *The Abuse of Casuistry,* 167–70.

29. DD, Bk. I, 168–69.

30. Ibid., 157.

31. Only once Taylor admits an equiprobabilistic position, Ibid, 141. For discussions of probabilism in casuistry, see Jonsen and Toulmin, *The Abuse of Casuistry,* 167–70, 175; John Mahoney, *The Making of Moral Theology: A Study of the Roman Catholic Tradition* (Oxford: Clarendon Press, 1987), 135–43; *The Westminster Dictionary of Christian Ethics,* 2d ed., s.v., "Casuistry" by Thomas Wood.

32. *DD,* Bk. I, 147.

33. Ibid., 209.

34. Ibid., 208.

35. Ibid., 217–18.

36. Ibid., 218.

37. Ibid., 180–81.

38. Ibid., 215.

39. Ibid., 219.

40. Ibid., Bk. II, 220, emphasis added.

41. Ibid., 221.

42. Ibid.

43. Ibid., 238.

44. Ibid., 221.

45. Ibid., 233.

46. Ibid., 233.

47. Ibid., 232.

48. Ibid., 230.

49. Ibid., 234–35.

50. See ns. 11, 12, 13 above.

51. The "Epistle Dedicatory" to *DD,* dedicated to Charles II, p. 1.

52. Ibid., Bk. I, 1.

53. This aspect of Taylor's moral theory is overlooked in Thomas Wood's account of Taylor's understanding of law in *English Casuistical Divinity*

During the Seventeenth Century, 80–92 (see n. 2). Wood overstates the parallels between Taylor and Aquinas's *De Legibus* in *Summa Theologiae,* I–II, Qq. 90–108, and omits Taylor's allusions to Ockham altogether.

54. Ibid., Bk. II, 240.

55. Ibid., 242.

56. Ibid., 238.

57. Ibid., 240.

58. Ibid., emphasis added.

59. Ibid., 369.

60. Ibid., 239.

61. Ibid., 269.

62. Ibid., 433.

63. Ibid., 437.

64. Ibid., Bk. I, 219.

65. Taylor, *Sources of the Self,* 211. Throughout this discussion I am drawing from Charles Taylor's discussion of the affirmation of ordinary life in the seventeenth century in *Sources of the Self,* sec. III (see n. 15). Taylor focuses largely on the emergence of an instrumental stance toward the world and the scientism of Bacon, calling attention to shifts in the fundamental moral horizons of Western thought in the early modern period. Jeremy Taylor's casuistry illustrates how the affirmation of ordinary life affected more specific problems in ethics during the seventeenth century.

66. Ibid., 211.

67. See, e.g., John Calvin, *Institutes of the Christian Religion,* bk. 3, chap. 14, pars. 18–19.

68. Ibid., 214.

69. Ibid., 231.

70. DD, Bk. IV, 446.

71. Ibid., Bk. III, 181.

72. Ibid.

73. Ibid., 193.

74. Ibid., 182.

75. Taylor, *Sources of the Self,* 224, and passim.

76. DD, Bk. IV, 518; cf. Bk. III, 181.

77. Ibid., Bk. IV, 445.

78. Ibid., Bk. III, 318.

79. Ibid., 109.

80. For discussions, see Jonsen and Toulmin, *The Abuse of Casuistry,* chap. 10; Johann P. Sommerville, "The 'New Art of Lying': Equivocation, Mental Reservation, and Casuistry," in *Conscience and Casuistry in Early Modern Europe,* ed. Leites, 159–84; Kenneth Kirk, *Conscience and Its Problems: An Introduction to Casuistry* (London: Longmans, Green and Co., 1948), 188–95.

81. Augustine, On Lying, in *The Nicene and Post-Nicene Fathers,* ed. Philip Schaff (Grand Rapids, Mich.: Eerdmans, 1956), 460.

82. Augustine, *Enchiridion on Faith, Hope, and Love,* trans. J. F. Shaw, ed., with an introduction by Henry Paolucci (Chicago: Henry Regnery Co., 1961), par. 22. Aquinas follows this line of argument in *Summa Theologiae,* II–II, Q. 110.

83. Augustine, *On Lying,* 458.

84. Ibid., 475.

85. Augustine, *City of God,* trans. Henry Bettenson, with an introduction by David Knowles (New York: Penguin Books, 1972), bk. 19.

86. Augustine, "On Free Will," I, 5, in *Fathers of the Church,* vol. 39, trans. Robert P. Russell (Washington, D.C.: Catholic University of America Press, 1968), 82.

87. These citations are as Taylor records them, not as they are in the RSV.

88. *DD,* Bk. III, 83.

89. Ibid.

90. Ibid., 84.

91. Taylor is not suggesting that his disagreements with Augustine are merely academic. Augustine's position serves as the foil against which Taylor develops his casuistry for perplexed consciences. As I remarked at the beginning of this chapter, circumstances of Taylor's day generated the need for casuistical inquiry. Unfortunately, the *Ductor* makes little mention of the actual circumstances or pastoral needs of Taylor's audience.

92. Ibid.

93. Ibid.

94. Ibid.

95. Ibid., 85.

96. Ibid.

97. Ibid., 85, 88.

98. Ibid., 86.

99. Ibid., 97.

100. Ibid., 93.

101. Ibid., 96.

102. Ibid., 94.

103. Ibid., 87.

104. Ibid.

105. In effect, Taylor produces something like the theory of proportionate reasoning, as that is understood in contemporary Catholic moral theology. Lies that undermine the good of life are disproportionate. Thus, the act in question should be redescribed. Taylor cites Andronicus Rhodius: "He does indeed deceive, but he is no deceiver; because not the cozening but the curing of his friend is the purpose of his false affirmative." See ibid., 91.

106. Ibid., 87.

107. Ibid., 97. In this case, and in the case of equivocation, Taylor's method operates by proceeding from a clear paradigm (lying) to analogous acts. As Jonsen and Toulmin note, "This gradual movement from clear and simple cases to the more complex and obscure ones was standard procedure for the casuist; indeed, it might be said to be the essence of the casuistic mode of thinking." See Jonsen and Toulmin, *The Abuse of Casuistry,* 251–52.

108. Ibid., 98.

109. Ibid., Bk. III, 130–74. For a discussion, see George Mosse, *Holy Pretence: A Study in Christianity and Reason of State from William Perkins to John Winthrop* (Oxford: Basil Blackwell, 1957), 132–141.

110. Jonsen and Toulmin, *The Abuse of Casuistry*, 201.
111. *DD*, Bk. III, 103.
112. Ibid.
113. Ibid., 101.
114. Ibid., 89.
115. Ibid.
116. I am grateful to Scott Ellis, Judy Granbois, Barbara Klinger, David H. Smith, and the editors of this volume for their assistance in producing this chapter.

Part Four

THE LEGACY OF CASUISTRY: Manuals and Development

The Manual and Casuistry of Aloysius Sabetti

CHARLES E. CURRAN

The American Catholic Church in the nineteenth century produced manuals of moral theology to serve as textbooks for its seminarians. These manuals prepared the future priests to serve as confessors, with special emphasis on their role as judge to determine what is sinful and the degree of sinfulness. This study will focus on the manual originally written by the Jesuit Aloysius Sabetti in 1884, *Compendium Theologiae Moralis,* which continued to go through subsequent updatings with newer editions put out by Sabetti's successors in teaching moral theology at Woodstock College, the Jesuit Scholasticate in Maryland.[1] Sabetti's Latin manual was the most influential and longlasting of the nineteenth-century moral manuals written in the United States, with over thirty editions published.[2] In a 1935 doctoral dissertation Theodore Heck, a Benedictine monk, examined the course of study in thirty-two seminaries training diocesan priests at that time. Ten of the seminaries reported using Sabetti as the textbook in moral theology, while the text of Jerome Noldin, an Austrian Jesuit, was the most popular textbook, used in twelve diocesan seminaries.[3]

OVERVIEW OF THE WORK AND THE AUTHOR

In accord with our contemporary understanding, Aloysius Sabetti is really not the author of probably 90 percent of the book which bears his name. This transplanted Neopolitan Jesuit rather has merely taken the John Peter Gury manual, edited by Anthony Ballerini, and redacted it for American use at Woodstock. The excellent quality of this older manual influenced him to adapt this book to the American context rather than try to write a new volume of his own.

His redaction of Gury–Ballerini involved a number of steps. First, he eliminated from the volume those aspects dealing specifically with the French situation. Second, he updated some of the material, especially on the matters of censures in the light of more recent Roman documents. Third, he included the pertinent realities from the

American scene. Since moral theology deals with practical applications, one must know the diverse local conditions. Fourth, Sabetti worked to improve the practical usefulness of the Gury–Ballerini manual. Subsequent updatings had increased the notes at the bottom of the page and added to the growing size of the manual. In fact, often the footnotes took up more space on the page than the text. Our American author did away with all the footnotes and put everything into the text in the same type of print. He also shortened the book and tried to make his points as clearly and concisely as possible.[4] Sabetti indicated that he was using the third edition of the Gury–Ballerini manual, so one can readily compare the original with the adaptation made by the American Jesuit.[5] The modern reader who reads the brief preface is still unprepared for the extent to which Sabetti depended on and used Gury–Ballerini.

The contemporary American reader and scholar comes from a very different perspective. The author presents one's own thought. Any material taken from another must be carefully cited and noted. The American academy today is very conscious of plagiarism and looks upon intellectual work as the private property of the individual scholar. Sabetti and all the manualists came out of a different tradition. Their writing is done in and for the church. Sabetti was merely trying to hand on to his own students the best possible textbook in moral theology. He made no claim to originality, but only wanted to help students from the common patrimony of the Catholic tradition. Sabetti closely follows the Gury–Ballerini manual not only in its general outline and development of particular issues, but even in its ideas and very words. A fellow professor at the Jesuit theologate at Woodstock has confirmed this judgment. "He never claimed any originality for his volume; I do not mean originality of principles for that would be a very dangerous claim for any theologian to make; but not even an originality of treatment. He simply took up Gury and applied his principles to changed circumstances of time and place."[6] Another commentator points out, that especially in his first fourteen years at Woodstock, Sabetti was very wary of giving his own opinions and even more so in defending them. However, after an encounter with a particularly articulate but unbalanced interlocutor, Sabetti gained confidence and began to speak more in his own voice.[7]

Sabetti's compendium fits squarely into the tradition of the manuals of moral theology. In his introduction to the work our Jesuit author makes no specific mention of the sacrament of penance, but it is evident that his whole purpose is to prepare seminarians and priests for their role as confessors in deciding about the morality and gravity of particular actions. According to the Council of Trent the faithful have to confess their sins according to number and species.[8] The manuals primarily focused on what was sinful and the gravity of the sin. For example, in the discussion of the obligation to hear Mass on Sundays and feast days, Sabetti's very first sentence asserts that all the faithful who have the use of reason are held sub gravi (under grave obligation) to be present at Mass, as is evident from various places in canon law and from all the catechisms in which the certain precept of hearing mass on these days is declared.[9]

Although the introductory note to the reader does not mention the sacrament of penance, Sabetti clearly states the nature of his work—a brief and practical manual with the intended audience of young students in our seminaries preparing themselves for priesthood and missionaries laboring in the Lord's vineyard. The students do not need dense dissertations, nor controversies, nor doubts, nor new and strange approaches, but brief and solid solutions provided by their professors. Missionaries (for Sabetti pastoral work in the United States was missionary work) will find a short treatment in which solutions that perhaps have been forgotten will at a moment's notice be perceived.[10]

Aloysius Sabetti was not an intellectual and really did not claim to be a scholar. Sabetti received the same education as other Jesuit priests and had no special graduate training in moral theology. The Italian Jesuit did not originally come to the United States to teach at Woodstock College, but to work among the Indians in New Mexico. However, after six months of preparing to go to New Mexico he was told that he was to teach at Woodstock College. He later affectionately referred to his Woodstock students on many occasions as "his Indians."[11]

The testimony of his colleagues and students confirms the impression from his writings that Father Sabetti was not really an intellectual or original scholar. Patrick Dooley in his discussion of the early Woodstock mentions the scholarly work of Fathers Meyer, Mazzella, and De Augustinis. "It does not detract in the least from his (Sabetti's) merit to say that in point of talent he could not equal any one of the three just mentioned, yet in point of achievement he surpassed them all in winning credit for the house. . . ."[12]

His personality seemed perfectly suited for the work he did in preparing ministers for the sacrament of penance. Almost all the published material we have about Sabetti the person comes from reminiscences from colleagues and students published in Woodstock Letters shortly after his death. One must approach these comments written on the occasion of his death with the proper hermeneutic, for such reminiscences usually filter out the negative and accentuate the positive. However, the various commentators paint a very similar picture of Aloysius Sabetti. Above all, he was a sympathetic person. Dooley describes him as a "loving and sympathetic personality."[13] A fellow professor maintained that Sabetti had in an eminent degree the quality of sympathy.[14] In one paragraph Father Ennis used the noun sympathy or its adjective five times to describe Sabetti.[15] Italians have the habit of calling a person "simpatico," a term of great respect and endearment which would seem to be a most appropriate description of this transported Southern Italian.

Sympathy is a very important virtue for one who is a moralist. One must be able to appreciate and feel for the people in their predicaments. A cold detached personality too often cannot appreciate the reality and experience of others. The confessor and the moral theologian should be sympathetic in order to truly help the penitent. The Jesuit students at Woodstock recognized the sympathy of their moral professor, for in times of their own doubts and problems they would go to him for help. The great majority of students chose him for their confessor rather than another member of the faculty.[16]

The term moralist used in a derogatory sense includes the connotation of puritanical and rigoristic. Neither Sabetti's writings nor his personality seemed to have such characteristics. There is also the tendency for moralists to take themselves and their own opinions too seriously and stress their own self-importance. Sabetti was not such a person. Sabetti was apparently an easy-going, lovable, somewhat heavyset Italian who was interested in helping other people and well liked by all. He was if anything somewhat naive and was often teased by fellow faculty members and students alike. However, he enjoyed being teased and would think something awry or that he had offended someone if he were not teased.[17] Sabetti did not take himself too seriously but could often laugh at himself and others, according to these reminiscences. Recall that for the first fourteen years he seldom ventured to even give his own opinions on a particular subject.[18] His humility, self-effacement, and ability not to take himself too seriously all helped him to be a good moral theologian in terms of preparing confessors for the sacrament of penance.

Another important characteristic for a good moralist is clarity. Anyone reading Sabetti's textbook can appreciate this virtue in the author. The clarity, order, conciseness, and preciseness of his written exposition indicate the same characteristics in his thinking. The testimony of his colleagues and friends underscores the clarity of his writing and of his thinking. Clarity and sympathy are the two words most used about Sabetti in the reminiscences at the time of his death. He was perfectly clear in his explanations. When a difficulty arose he was never satisfied until his questioners understood and accepted the answer.[19] Father Ennis acknowledges that there are probably works wherein questions are treated more extensively and with greater erudition, but none are clearer or of easier application than Sabetti.[20] Precision is closely allied to clarity. Sabetti was precise in his thinking and his writing. In his writing he adapted the material of Gury–Ballerini to his students by reducing its length and sharpening its force. In the introduction to his compendium, Sabetti claims that the students do not need long disquistions but brief and solid solutions.[21] Precision in analyzing the situation, in describing what is the heart of the problem, and in proposing solutions is a most important characteristic for the manualist. Sabetti's precision is evident throughout his work.

The moral theologian following the path of Alphonsus Liguori strives to avoid the twofold extremes of rigorism and laxism. Such a person needs a good pastoral and common sense. Beware of the zealot or the one who acts too hastily. A fellow professor lauded Sabetti for his "mental stability and equipoise."[22] This clearheaded common sense comes through in his writing and helps give him his reputation.

Sabetti had no ambition to be a scholar or an original thinker, but wrote for the needs of the church. As such he had to be aware of the realities that people lived and experienced in their lives. His sympathetic nature was a big help in this matter. But Sabetti knew that he had to be familiar with the problems and issues of people. He often spent his vacations hearing confessions and working in a parish so that he would be in touch with what was happening and never become one who taught but never practiced what he taught.[23]

THE MORAL MODEL

Contemporary theologians talk about three different models for moral theology—the deontological, the teleological, and the relationality–responsibility model.[24] Not all moral theologians even on the contemporary scene deal explicitly with the question of the ethical model they are using, but in reality all approaches will use one or another of these models as the primary way of understanding the moral life.

Sabetti does not explicitly consider the question of models, but he obviously follows the deontological model. The deontological model sees the moral life primarily in terms of duty and obligation. Sabetti structures his development of moral theology on the basis of a law model. This legal model common to all the manuals coheres very well with the purpose of the manuals, to point out what acts are sinful and their degree of sinfulness. The manuals of moral theology first treated fundamental moral theology, which discussed what was basic and common to all moral issues. The manuals then developed at much greater length special moral theology, which considered specific moral actions, generally following the schema of the commandments and the sacraments.

Fundamental Moral Theology

The first three short treatises in the compendium clearly show forth the legal model at work in this manual as in all manuals. The first treatise discusses human acts; the second, conscience; and the third, laws. The very nature of the matters discussed here, as well as the fact they are the first three matters considered, shows the legal model at work. However, Sabetti would have been even more explicit about the model he is using had he not chosen to eliminate the very first introductory paragraphs found in Gury–Ballerini in the discussion of both human acts and laws. Sabetti apparently left them out in his attempt to shorten the discussion, but they are very important short paragraphs because they explain the basic framework of the approach taken. Gury–Ballerini's first paragraph introducing human acts maintains that since moral theology concerns the proper evaluation of human acts, the nature of things and the common custom call for the book to begin with a discussion of human acts.[25] The introductory paragraph on law succinctly states that law is the external and remote rule of human acts, just as conscience as the dictate of reason is the internal and proximate rule of human acts.[26] Sabetti, with his penchant for clarity, might have been better to retain these two short introductions which explicitly give the reason for treating these three topics at the very beginning of the manual and explain the legal model employed. Sabetti himself, near the beginning of his discussion of conscience, points out that conscience is the proximate rule of the will.[27] The fourth tract treats sins and on the basis of the legal model defines sin as the free transgression of any law binding in conscience.[28]

The Commandments

This legal model dictates the basic approach taken not only in the short discussion of the fundamentals of morality but also in the consideration of particular moral acts. The major discussion of the morality of human acts common to all employs the schema of the ten commandments, with each commandment developed on the basis of the sins opposed to the commandment. In discussing the first commandment, for example, Sabetti begins by pointing out that this commandment, insofar as it is affirmative, prescribes the acts of the virtue of religion, specifically the obligations of adoration and prayer. The purpose and model of the manual dictate how these realities are treated. Prayer must constitute an important part of the life of the Christian person, and one would expect to see both adoration and prayer as the response of the Christian to the gift of God's loving self in Jesus through the Spirit. But the one-page consideration is only interested in the legal and minimal aspects. Sabetti makes two comments about prayer. The first treats the necessity of prayer. Prayer is certainly necessary for all adults by a necessity of precept, as is evident from many texts in the Scriptures. In addition, according to most authorities, prayer is also necessary by a necessity of means because it is the ordinary way instituted by God for attaining graces.[29]

This first statement made by Sabetti about prayer deserves some comment. Something is necessary by a necessity of means if it is required by the nature of things to achieve a necessary goal. Something is required by a necessity of precept if one is commanded to do it by a competent authority. In this case the first reason for the necessity of prayer is the precept found in the Bible. A legal model tends to make the will of the legislator the primary source of obligation. Sabetti does mention that most authorities hold to the obligation of prayer as a necessity of means, but the emphasis here is not on the internal reasons why prayer is necessary as a means to the end, but simply that most authorities hold it to be so. The one and only reason given why prayer is considered by most to be required by a necessity of means concerns the need to obtain the necessary graces. But even at this time Catholic theology did not reduce prayer just to supplication for the necessary graces to live a Christian life. Prayer involves adoration, contrition, and thanksgiving, as well as supplication. In the light of the narrow purpose of the manuals, these other aspects of prayer are not mentioned. Prayer becomes merely a means to obtain the necessary grace to obey the law.

Today one rightly rejects such an approach and understanding. The Christian life involves our loving union with a gracious God who comes to us. Prayer is an absolutely necessary means to receive, perceive, and grow in that union with God. The very nature of the Christian life calls for prayer. Prayer is not something established primarily by a precept or command coming from the outside but arises from the very nature of the Christian life itself. A legalistic approach easily becomes extrinsic and sees something to be good because it is commanded. However, prayer is commanded because it itself is good and necessary for the Christian life. The Christian life is distorted if its obligations are seen primarily as coming from an external power and not based on the intrinsic meaning and enfolding of the reality itself. Sabetti and the manualists in general put heavy emphasis on morality as obeying an external authority, who in this case is God who commands us to do certain things.

The legal model in moral theology tends to emphasize the role of human acts in salvation and forgets that salvation is primarily God's gracious gift. Historically such an approach has been identified with the heresies of pelagianism and semipelagianism. We save ourselves by our own works. According to the brief sections in this text we should do the act of human praying in order to obtain the divine grace to avoid sins and be saved. Note that the human act of prayer comes before divine graces! One thus sees in this discussion of prayer the dangers of legalism, extrinsicism, and a tendency to downplay and subordinate the divine gift and God's grace.

Sabetti's second comment about prayer records the need to pray frequently, but that does not mean without interruption, for that is impossible given human weakness. The biblical words from Luke 18 about praying always mean to pray frequently and at the opportune time. The two questions raised in this one-page discussion of prayer have to do with when the precept to pray obliges. *Per accidens*, the obligation to pray arises whenever prayer is necessary to attain a certain end. Clearly the precept to pray obliges per se often and frequently in our life. However, the experts are greatly divided over precisely when this obligation arises. In practice one can hold the opinion maintaining that one who prays at least once a year does not commit a grave sin. Notice here the tendency to become minimalistic because of a hesitancy to convict a certain act of being a mortal sin. To his credit, Sabetti, following Gury–Ballerini, points out that the confessor should be more solicitous about inculcating in the penitent the necessity of praying frequently than in determining a grave fault when prayer is omitted. Sabetti, following his guide, also raises a question that was still common among Catholic children (and even adults) in the pre-Vatican II American church—does one sin at least venially by not saying morning and night prayers? The short, precise, and clear response is: per se one does not sin because there is no law which prescribes determined prayers at particular times or days. Here again, the primacy is on the law as the force of obligation and law understood as something external to the lived reality.[30]

The first commandment, in addition to prescribing certain acts, also forbids certain acts which are then discussed under the two headings of superstition and irreligiosity. In keeping with the precision of the manuals these terms are first defined and the various types of superstition and irreligiosity are discussed. Superstition is, according to Aquinas, the vice opposed to the virtue of religion by excess either because it gives divine worship to someone or thing to which it is not due (the more common form) or gives divine worship in an inappropriate way or manner. Four species of superstition are succinctly defined and discussed. Idolatry is the action by which the worship due to God alone is given to a creature. Vain observance is a superstition by which means that are neither proportionate nor instituted by God are used to achieve a certain effect. The three types of vain observance are: seeking knowledge without labor, seeking health by inappropriate means, or seeking from the observance of fortuitous events that one will have good or bad luck in the future. The above is a paraphrase of Sabetti but shows the clear mind at work and the concise and precise way in which the material is discussed. These same attributes are present in the discussion of the nature and gravity of vain observance. Vain observance is a grave sin because it gives divine honor to a creature while expecting from the creature what one should expect from God alone and because it is based on an implicit pact with the devil. However, often it will only be a venial sin because of the imperfection of the act, simplicity of the person, or a certain ignorance or timidity as often happens among uneducated people.[31] Here the author prudently recognizes the many factors that in practice diminish culpability and make this only a light or venial sin. In a similar way Sabetti discusses divination and magic.[32] The contemporary reader is struck by the frequency with which these considerations involve the work of the devil. Belief in good and evil spirits still retains an important role in Sabetti's manual in the late nineteenth-century United States.

The entire elaboration of the ten commandments, consuming almost one hundred pages, follows the legal model and clearly illustrates this method at work. After the ten commandments Sabetti treats in the customary way of the manuals the commandments or precepts of the church. Sabetti mentions in the beginning that different enumerations of these commands binding on all the faithful are found in different sources, but there is not that much difference with regard to substance. Sabetti here follows the number and wording of the commandments of the church which had been formally adopted by the Third Plenary Council of Baltimore in 1884. The six precepts of the church are: (1) To hear Mass on Sundays and feast days. (2) To observe fasting and abstinence on certain days. (3) To confess sacramentally at least once a year. (4) To receive the eucharist (communion) in paschal time. (5) To contribute to the fitting support of the pastor. (6) To abstain from the celebration of marriage in those circumstances forbidden by the church.[33] This discussion takes up almost twenty pages, but the material about marriage is discussed in the later section on the sacraments and not here.[34] The legal model certainly encouraged the development of such a list of commandments of the church to go along with the ten commandments of God. These commandments then become the means that the faithful use to examine their consciences before going to the sacrament of penance.[35]

The tenth and last tract before the long discussion of the sacraments continues to flesh out and illustrate the legal model by discussing particular obligations. The first part, comprising eight pages, deals with the particular obligations of lay people.[36] Sabetti notes that he will treat primarily those obligations relating to the public good and especially legal matters. Other roles of the laity such as workers, merchants, and teachers are discussed elsewhere in the book. Thus he discusses the obligations of judges, lawyers, defendants, and witnesses. A final short section discusses the obligations of doctors. Here again, for example, he states the general obligations of doctors clearly and concisely, and then develops further ramifications. Doctors are held above all under grave obligation to have sufficient knowledge and skill and to use diligence proportionate to the gravity of the matter. If doctors are deficient in these things, they are held to all the damage that follows from their acts. In addition, doctors are to help gratuitously the poor who are in need.[37] Much of the discussion focuses on the obligations of clerics and religious.[38] The short discussion given to the particular obligations of the laity in comparison to clerics and religious indicates the greater importance and emphasis given to the clerical and religious life as well as the tendency of the manuals to emphasize church laws, which are quite numerous with regard to religious and clerics.

Other Treatises

There are two tracts in the entire book apart from the treatment of the sacraments which do not at first sight seem to follow from and be structured by the legal model. The fifth tract deals with the virtues. Virtue is defined as the habit of acting according to right order. Theological virtues (faith, hope, and charity) have God as their immediate formal object, whereas the moral virtues have the correctness of the action as their immediate formal object. The moral virtues can be reduced to the four cardinal virtues of prudence, justice, fortitude, and temperance. This section, however, discusses only the theological virtues because the moral virtues are discussed throughout the other parts of the compendium.[39] In the beginning of the discussion of faith, Sabetti mentions that he will not consider the many things treated about faith in dogmatic theology but will discuss only the necessity of faith, the formal logic of faith, and the vices opposed to faith. Thus the treatise is not at all about the virtue of faith but about the acts of faith. The necessity of faith discusses both the internal and external acts of faith that are required. The material object again deals with the act of faith. The vices opposed to faith are the two acts of infidelity and heresy.[40] Thus the discussion of the virtue of faith is really a discussion of the acts of faith precisely under the legal rubric of what is required and when, and also the acts opposed to faith. Sabetti discusses hope and charity in the same way.[41] So despite the titles dealing with virtue the tract deals with acts in the light of what is prescribed or prohibited. The legal model has totally influenced the way that Sabetti treats the theological virtues.

Tract VIII on justice and rights constitutes the longest discussion on strictly ethical matters, prescinding from the sacraments.[42] The discussion begins with the definition of justice and a description of the four kinds of justice. Legal justice inclines one to render to society what is required for the common good. Distributive justice regulates how the honor, offices, and common burdens are to be distributed among the members of the society according to a due proportion of merits and abilities. Vindictive justice inclines the ruler (for the good of society to inflict on the guilty appropriate punishments Sabetti here has not made the transition to the American scene but merely repeats the word *princeps*, used by Gury–Ballerini,[43] which is not accurate in the American scene). Commutative justice inclines the will to render a strict right to a private individual, observing a strict arithmetic equality. By that is meant that commutative justice deals with the inherent arithmetic equality which is the same for all, no matter who the persons are. After this discussion of the four kinds of justice, Sabetti concludes that his book will treat only commutative justice, because in the strict sense commutative justice alone merits to be called justice.[44]

The reason proposed by Sabetti for treating only commutative justice is traditional within Catholicism. Commutative justice involves a strict mathematical equality of what is due and what is given. The other types of justice aim at a proportional equality and therefore in theory are not strict justice. However, the real reason for not treating the other aspects of justice comes from the very nature of the manuals. They are geared to the confessor and the penitent and hence deal primarily with individual morality. The entire aspect of social ethics as distinguished from individual ethics is missing in these textbooks. Thus in Sabetti there is no discussion of the state, the political order, the economic order, or the cultural realities. All these aspects lie outside the parameters of the manuals of moral theology.

This individualistic orientation coheres very well with a legal model. The law determines what the individual should and should not do. Thus the discussion on justice does not consider all the ramifications of justice, especially in terms of the relationship of society to the individual. For all practical purposes the discussion on the virtue of justice really amounts to a discussion of the seventh and tenth commandments. Sabetti signaled this reality earlier in his treatment of the ten commandments. He skips the seventh and tenth commandments because the tract on justice and rights will discuss the "various sins of injustice" concerning property and possessions.[45]

The Sacraments

Sabetti devotes over 300 pages to the discussion of the sacraments. The opening tract on the sacraments in general introduces separate tracts on each of the seven sacraments—baptism, confirmation, eucharist, penance, extreme unction, orders, and matrimony. The fundamental definitions are developed on the basis of a legal model. A sacrament is a sign permanently instituted by Christ to sanctify and confer grace.[46] The very definition is geared to examine the validity of the sacrament from a legal perspective. The primary question concerns what is required to truly constitute the sign. Contemporary theologians often speak of sacraments as encounters with God and the community, but such understandings are difficult to analyze from a legal perspective.

The basic questions concern what is required for a valid sacrament (what is required so that the church acknowledges this reality as a true sacrament) and a licit or lawful sacrament (what is in keeping with the laws of the church but not affecting the basic validity of the sacrament). For example, the wearing of certain vestments might be required for liceity or the lawfulness of the sacrament but not for its validity. The discussion of the sacraments in general and of each of the individual sacraments follows the same general outline. The role of the sacraments in the life of the community and of the individual Christian is not mentioned. The whole spirituality of the sacramental life is missing. The legal perspective by definition deals with the minimum and with the minimum understood primarily in the light of visible external criteria. Sabetti and the manualists first discuss the matter and form of the sacraments. The matter is the sensible reality determined by its form to become a sacrament. The form which determines the significance of the matter regularly consists in the words of the minister.[47] Thus, for example, in baptism the matter is the ablution with water and the form involves the words spoken by the minister, "I baptize you in the name of the Father and of the Son and of the Holy Ghost." The questions raised in this section concern what words are required for validity (e.g., is "I christen" a valid form?) and what material is truly water (e.g., what about snow?).[48]

The discussion next considers the minister of the sacrament, who in general must have the proper attention (the attention required for a truly human act, which is compatible with some distractions) and intention (a virtual intention but not an habitual or interpretive intention suffices for validity). Under this heading Sabetti repeats the general teaching that neither faith, nor probity of life, nor the state of grace is required on the part of the minister for a valid sacrament although they are required for a licit administration, at least if the minister is consecrated to confer the sacrament and confers it solemnly in accord with the prescribed ritual.[49] Sabetti earlier mentioned the famous reason why the sacrament is valid without faith or the state of grace in the minister—the sacraments are said to work *ex opere operato*—by the very fact that the work or the sacrament has been done.[50] Thus if the matter and the form are present with the necessary attention and intention, there is a valid sacrament. The discussion of each sacrament goes more specifically into the question of the minister of that particular sacrament. For example, the ordinary minister of confirmation is the bishop while a simple priest is the extraordinary minister.[51]

Sacraments in general then treat the subject in terms of both validity and lawfulness. In penance, for example, the discussion of the subject treats the three acts of the penitent—contrition, confession (with the requirement of the integral confession of sins according to number and species), and satisfaction.[52] The last part of the sacraments in general discusses the ceremonies in the administration of the sacraments.[53] Thus the discussion of the sacraments in general and of each individual sacrament follows the same basic approach about the requirements of validity and lawfulness with regard to matter and form, the minister, the subject of the sacrament, and the ceremonies.

The legal influence on the understanding of sacraments is even more pronounced with regard to marriage. Marriage is both a contract and a sacrament. As a contract, marriage is an agreement by which a man and a woman legitimately give to each other dominion over their bodies for acts that are per se apt for the generation of offspring and obligate themselves to an indivisible partnership of life. As a sacrament marriage is a sacrament of the new law conferring grace for sanctifying the legitimate union of husband and wife and for faithfully undertaking progeny and educating them piously and virtuously.[54] However, the sacrament is understood primarily as a contract, and the concept of contract pervades the whole treatise.

The Catholic Church has developed an elaborate legal system to deal with marriage, and the centrality of the concept of contract underscores this legal approach. What is required for a valid contract? Church law developed a long list of impediments. Prohibitive impediments render the marriage contract unlawful but not invalid. Diriment impediments, which render the marriage null and void, include substantial error, consanguinity, etc. Note that one can attain a dispensation from some impediments.[55] The church court system has been developed to deal with annulments of marriage. The official Catholic position then and now holds to the indissolubility of marriage, thus forbidding divorce and remarriage, but marriage can be declared null and void if there is no true contract from the very beginning.

After the long treatment on the sacraments, Sabetti has two tracts (XIX and XX) on censures (spiritual and medicinal penalties) and irregularities (impediments to the reception or exercise of holy orders). By definition these are legal realities discussed in canon law and developed accordingly by Sabetti and all the manualists.[56]

Thus Sabetti, in keeping with all the manualists, emphasizes a legal model and consistently and coherently develops the entire book on that basis. From the ethical perspective, some of the negative aspects of such an approach have been mentioned—the emphasis on the minimal, the extrinsic, and human effort as distinguished from divine grace. The legal model also distorts the understanding of God and of the church. God is seen primarily as the lawgiver. The love, mercy, and forgiveness of God are mentioned, but they are subordinated to the role of God as lawgiver. God the lawgiver also provides the reward and sanction for the law. Often the fear of the sanction becomes more important than our love for God. The justice of God assumes a greater significance than the mercy of God. God's grace, the primary reality in the Christian life, is reduced to a means to obey the law. The legal model coheres well with the ultramontanist ecclesiology, which stresses the church as a hierarchical society with the pope enjoying the fullness of power. Such a model downplays the church as the people of God or even the body of Christ.

Positive features of the legal model also deserve mention. The legal mind at work in Sabetti and other manualists results in a very precise and concise approach. Definitions and concepts are clearly given. Important distinctions are delineated so that one can classify the different types of actions. Principles are enumerated in a very accurate and concise manner. The manuals stand out for their clear and orderly presentation. Such an approach has much to recommend it, especially to the beginning student who is trying to learn a discipline for the first time.

SPECIFIC MORAL REASONING ABOUT HUMAN ACTS

Human reason occupies a central place in the approach of Sabetti and the manualists to evaluate the morality of particular acts. Sometimes this reason will employ arguments from Scripture and church authority, but these fit within the larger framework of human reason enlightened from other sources going about its work. The legal model influences how reason goes about its task of evaluating human actions. This section will discuss how Sabetti develops his casuistry or moral analysis of particular cases.

The Method of the Compendium

Every consideration begins with a definition, which is characterized by a very precise and concise formulation. For example, scandal is defined as a word or deed less upright, giving to another the occasion of a spiritual fall. These terms are then briefly explained. "Word or deed" includes also omissions. "Less upright" refers to something which is evil in itself or has the appearance of evil. "Giving the occasion" recognizes that the proper cause of sin is the will of the primary agent. "Spiritual fall" includes either mortal or venial sin.[57] Dominion, for example, is defined as the right of disposing of a certain thing as one's own in every use which is not prohibited by law or agreement.[58] Another example: drunkenness is voluntary excess in drinking to the point of losing reason.[59] Such succinct definitions clearly delineate what is being talked about.

After the definition Sabetti ordinarily strives for precision and further classification by presenting the important distinctions or types of what is being considered. Such classification enables the student to discern precisely what is involved in a particular case. Sabetti, for example, accepts the classical distinction of lying as speech against what is in the mind. There are three types of lies: a malicious lie inflicts unjust harm on another; an officious lie is told for the advantage of oneself or another; a jocose lie is told for the sake of a joke or amusement. This threefold distinction obviously paves the way for the judgment about the morality and the gravity of lying. A lie differs from a mental reservation, which is an act of the mind distorting or restricting the words of a certain proposition to a meaning different from the natural and obvious meaning. There are two types of mental reservations. A pure mental reservation means that the true meaning of what is spoken can in no way be perceived by the hearer. A broad or improper mental reservation occurs when the true sense of the speaker can be perceived from the circumstances. Sabetti illustrates a broad mental reservation with the classical case of the servant who tells a caller that the master is not home when in reality the master is home. People generally understand such speech to mean that the master is not home for the purpose of visiting or talking.[60]

Such careful distinctions help the student and the priest in the confessional to sort out and classify the matter under discussion. These distinctions supply one with a grid of classifications so that one can determine exactly what is the particular reality under discussion. Is this a lie, a pure mental reservation, or a broad mental reservation? If it is a lie, what kind of lie is it? The legal approach tends to classify, compare, contrast, and differentiate. All this abets an orderly and clear process. The first step in ethical analysis is to determine what is occurring. What is the reality that must be morally analyzed?

The example of almsgiving also illustrates this method.[61] A true precept of giving alms to the needy exists, as is proved from the general law of charity obliging us to love our neighbor and from Scripture which is supported by two proof texts—Ecclesiasticus 4:1 and Matthew 25:42. The precept of giving alms includes two presuppositions—indigence or necessity on the part of one receiving the alms and a superfluity on the part of the giver. Necessity can be of three different types: extreme necessity means that the danger of death or of another evil almost equal to death is so proximate that it cannot be avoided except with the help of another. Grave necessity renders one's temporal existence very burdensome. Ordinary and common necessity is that state in which one is able to provide for herself without grave difficulty. Poor beggars on the street generally fall into this category, for their life, according to their condition, is not too burdensome or miserable. Superfluous goods are of two types. Superfluous for life are those goods which one is able to live without. Superfluous to one's state in life are those goods which are not necessary for honestly and decently living according to one's state in life; e.g., having servants, entertaining guests. (This discussion well illustrates the class differences found throughout Sabetti.)

Three practical and succinct rules follow. (1) I am obliged to come to the assistance of my neighbor in extreme necessity certainly and only with goods necessary for my own state in life. Certainly, because the right order of charity demands that the life of the neighbor take precedence over my own far inferior goods; only, however, because my life is nearer to me than the life of my neighbor and therefore I do not have to sacrifice what is necessary for my life. (2) In grave necessity which comes close to extreme necessity, I should help the neighbor with goods that are somewhat necessary for my state in life or with a slight harm to my state in life. Notice the attempt to find another category between the categories of extreme and grave. In a grave necessity which is not bordering on the extreme, it is enough to assist the neighbor from those goods which are superfluous for my state in life. (3) In common necessity, although there is no obligation of giving alms to this or that person in particular, the common opinion of the theologians maintains that the person having goods superfluous to one's state and never giving any alms cannot be excused from sin.

What about the gravity of this precept to give alms? Almsgiving, like the precept of charity, per se constitutes a grave obligation, but it does not oblige gravely in every necessity. In extreme and grave necessity touching on the extreme, the obligation is grave. The theologians are divided not only about whether there is a grave obligation to give alms to a particular poor person who labors under a simply grave necessity but whether there is a grave obligation for helping poor people in general who are in common need.

How much should be given to the poor? In extreme need or grave touching on extreme, one must give what suffices to take away the need here and now unless there are others willing to help. No one is held, however, to give a large sum of money for freeing a poor person from the danger of death or for obtaining extraordinary and very expensive remedies. In common need, a determined quantity cannot be assigned but more probably it suffices to give 50 percent of the goods which are superfluous to one's state.

The discussion of killing an unjust aggressor moves in the same direction. After justifying the killing of an unjust aggressor in order to save one's own life, Sabetti offers five legitimate instances: if the aggressor is out of her mind or drunk, for such a person is a materially unjust aggressor; in defense of material goods of great value; a woman in defense of her chastity; and killing the unjust aggressor to save the life of a neighbor. Sabetti gives a negative response to the case of killing an unjust aggressor of one's honor. Such a position is in keeping with the condemnation of this act by Innocent XI. If the injury is already done, then the act is not defense. If the injury is in the process of being done, it can be repelled by means less than the death of the attacker. In this example of killing in self-defense, one sees how the case of defense of honor differs from the other cases and therefore is not permitted.[62]

In the context of the compendium Sabetti approaches particular cases by going from principles to rules to the cases. However, this method is obviously dictated by the very purpose, method, and approach of the manuals themselves. The compendium does not pretend to be solving cases for the first time. The compendium's format comes from its pedagogical purpose of preparing seminarians and priests for the ministry of the confessional. Logically, the cases are seen as applications of principles and rules to the particular issue, but is this how Sabetti would deal with the morality of a case when it is first presented to him?

The Logic of Sabetti's Casuistry

We know that bishops, priests, and others frequently consulted him about moral cases. He discussed a case of conscience each week at

Woodstock. Before he fell ill near the end of his life he apparently was planning on putting together a book on cases of conscience based on his previous work.[63] Sabetti published a number of solutions to cases of conscience in the *American Ecclesiastical Review*. However, the vast majority of these cases do not deal with moral issues as such but with canonical issues such as baptismal cases, marriage and its invalidity, confession, nuptial blessing, generic confession, matrimonial impediments, and the sanation of marriages.[64] A few moral issues are discussed but the most in-depth discussion concerns ectopic pregnancy. An examination of this discussion should shed some light on his casuistry.

The *American Ecclesiastical Review* presented a discussion beginning in 1893 among many doctors and some theologians on the question of ectopic pregnancy. Three theologians took part in the discussion—August Lehmkuhl, the German Jesuit; Joseph Aertnys, a Dutch Redemptorist; and Sabetti. The original case had a number of parts dealing with different ways of removing the ectopic pregnancy which was threatening the life of the mother. Sabetti and Lehmkuhl both agreed that the ectopic pregnancy (i.e., the immature fetus outside the womb) which is threatening the life of the mother could be removed, but they gave very different justifications for it.[65]

Sabetti himself begins his discussion with a reference to his own methodology in solving cases. It is easier and more intelligible to proceed from the certain to the uncertain.[66] The discussion also illustrates how his case method involved trying to find parallels with other aspects and why parallels did not exist in certain cases. One might speak here of what some contemporary authors call paradigm cases.[67] The crux of the method was to show that the case is permitted or not by comparing it with principles and with other cases.

Parameters of the discussion must be kept in mind. Sabetti had always opposed craniotomy to save the life of the mother and, after the congregation of the Holy Office's condemnation, he maintained that all Catholic theologians would agree. Direct abortion, including craniotomy, was always wrong even if it was done to save the life of the mother. Sabetti strongly insisted on the principle that the end does not justify the means and cited this axiom at the end of his discussions of abortion and craniotomy.[68]

Sabetti clearly recognizes he has to prove two points to make his argument that the ectopic fetus threatening the life of the mother can be killed to save the mother.[69] First, it is licit to kill even directly a materially unjust aggressor against one's life. In its own way this constitutes an exception to the principle that one can never directly kill another human being and somewhat modifies the principle that the end does not justify the means. But Sabetti does not go into these aspects. Sabetti understands direct as that which is a means to obtain the end. Killing the fetus is the means by which the mother is saved. The right to life implies that the individual has all the means necessary for protecting that right, provided the means do not in some way contradict nature or the natural law. Since the aggressor is acting unjustly, he cannot claim any rights. Since the aggressor has lost the right to life by what he does unjustly, the one who kills him in self-defense does nothing wrong. But is this also true of the materially unjust aggressor, that is, the one who does not knowingly and willingly do the injustice against another's life? The ultimate reason why it is permitted to kill an unjust aggressor, observing the proper limits, does not come from the actual malice of the aggression but from the right to defend one's self, which is the same whether the aggression is formal or material. The classic example here concerns the aggressor who is drunk or insane.

Second, is the ectopic fetus threatening the life of the mother a materially unjust aggressor? The presupposition of its threatening the life of the mother proves it is an aggressor. But is it unjust? Yes, the fetus is disturbing the order of nature by being present where it should not be. The ectopic fetus, by being where it should not be, is disturbing the course of nature and severely endangering the certain and persisting right of an innocent party.

Sabetti accepts as a general principle that whenever we find something unnatural and strange, one cannot say that removing it goes against the law of nature because nature does not contradict itself. Thus if a person is born with two noses or six fingers, one can legitimately cut off the extra members. The person in this case does not commit a forbidden mutilation against the fifth commandment because the body is not deprived of its natural integrity. Since the fetus is acting against nature by being where it should not be, it is unjust in its aggression and, therefore, can be directly removed. But Sabetti recognizes an objection that can be raised against him. Logically, if the head of the fetus is too large and cannot be removed from the mother whose life is being threatened, one then can do a craniotomy to save the life of the mother. But the size of the head is not the same unnaturality as two noses, six fingers, or a fetus outside its natural place in the womb. The greater size of the head is an accidental and not a substantial unnaturality. Sabetti recognizes that his approach would justify a craniotomy in this one case if necessary to save the life of the mother threatened by an ectopic pregnancy. But such is his fear and horror of craniotomy that he would repudiate his position in the case of the ectopic pregnancy if the proponents of craniotomy in other cases were to use it to justify themselves.[70] Precisely because Sabetti justifies direct killing of the unjust aggressor, it makes no moral difference to him if the fetus is killed in the womb or outside the womb. In fact, he maintains the decision of what means to use belongs in this case to the doctor and not to the theologian.[71]

While defending his own position, Sabetti strongly rejects the justifying position proposed by Lehmkuhl. Lehmkuhl rightly points out that the primary difference between them is whether the removal of the fetus is a direct or indirect killing and secondarily whether or not the ectopic fetus is an unjust aggressor. Lehmkuhl argues that the removal of the fetus in this case is indirect and not a direct killing. Unlike Sabetti, Lehmkuhl does not allow the fetus to be killed in the womb. Lehmkuhl maintains that the removal of the fetus comes first and with it comes the saving of the mother. The death of the fetus only comes later. Hence the killing is indirect. The death of the fetus is not the means by which the mother is saved. This differs from craniotomy, since the death of the fetus is the means by which the mother is saved. Lehmkuhl appeals to other similar cases to show that the killing here is indirect. His main analogy comes from two shipwrecked people holding onto a plank to save themselves. Knowing that the plank cannot hold both, one person willingly gives up the plank even though she can't swim and will soon drown. Many prominent theologians agree with this approach. Lehmkuhl also appeals to the famous cases of Eleazar and Samson in the Hebrew bible. Eleazar (I Maccabees 6:43 ff.) walked under the elephant carrying the enemy king and slew the elephant, which fell on him and killed him, but the king died too. Many theologians see that as an indirect killing. His action killed the elephant and equally immediately Eleazar and the king died. The death of Eleazar was not the means by which the king was killed.[72]

Sabetti admits the three other examples given by Lehmkuhl. In the case of the shipwreck, Eleazar, and Samson the killing is indirect. The action is good or indifferent, and from this action there follows equally immediately the good effect and bad effect. But the removal of the fetus is not a good or indifferent act. You are depriving the fetus of what is absolutely necessary for its life. This is directly killing. Sabetti appeals to the analogy of taking a fish out of water or cutting off a human being's supply of air. The removal of the fetus is a death-bearing means which brings about the good effect. The killing act is the means by which the good is accomplished. In Sabetti's mind there is an even more important factor at work in this analysis. Sabetti correctly recognizes that the theory proposed by Lehmkuhl would permit the acceleration of birth of an immature fetus which is not ectopic, in order to save the life of the mother. The American Jesuit steadfastly opposes such an action.[73]

Who is correct on this point? In accord with the understanding of the meaning of direct and of the condition of the double effect that the good effect must occur equally immediately as the evil effect and the evil cannot be the means by which the good effect occurs, I think the case could be made for Lehmkuhl. If there were an artificial womb available, the fetus would not have to die. This shows that the good effect of saving the mother is not achieved by means of the bad effect of the death of the fetus. However, this position would definitely have resulted in a different approach to conflict situations involving abortion. The problem revolves around how you define the object of the act. Here the object of the act is the removal of the fetus. The act itself does not kill the fetus. Sabetti adds a circumstance to the object of the act. Lehmkuhl's argument has weaknesses of its own. For example, he maintains that one can think of certain actions which in ordinary circumstances are directly killing or the equivalent of it but in extraordinary circumstances there is no malice and the death is only permitted.[74] Logically, Lehmkuhl should not say that circumstances change the object. The act would be the same—that is, indirect killing in all circumstances—but in the normal circumstances no proportionate reason justifies the indirect killing.

At the end of the nineteenth century, both authors agreed on what was meant by direct and the conditions of the principle of the double effect. Direct is referred both to the intention of the agent and to the nature of the act, especially the causality of the act. You could not directly intend and directly do the evil deed. Sabetti saw the act as directly killing because the act takes away what is absolutely essential for the life of the fetus. Lehmkuhl understood the causality and the object of the act to be the removal of the fetus and not the death which would follow later.

Although Sabetti recognizes that the removal or killing of an ectopic pregnancy in the womb is a direct killing, he still wants to justify such an action when the life of the mother is threatened. He appeals to the principle that one can directly kill a materially unjust aggressor. His argument here is somewhat weak. The ectopic pregnancy is not where nature wants it to be. Therefore, it is an unjust aggressor because it is disturbing the course of nature and threatening the life of the mother. The fetus should not be doing what it is doing, just like the drunk or mentally deranged attacker.[75] One could argue, as Lehmkuhl does, that the ectopic fetus is really not an unjust aggressor because, unlike the drunk or deranged person, the fetus is doing nothing. The fetus' own condition is not caused by itself but by its parents and natural causes.[76]

The hierarchical magisterium soon condemned both Lehmkuhl's defense of indirect abortion and Sabetti's defense of direct abortion in the case of the ectopic pregnancy threatening the mother's life.[77] Later Catholic theologians developed the understanding that the tube or organ containing the fetus becomes infected and hence one could remove the infected tube or organ which happens to contain the fetus. The action does not constitute a direct killing because the act is directed at the diseased or infected organ, even though the fetus is contained in it and will die.[78]

The extended debate on the ectopic pregnancy sheds some light on the nature of Sabetti's casuistry. Sabetti's approach to solving moral cases was more complex than the compendium's approach of seeing it as the application of principles and norms to particular cases. This case history shows a comparative and contrasting analysis with other cases to determine the morality of the case under discussion. Lehmkuhl and Sabetti make different claims in this area even though they come to somewhat the same conclusion.

Another important factor is also at work in Sabetti's casuistry. Sabetti seems to have a basic intuitive moral judgment that the action is good or bad. This intuitive or nondiscursive judgment is part of the whole process. A positive judgment about a particular act looks for a way, if possible, to justify such a conclusion. In this case Sabetti used the principle of repelling a materially unjust aggressor to justify aborting the ectopic pregnancy. One of his students indicated the very significant role of intuitive and nondiscursive judgments in Sabetti's approach, which cannot be found or discovered in the manual itself. When asked a question in class, he would often give an answer without seeing clearly the intermediate steps. On several occasions he replied, "Here is the answer, I'll give the reasons tomorrow; I don't see them clearly now." The student reporting this noted that such a jump to a solution with the frank recognition that Sabetti could not now give his reasons increased rather than decreased one's confidence in him.[79] Such testimony sheds light on how Sabetti's mind worked, but even the genre of cases of conscience does not reveal this factor at work. Sabetti's casuistry certainly recognizes a great role for principles and norms and their applications; but a comparative and contrasting analysis with other cases takes place, and also the intuitive judgment about the morality of the act plays a significant role.

The question arises: Can the judgment about a particular case through this more inductive approach ever cause the theologian to modify or change a very specific principle or norm? Sabetti never recognizes this in any of his cases. For him the insistence on eternal, immutable principles and norms appears to argue against such a modification. This more inductive approach to principles also goes against the heavy emphasis on deduction throughout his work. His classicist approach with little or no historical consciousness would not be open to such changes or modifications in principles and norms. However, in reality such changes have occurred in the history of Catholic moral theology, and John B. Hogan, a French-born American contemporary of Sabetti, recognized the possibility of such modifications.[80]

Another important factor in casuistry for Sabetti and the Catholic manualists of the time was the intervention of the hierarchical teaching office. Sabetti believed that once Rome had spoken, even through a curial congregation, the debate was finished. Sabetti not only did not resent this Roman involvement but warmly welcomed it.[81] The nineteenth century witnessed growing emphasis on the power, authority, and prerogatives of the role of the papacy in the church. In the case of morals the papal teaching office intervened more than ever before to settle disputes among theologians, as well exemplified in the case of direct abortion, craniotomy, the acceleration of birth, and ectopic pregnancy.[82] Aloysius Sabetti, in the tradition of the Neapolitan Jesuits and the Woodstock faculty, was a staunch ultramontanist in his support of the papacy.[83]

Here again one notices an extrinsicism at work. The practical cases deal with what Sabetti in theory called the somewhat distant and remote conclusions from the first principles of the natural law, where different positions exist and theologians often held different sides. But Roman authority could intervene and decide the case once and for all, despite this apparent lack of certitude. Where does that certitude come from?

Sabetti's casuistry recognized a role for comparisons with other cases and for intuitive, nondiscursive moral judgments, but these were always subordinated to and controlled by the accepted principles and rules. No matter how strong and sharp the debate about particular cases, the papal teaching office through the Roman Congregations could and should intervene to solve the question and put an end to all debate.

Aloysius Sabetti was not an original thinker, nor did he make significant contributions to moral theology. However, his work well illustrates the general approach, method, and casuistry of the teachers of moral theology at the end of the nineteenth century.

NOTES

1. Aloysius Sabetti, *Compendium Theologiae Moralis* (Woodstock, MD: Woodstock College Press, 1884). In 1882 Sabetti published 100 copies of a trial edition, which he used with his students at Woodstock and submitted to others for their evaluation and responses. See Edmund G. Ryan, S.J., "An Academic History of Woodstock College in Maryland (1869–1944): The First Jesuit Seminary in North America" (Ph. D. Diss., Catholic University of America, 1964), 64. Thirteen editions were published in his lifetime. This chapter uses the seventh edition published by Fr. Pustet in Germany and New York in 1892. References will be given to the paragraph numbers (n.), which are basically the same in the earlier editions, as well as to the page number of this particular edition used here.

2. Francis J. Connell, "The Theological School in America," in Roy J. Deferrari, ed., *Essays on Catholic Education in the United States* (Washington, DC: Catholic University of America Press, 1942), 224. Paul E. McKeever, "Seventy-Five Years of Moral Theology in America," *American Ecclesiastical Review* 152 (1965): 19, 20; John P. Boyle, "The American Experience in Moral Theology," *Proceedings of the Catholic Theological Society of America* 41 (1986): 26.

3. Theodore H. Heck, *The Curriculum of the Major Seminary in Relation to Contemporary Conditions* (Washington, DC: National Catholic Welfare Conference, 1935), 46, 47.

4. Sabetti, *Compendium*, "*Lectori*," v-vii.

5. Ibid., "*Notandum*," facing 1.

6. "Father Aloysius Sabetti: A Fellow Professor's Reminiscences," *Woodstock Letters* 29 (1900): 216.

7. Patrick J. Dooley, *Woodstock and Its Makers* (Woodstock, MD: The College Press, 1927), 87.

8. Sabetti, *Compendium*, nn. 741-743, 535-538.

9. Ibid., n. 240, 179.

10. Ibid., "*Lectori*," vii.

11. "Father Aloysius Sabetti," *Woodstock Letters* 29 (1900): 215-217; Dooley, *Woodstock and Its Makers*, 86-89.

12. Dooley, 86.

13. Ibid.

14. "Father Aloysius Sabetti," *Woodstock Letters* 29 (1900): 216.

15. "Father Aloysius Sabetti: Reminiscences of Father Ennis," *Woodstock Letters* 29 (1900): 221

16. "Father Aloysius Sabetti: A Pen Picture of Father Finn," *Woodstock Letters* 29 (1900): 223; also 217.

17. "Father Aloysius Sabetti," *Woodstock Letters* 29 (1900): 221; 213. Dooley, 86.

18. Dooley, 87.

19. "Father Aloysius Sabetti," *Woodstock Letters* 29 (1900): 217.

20. Ibid., 219.

21. Sabetti, *Compendium*, vii.

22. "Father Aloysius Sabetti," *Woodstock Letters* 29 (1900): 218.

23. Dooley, 87, 88.

24. For my approach, see my *Directions in Fundamental Moral Theology* (Notre Dame, IN: University of Notre Dame Press, 1985), 11-14; 188-190.

25. Gury–Ballerini, *Compendium*, above n. 1., 1.

26. Ibid., above n. 81, 77.

27. Sabetti, *Compendium*, n. 30, 21.

28. Ibid., n. 124, 85.

29. Ibid., n. 202, 143.

30. Ibid., nn. 202, 203, 143.

31. Ibid., nn. 204-206, 144,145.

32. Ibid., nn. 207-211, 146-150.

33. Ibid., n. 326, 233.

34. Ibid., nn. 326-344, 233-251.

35. Ibid., n. 757, 552.

36. Ibid., nn. 558-566, 365-373.

37. Ibid., nn. 565, 566, 372, 373.

38. Ibid., nn. 567-627, 374-417.

39. Ibid., n. 151, 107.

40. Ibid., nn. 152-161, 107-115.

41. Ibid., nn. 162-199, 115-139.

42. Ibid., nn. 345-557, 252-364.

43. Gury–Ballerini, *Compendium*, n. 518, 475.

44. Sabetti, *Compendium*, nn. 345-346, 252-254.

45. Ibid., n. 309, 220.

46. Ibid., n. 628, 418.

47. Ibid., n. 631, 420.

48. Ibid., nn. 654-657, 438-441.

49. Ibid., nn. 634-636, 421-423.

50. Ibid., n. 628, 418.

51. Ibid., n. 672, 454.

52. Ibid., nn. 729-767, 523-562.

53. Ibid., nn. 649, 650, 432, 433.

54. Ibid., n. 852, 653.

55. Ibid., nn. 867-928, 668-722.

56. Ibid., nn. 944-1061, 738-840.

57. Ibid., n. 182, 128.

58. Ibid., n. 350, 256.

59. Ibid., n. 147, 104.

60. Ibid., nn. 310-313, 221-223.

61. Ibid., nn. 175-177, 124, 125.

62. Ibid., nn. 268, 289, 200-202.

63. "Father Aloysius Sabetti," *Woodstock Letters* 29 (1900): 228.

64. "Sabetti, S. J., The Rev. Aloysius," *American Ecclesiastical Review Index, Vol. 1-50*, 283.

65. Augustinus Lehmkuhl, Josephus Aertnys, Aloysius Sabetti, "*Solutiones Theologorum*," *American Ecclesiastical Review* 9 (1893): 347-360.

66. Sabetti, *American Ecclesiastical Review* 9 (1893): 354.

67. Albert R. Jonsen and Stephen Toulmin, *The Abuse of Casuistry: A History of Moral Reasoning* (Berkeley, University of California Press, 1988), 251-253, 321-325.

68. Aloysius Sabetti, "*Animadversiones in Casum*," *American Ecclesiastical Review* 9 (1893): 433.; Aloysius Sabetti, "The Catholic Church and Obstetrical Science," *American Ecclesiastical Review* 13 (1895): 132.

69. Sabetti, *American Ecclesiastical Review* 9 (1893): 354-357.

70. Aloysius Sabetti, "*Animadversiones in Controversia de Ectopicis Conceptibus*," *American Ecclesiastical Review* 11 (1894): 434.

71. Sabetti, *American Ecclesiastical Review* 9 (1893): 358.

72. Augustinus Lehmkuhl, "*Excisio foetus atque eius directa occisio*," *American Ecclesiastical Review* 10 (1894): 64-67.

73. Sabetti, *American Ecclesiastical Review* 10 (1894): 131-134.

74. Lehmkuhl, *American Ecclesiastical Review* 10 (1894): 65.

75. Sabetti, *American Ecclesiastical Review* 9 (1893): 356.

76. Lehmkuhl, *American Ecclesiastical Review* 10 (1894): 67.

77. Decree of the Holy Office, May 5, 1902 in T. Lincoln Bouscaren, *Ethics of Ectopic Operations*, 2nd ed. (Milwaukee: Bruce, 1943), 22.

78. Bouscaren, *Ethics of Ectopic Operations*.

79. "Father Aloysius Sabetti," *Woodstock Letters* 29 (1900): 218, 219.

80. John Hogan, "Clerical Studies: Moral Theology III, Casuistry," *American Ecclesiastical Review* 10 (1894): 1-12. This article and others in the series published in the *American Ecclesiastical Review* appeared later as a book—John B. Hogan, *Clerical Studies* (Boston: 1898), 223-235.

81. Sabetti, *American Ecclesiastical Review* 6 (1892): 165, 166; 7 (1895): 130, 131.

82. For the story of these interventions, see Bouscaren, *Ethics of Ectopic Operations*.

83. John L. Ciani, "Metal Statue, Granite Base: The Jesuits' Woodstock College, Maryland, 1869-1891," a paper delivered at the Cushwa Center of Notre Dame University in 1983.

Development in Moral Doctrine

JOHN T. NOONAN, JR.

That the moral teachings of the Catholic Church have changed over time will, I suppose, be denied by almost no one today. To refresh memories and confirm the point, I will describe four large examples of such change in the areas of usury, marriage, slavery, and religious freedom, and then analyze how Catholic theology has dealt with them.

USURY

The first is the teaching of the church on usury. Once upon a time, certainly from at least 1150 to 1550, seeking, receiving, or hoping for anything beyond one's principal—in other words, looking for profit—on a loan constituted the mortal sin of usury. The doctrine was enunciated by popes, expressed by three ecumenical councils, proclaimed by bishops, and taught unanimously by theologians. The doctrine was not some obscure, hole-in-the-corner affection, but stood astride the European credit markets, at least as much as the parallel Islamic ban of usury governs Moslem countries today. There were lawful ways of profiting from the extension of credit, but these ways had been carefully constructed to respect the basic prohibition; it was a debated question at what point they crossed the line and were themselves sinfully usurious. The great central moral fact was that usury, understood as profit on a loan, was forbidden as contrary to the natural law, as contrary to the law of the church, and as contrary to the law of the gospel.[1]

All that, we know, has changed. The change can be exaggerated. Even at the height of the prohibition of usury not every form of credit transaction was classified as a loan from which no profit might be sought. The idea of legitimate interest was also not absent. Formally it can be argued that the old usury rule, narrowly construed, still stands: namely, that no profit on a loan may be taken without a just title to that profit. But in terms of emphasis, perspective, and practice, the old usury rule has disappeared; the just title to profit is assumed to exist.

The centrality of "Lend freely, hoping nothing thereby," construed as a command, has disappeared. We take interest as profit on our banking accounts. We expect our banks to profit from their lending business. Our entire financial world is built on profitable charges for credit. The idea that it is against nature for money to breed money, or that it is contrary to church law to deposit in a savings institution with the hope of a profit, or that hoping for profit at all from a loan breaks a command of Christ—all these ideas, once unanimously inculcated with the utmost seriousness by the teaching authority of the church, are now so obsolete that one invites incredulity by reciting them.

MARRIAGE

Usury was a moral doctrine dependent on economic conditions that could change. Let us now consider, as something related to fundamental unchanging human nature, moral doctrine on adultery, bigamy, and marriage. Monogamy without divorce is the law of the gospel, established by words attributed to Jesus himself and related by him to the primordial order established by God (Matt 19:2–9). Within the New Testament, however, a perceptible change occurs. If, of two married unbelievers, one converts and the other does not but deserts the convert, St. Paul teaches that the convert is free: "Neither a brother nor a sister is a slave in these matters" (1 Cor 7:10–16). The implication, teased out in patristic times, is that the convert can commit what otherwise would be adultery and bigamy and enter a second marriage in the Lord.[2]

Until the sixteenth century, this so-called Pauline privilege remained the solitary exception to Christian monogamy. Then, on behalf of African slaves torn from their African spouses and shipped to South America, the privilege was radically extended. The slave who wanted to convert could not know whether his absent spouse would abandon him or not. No matter, Gregory XIII ruled in 1585, it was important that such converts be free to remarry "lest they not persist in their faith." On their behalf, the pope dissolved their old marriages and declared them free to enter a second marriage that would otherwise have been adulterous and bigamous.[3]

The next step in this direction was taken under the impetus of the great canonist Cardinal Pietro Gasparri in the 1920s. In a case from Helena, Montana, Gerard G. Marsh, unbaptized, had married Frances F. Groom, an Anglican. They divorced; Groom remarried. Two years later Marsh sought to marry a Catholic, Lulu La Hood;

Pius XI dissolved Marsh's marriage to Groom "in favor of the faith" of Miss La Hood. Apparently exercising jurisdiction over the marriage of two non-Catholics (Groom and Marsh), the Pope authorized Marsh to marry a Catholic under circumstances that but for the papal action would (morally, not civilly) have constituted bigamy for Marsh and adultery for La Hood.[4] Prior to 1924 the teaching of the church, expressly grounded both on the commandment of the Lord and on the natural law, was that marriage was indissoluble except in the special case of conversion of an unbeliever. The teaching was unanimously expressed by papal encyclicals and by the body of bishops in their universal ordinary teaching. Then, in 1924, by the exercise of papal authority, the meaning of the commandment against adultery was altered; what was bigamy was revised; and a substantial gloss was written on the Lord's words, "What God has joined together let no man put asunder."

SLAVERY

Let us now examine two examples taken from an area more fundamental than justice in lending, more fundamental than rectitude in sexual relations—examples that bear on the basic conditions of moral autonomy. I mean moral doctrine on human liberty. And first, moral doctrine on a human being's right to be free from ownership by another human being.

Once upon a time, certainly as late as 1860, the church taught that it was no sin for a Catholic to own another human being; to command the labor of that other human being without paying compensation; to determine where he or she lived and how much he or she was fed and clothed; to restrict his or her education; to pledge him or her for a loan, forfeit him or her for a default, sell him or her for cash; to do the same to his or her offspring; and to discipline him or her by physical punishments if he or she were rude or boisterous or slack in service. I refer, of course, to some of the features of chattel slavery as it existed in the United States, as it was upheld by American law, and as it was applied by Catholic laymen, bishops, and religious orders with the approval of ecclesiastical authority. No qualm of conscience troubled that leading Catholic jurist, Chief Justice Roger Taney, as he wrote Dred Scott, or disturbed the slaveholding Maryland Province of the Society of Jesus.[5] That loving one's neighbor as one's self was observed only in a Pickwickian way by holding one's neighbor in bondage was not a commonplace of Catholic moral thought.

It was Catholic moral doctrine that slaves should be treated humanely, and that it was good to give slaves freedom. With some qualifications it was Catholic moral doctrine that slaves should be allowed to marry.[6] But Catholic moral doctrine considered the institution of slavery acceptable. St. Paul had accepted it, returning Onesimus to his master (Phlm 11–19) and instructing the Christian slaves of Corinth to obey their masters (1 Cor 7:21).

The premier moralist of the West, St. Augustine, said succinctly that Christ "did not make men free from being slaves." The greatest of reforming popes, Gregory I, accepted a young boy as a slave and gave him as a gift to another bishop; his famous decision to send missionaries to England is said to have arisen from his musings as he browsed in a slave market in Rome.[7]

The greatest of Catholic jurisprudents, Henri de Bracton, thought slavery was contrary to natural law, but accepted it as an institution of the law of nations; he merely copied the great Catholic lawgiver, Justinian. St. Antoninus of Florince followed St. Thomas in acquiescing in the civil law permitting slave status to follow birth to a slave woman. Paul III praised the benevolent effects of slavery on agriculture while approving the traffic in slaves in Rome. The eminent Jesuit moralist Cardinal Juan De Lugo was in harmony with the moralists' tradition when he found slavery "beyond the intention of nature," but "introduced to prevent greater evils." Near the end of the seventeenth century, the master French theologian, Bishop Bossuet, declared that to condemn slavery would be "to condemn the Holy Spirit, who by the mouth of St. Paul orders slaves to remain in their state."[8]

In 1839 Gregory XVI condemned the slave trade, but not so explicitly that the condemnation covered occasional sales by owners of surplus stock.[9] In the first treatise on moral theology written for Americans, Bishop Francis Kenrick in 1841 declared it no sin against nature to own slaves treated in a humane way and added that, even if Africans had been brought to America unjustly, long lapse of time had cured any defect in title on the part of those who had inherited them.[10] Up until actual abolition occurred, the church was mute on the institution. Or, rather, the church endorsed the institution as compatible with Christianity, indeed as Bossuet observed, expressly approved in Christian Scripture.

Again, all that has changed. In the face of the repeated teachings of modern popes, beginning with Leo XIII, on the rights of labor, uncompensated slave labor is seen as a moral outrage. In the light of the teachings of the modern popes and the Second Vatican Council on the dignity of the human person, it is morally unthinkable that one person be allowed to buy, sell, hypothecate, or lease another or dispose of that person's children.[11] And all the usual and inevitable corollaries of chattel slavery (the denial of education, the denial of vocational opportunity, the destruction of the family) have been so long and so vigorously denounced by bishops and moral theologians that today there is a rampart of authority condemning the conditions without which such slavery could not exist. Slavery has disappeared from most of the world. The Catholic Church stands as one of the great modern teachers excoriating it as evil.

RELIGIOUS FREEDOM

Finally, I turn to moral doctrine on the freedom that should attend religious belief. Once upon a time, no later than the time of St. Augustine, it was considered virtuous for bishops to invoke imperial force to compel heretics to return to the church. Augustine's position was expressly grounded in the gospels.[12] At a later point in time (the rule is well-established in St. Thomas Aquinas) it is doctrine that a relapsed heretic will be judged by the ecclesiastical authorities and remanded to the secular authorities for execution. Forgers are put to death for debasing the currency. Why should not those disloyal to the faith be killed for falsifying it? God may pardon them; the church and the state should not.[13]

For a period of over 1,200 years, during much of which the Catholic Church was dominant in Europe, popes, bishops, and theologians regularly and unanimously denied the religious liberty of heretics. No theologian taught that faith may be freely repudiated without physical consequences; no pope extended the mantle of charitable tolerance to those who departed from orthodox belief. On the contrary, it was universally taught that the duty of a good ruler was to extirpate not only heresy but heretics.[14] The vast institutional apparatus of the church was put at the service of detecting heretics, who, if they persevered in their heresy or relapsed into it, would be executed at the stake. Hand and glove, church and state collaborated in the terror by which the heretics were purged.

Nor did doctrine change markedly as the Protestant Reformation led to the acceptance not of religious liberty but of religious toleration in parts of Europe. Tolerance is permission of what is frankly described as an evil, but a lesser evil. Eventually, as religious peace became the norm in eighteenth- and nineteenth-century Europe, the hypothesis was advanced and accepted that in such circumstances it was for the common good to refrain from religious persecution.[15] The thesis required that in ideal circumstances the state be the physical guarantor of orthodoxy.

All that changed quite recently—only 30 years ago. Then the Second Vatican Council taught that freedom to believe was a sacred human right; that this freedom was founded on the requirements of the human person; that this freedom was at the same time conveyed by Christian revelation; and that the kind of respect that must be shown for human freedom of belief had been taught from the beginning by Jesus and his Apostles, who sought not to coerce any human will but to persuade it. No distinction was now drawn between the religious freedom of infidels (in theory always respected) and the religious freedom of heretics, once trampled on in theory and practice. Now each human being was seen as the possessor of a precious right to believe and to practice in accordance with belief. Religious liberty was established. The state's interference with conscience was denounced.[16]

The minority in opposition strenuously maintained that the teaching of the magisterium was being abandoned; they cited express texts and hitherto unchallenged papal statements. Archbishop Marcel Lefebvre, a leader of the minority, debating the document at the council, said sarcastically that what was proposed was "a new law," which had been condemned many times by the church. What was being taught did not come from the tradition of the church, but from "Hobbes, Locke and Rousseau," followed by rejected Catholic liberals such as Lamennais. Pius IX had rejected it. Leo XIII had "solemnly condemned it" as contrary "to Sacred Scripture and Tradition."[17] A commentator after the fact calmly observed that the council had "reversed the teaching of the ordinary papal magisterium."[18] The doctrine regnant from 350 to 1964 was, in a cryptic phrase, reclassified as conduct occurring through "the vicissitudes of history."[19]

ANALYSIS

Enough has been said, I trust, to suggest the nature of the problem. Wide shifts in the teaching of moral duties, once presented as part of Christian doctrine by the magisterium, have occurred. In each case one can see the displacement of a principle or principles that had been taken as dispositive—in the case of usury, that a loan confers no right to profit; in the case of marriage, that all marriages are indissoluble; in the case of slavery, that war gives a right to enslave and that ownership of a slave gives title to the slave's offspring; in the case of religious liberty, that error has no rights and that fidelity to the Christian faith may be physically enforced. These principles were replaced by principles already part of Christian teaching: in the case of usury, that the person of the lender, not the loan, should be the focus of evaluation; in the case of marriage, that preservation of faith is more important than preservation of a human relationship; in the case of slavery, that in Christ there is "neither free nor slave" (Gal 3:28); and in the case of religious liberty, that faith must be free. In the course of this displacement of one set of principles, what was forbidden became lawful (the cases of usury and marriage); what was permissible became unlawful (the case of slavery); and what was required became forbidden (the persecution of heretics).

It is true that the moral doctrine of the Catholic Church can be seen as *sui generis*; it belongs to no type and so yields no laws. Change depends on two free agencies: human will and the Holy Spirit. No *a priori* rules can bind or predict their course.[20] Nonetheless, when a palpable change has taken place (and surely usury, slavery, religious liberty, and divorce are cases in point) it should be possible to look back and determine what the conditions of change were; to observe the extent of the change that was possible; and to construct a provisional theory as to the limits to change. At least, in Newman's words, one might propose "an hypothesis to account for a difficulty."[21]

While a large literature exists on the development of doctrine, examination reveals that this literature is focused on changes in theological propositions as to the Trinity, the nature of Christ, the Petrine office, or Marian dogma. I have found no well-known writer on development who has addressed the kinds of change I have described; no great theologians have immersed themselves deeply in these mutations of morals. One exception, as will be noted, is Bernard Häring, but he does not theorize at length. But perhaps we can profit by analogy if we look at what theologians have had to say about changes in propositions of faith.[22]

One approach, of which Bishop Bossuet and Orestes Brownson are representative, has been to deny that any real change has ever occurred; there has only been an improvement in expression. For Bossuet and Brownson the invariance of Catholic teaching was a mark of the true church, to be triumphantly contrasted with "the variations" found among Protestants. A second approach, of which Spanish seventeenth-century theology affords an example, took the position that it is possible for the church to work out the logical implications of Scripture and so reach, and declare as true, propositions not contained in Scripture; real advances occur.[23]

A third, and highly influential, theory was put forward in 1843 by John Henry Newman. Writing still as an Anglican, yet as one about to become a Catholic, Newman produced a work that is part detective story (what is the true church?) and part apologia (all the apparent defects of the true church are defensible). His mind, teeming with images, offered a variety of ways of understanding how the church's doctrine of today was not literally the same as the church's doctrine of yesterday, but yet the church was faithful to her Founder. Doctrine, he declared, developed. In the later *Apologia pro vita sua,* development became one of the "principles" of Catholic Christianity.[24] What was meant by development was illustrated in the *Essay on Development* by analogy: by analogy to the beliefs of a child as these beliefs matured in the mind of the child become adult; by analogy with the thought of a poet, whose verse contained more than was explicit in his mind as he composed; by analogy with any organic life as it grows from bud to flower; and by analogy to the course of an idea embraced by a society, an idea whose detailed consequences can be grasped only as the idea is lived out in the society. By all these comparisons Newman confessed that changes had occurred in the doctrine of the church, but he maintained that the changes had been rooted in the original revelation and were a perfection, not a distortion, of it. True development, he wrote, "corroborates, not corrects, the body of the thought from which it proceeds."[25]

The Modernists took the idea of development and ran away with it. Doctrine became the projection of human needs, changing in response to those needs. Control of doctrine by the objective content of revelation disappeared.[26] The church rejected Modernism and retained Newman's conclusion that there was genuine growth in doctrine from unchanged foundations. Vatican II put it tersely: "Insight grows both into the words and the realities that have been handed on."[27] Change, that was in fact doctrinal progress, was celebrated. The central reality, in relation to which insight grew, was Jesus Christ, himself "both the mediator and the plenitude of the whole revelation."[28]

How would any of these approaches work if applied to moral doctrine? To deny that real change had occurred, as Bossuet and Brownson did, would be an apologetic tactic incapable of execution and unworthy of belief. To say, as did the seventeenth-century Spanish, that the unfolding had been by logical implication would be equally incredible. The acceptance of slavery did not imply freedom;

the endorsement of religious persecution did not entail respect for religious freedom. The method might indeed be used if the most basic principles, such as "Love your neighbor as yourself," were the starting point. But would logic alone suffice?

Newman's complex set of analogies is different. At one level of doctrine, of course, one cannot maintain that the church's present championing of freedom, personal and religious, "corroborates" an earlier stage in which the church defended chattel slavery and religious persecution. At another level, Newman's notion of an idea maturing can be criticized by taking his analogy with organic life literally; he can then be caricatured as supposing that spiritual growth is similar to vegetative growth.[29] But Newman's rich range of arguments and metaphors cannot be so neatly written off. In a passage dealing with the nature of development in general that I read as decisive, he declares:

> The development then of an idea is not like investigation worked out on paper, in which each successive advance is a pure evolution from a foregoing, but it is carried on through and by means of communities of men and their leaders and guides; and it employs their minds as its instruments and depends upon them while it uses them. . . . It is the warfare of ideas under their varying aspects striving for the mastery. . . .[30]

This passage acknowledges an objectivity in the idea or ideas at issue; at the same time it fully recognizes that development occurs by conflict, in which the leading idea will effect the "throwing off" of earlier views now found to be incompatible with the leading idea more fully realized.[31] Principles, broadly understood, underlie and control specific changes.[32] Newman's approach is adaptable to the development of moral doctrine.

The Modernist position that human needs will shape doctrine carries the cost of eliminating any objective content; it is, as Pius X put it, "the synthesis of all the heresies."[33]

Finally, there is the position of Vatican II: there can be and is a growth in insight into a reality that is Jesus Christ. It comes from "the contemplation of believers, the experience of spiritual realities, and the preaching of the church."[34] As Bernard Häring has amplified the words of *Dei verbum*: "Christ does not become greater through ongoing history, but our knowledge of the plan of salvation which is revealed in the world in Christ does become more complete and close to life in our hearts through the working of the Spirit in the history of the Church and above all in the saints."[35]

To hold that moral doctrine changes with increased insight into Christ is an attractive proposition. It entails one obvious danger. When one sees more deeply into Christ, is one looking into a mirror merely reflecting one's own deepest feeling? The answer must be that the church has the mission of determining what is only the projection of subjective feelings and what is an authentic response to Christ as revealed.

If insight into Christ is taken from the realm of faith to that of morals and applied to our four examples, it will be found to afford at least a partial explanation of what has happened. On the great question of religious liberty, a stronger appreciation of Christ's own methods has led to repudiation of all violence in the enforcement of belief. On the great question of human slavery, a better grasp of the fellowship effected by Christ has made the holding of any person in bondage intolerable.

In the other cases one factor facilitating change was a deeper, less literal, reading of the words of Christ. Where "Lend freely, hoping nothing thereby" had been understood as a peremptory command, it came to be understood as an exemplary exhortation.[36] Where "What God has joined together, let no man put asunder" had been read as absolute, the possibility of exception has been eventually envisaged and expanded. In these cases, too, one could say that the reality of Christ was better reached by the abandonment of the letter.

Yet it would be preposterous to imagine that all these profound changes occurred simply by the acquiring of deeper insights into Christ. Human beings do not reach moral conclusions in a vacuum apart from the whole web of language, custom, and social structure surrounding them. A society composed entirely of free human beings was unknown in the Mediterranean world of the first centuries; a society where the state did not support religion was equally unknown. Only as social structures changed did moral mutation become possible, even if the change in social structures, as it might reasonably be argued, was owed at least in part to the perception that structures fostering liberty were more congruent with deeper insight into Christ.[37]

Those structures could not have shifted without experience. The central European experience leading first to religious tolerance and then to religious liberty was the experience of the evil of religious persecution. The experience was long and bloody and sufficient to demonstrate how demoralizing the enforcement of religion by force was. Equally, I would argue, it was the centuries-old experience of slavery that led to the conclusion that slavery was destructive both for the slaves and for the masters.[38]

Experience as such, taken as "raw experience," the mere participation in this or that phenomenon, is, however, not the key. Raw experience carries with it no evaluation. But experience, suffered or perceived in the light of human nature and of the gospel, can be judged good or bad. It was the experience of unfreedom, in the gospel's light, that made the contrary shine clear.[39]

The negative experience of religious persecution was reinforced by the American experience of religious freedom, for America launched the great experiment of a nation committed to the nonestablishment of any national religion and the free exercise of religion. The American experiment had blemishes, such as the persecution of the Mormons and of the Jehovah's Witnesses, and the denial of constitutional freedom to conscientious objectors to unjust war. But the American ideal and its relative success were clear and were taught to Europe by Tocqueville, Lamennais, and Lacordaire. In the end, the theologians built on the American experience, guided in no small part by an American theologian, John Courtney Murray. Finally, sealing all by fire, was the experience of religious unfreedom under the terrible dictatorships of the twentieth century. Without those experiences, negative and positive, and without the elaboration of the ideal by Tocqueville and Murray, the changes made by Vatican II could not have occurred.[40]

The advance on slavery also depended on articulation by individuals who were ahead of the theologians and the church. In Catholic France, Montesquieu challenged the morality of slavery, writing with fine irony of blacks: "It is impossible that we should suppose those people to be men, because if we should suppose them to be men, we would begin to believe that we ourselves are not Christians."[41] It was eighteenth-century Quakers and Baptists and Methodists and nineteenth-century Congregationalists who led the fight against slavery in the English-speaking world, and it was the French Revolution that led to its abolition in the French empire. The gospel, as interpreted by Protestants and as mediated by Rousseau and the revolutionaries of 1789, achieved much.[42] Only after the cultures of Europe and America changed through the abolitionists' agency, and only after the laws of every civilized land eliminated the practice, did Catholic moral doctrine decisively repudiate slavery as immoral. Only in 1890 did Pope

Leo XIII attack the institution itself, noting that slavery was incompatible "with the brotherhood that unites all men."[43] At the end of the argument and articulation and legal upheaval that had gone on for two centuries, the requirement of Christ was clear.

In contrast, the change regarding divorce and remarriage, adultery and bigamy, appears to have been almost entirely an internal process. But was it? St. Paul's original modification of monogamy responded to conditions he encountered affecting conversion. His rule worked well enough until the extreme conditions of African slavery in South America suggested the need for radical expansion. And that change was not improved upon until, in modern religiously mixed societies, it became common for unbaptized persons and Catholics to fall in love and want to be married. Then a new expansion was made. Canonistic ingenuity and exaltation of papal power played a dominant part. The canonists responded to changed external conditions as they discovered the true meaning of Christ's command.

The change with regard to usury, basically effected in the course of the sixteenth century although formally acknowledged only in the nineteenth, came from the convergence of several factors. Europe moved from an agricultural to a commercial economy. Moral theologians began to give weight to the experience of otherwise decent Christians who were bankers and who claimed banking was compatible with Christianity. The morality of certain types of credit transactions (the so-called triple contract and the personal annuity and the foreign exchange contract) were all reexamined and reevaluated in the light of credit transactions already accepted as legitimate. Perhaps above all, the perspective of moral analysis shifted from focus on the loan in itself to focus on the lender and the investment opportunity the lender lost by lending. All these factors—commercial developments, attention to experience, new analyses, and shift in perspective—produced a moral doctrine on usury that was substantially different from that taught throughout the Middle Ages and substantially similar in practice to what is accepted today. All these factors, plus reevaluation of the words of Christ, created the new moral doctrine.[44]

CONCLUSION

Where morals are at issue, the process of change requires a complex constellation of elements. Every society, including the church, lives by rules that keep its vital balance. Change one, and the balance is jeopardized. Hence there is a conservative tendency to keep the rules as they are, there is fear when they are given up, and sometimes nostalgia for the loss.

Change is also resisted for other reasons. There is a praiseworthy desire to maintain intellectual consistency. There is a longing in the human mind for repose, for fixed points of reference, for absolute certainty. There is alarm about the future: What else can change? There is the theological conviction that as God is unchanging, divine demands must also be unchanging. How could one have gone to hell yesterday for what today one would be held virtuous in doing? How could one have done virtuously yesterday what one would by damned for doing today? How could one once have been bound to a high and demanding standard that later is said to be unnecessary? How could one once have been permitted to engage in conduct that is later condemned as uncharitable? A mutation in morals bewilders. Hence there is a presumption of rightness attending the present rules, and authority is rightly vigilant to preserve them. Not every proposed mutation is good; the majority, it could be guessed, might be harmful.

But a new balance can be struck. The consistency sought should not be verbal nor literal; nor can conformity to every past rule be required. The consistency to be sought is consistency with Christ. The human desire for mental repose is not to be satisfied in this life. One cannot predict future changes; one can only follow present light and in that light be morally certain that some moral obligations will never alter. The great commandments of love of God and of neighbor, the great principles of justice and charity continue to govern all development. God is unchanging, but the demands of the New Testament are different from those of the Old, and while no other revelation supplements the New Testament, it is evident from the case of slavery alone that it has taken time to ascertain what the demands of the New Testament really are. All will be judged by the demands of the day in which they live. It is not within human competence to say with certainty who was or will be saved; all will be judged as they have conscientiously acted. In new conditions, with new insight, an old rule need not be preserved in order to honor a past discipline.

Another response to change is to ignore it, to deny explicitly or implicitly that it has occurred, to be aware of the mutations described here and find them without significance—just so many well-established and well-known historical facts. Denial of that sort also betrays fear of change, fear that change is simply chance. Mutations are muted. But why should believers in Christ have such a fear? The Spirit guides the church. The acts of development have a significance beyond themselves. "The idea of development was the most important single idea Newman contributed to the thought of the Christian Church."[45] The idea of development had this importance because it contained an explanation of the passage from the past and a Delphic prophecy of the future.

In the church there can always be fresh appeal to Christ, there is always the possibility of probing new depths of insight. To grow is to change, and the gospel parable of the mustard seed promises growth (Matt 13:31–32). The kingdom of heaven, we are told, is like a householder who from his storeroom brings forth things old and new (Matt 13:52). Our world has grown by mutation; should not our morals, especially when the direction and the goal are provided by the Lord? "[H]ere below to live is to change. And to be perfect is to have changed often."[46] Must we not, then, frankly admit that change is something that plays a role in Catholic moral teaching? Must not the traditional motto *semper idem* be modified, however unsettling that might be, in the direction of *plus ca change, plus c'est la même chose*? Yes, if the principle of change is the person of Christ.

NOTES

*A more developed form of the Thomas Verner Moore Lecture sponsored by St. Anselm's Abbey, September 29, 1990, at the Catholic University of America.

1. On the whole topic, see John T. Noonan, Jr., "Authority on Usury and on Contraception," *Tijdschrift voor Theologie* 6 (1966) 26-50, republished in *Cross Currents* 16 (1966) 55-79 and *The Wiseman Review* (Summer, 1966) 201-29. The standard definition of usury was given by Gratian, *Decretum, Corpus iuris canonici*, ed. E. Friedberg (Leipzig, 1879-1881) 2.14.3.1. The Second Council of the Lateran condemned usury (G.D. Mansi, *Sacrorum conciliorum nova et amplissima collectio* [Paris, 1901-1920] 21.529-30); the Third Council of the Lateran declared usury to be condemned "by the pages of both Testaments" (Mansi 22.231). The Council of Vienne declared that anyone "pertinaciously affirming that to practice usury is no sin should be punished as a heretic" (Clement, *Constitutiones* 5.5, *Corpus iuris canonici*, ed. E. Friedberg).

2. See John T. Noonan, Jr., *Power to Dissolve* (Cambridge: Harvard Univ., 1972) 343.

3. Ibid. 356, citing Gregory XIII, *Populis et nationibus*, reprinted as Document VII in the appendix to *Codex iuris canonici* (Rome: Vatican, 1917).

4. *Power to Dissolve* 370-371.

5. According to Ambrose Marechal, Archbishop of Baltimore, the province in 1826 owned as personal property "about 500 African men" (Marechal to Cardinal Della Somaglia, January 15, 1826, in Thomas Hughes, S.J., *History of the Society of Jesus in North America: Documents* [New York: Longmans, Green, 1908] 1.1544). Anthony Kohlmann, S.J., commenting on this assertion, put the number of slaves at half this figure; he added that their value was less than Marechal supposed because "those over 45 cannot be alienated," the clear inference being that those under 45 could be sold (ibid. 545).

6. Gratian, Decretum 2.29.2.8 upheld the validity of slave marriages but required the consent of the slaves' owners. In the U.S., Bishop Francis Kenrick thought that "the majority" of slave agreements did not have "the force of marriage" since "the intention of contracting a perpetual bond is lacking to them" (Francis P. Kenrick, *Theologia moralis* [Philadelphia, 1843] 3.333).

7. Augustine, *On Psalm 125* no. 7 (J.P. Migne, *Patrologiae cursus completus. Series latina* [hereafter *PL*] (Paris, 1844-1891) 37.1653; Gregory, *Epist*. 7.30 (PL 77.887 [accepts slave]). For the story of the slave market, see Bede, *Historia ecclesiastica gentis anglorum*, ed. George H. Moberley (Oxford: Clarendon, 1869) 2.1; cf. Anon., *The Earliest Life of Gregory the Great*, ed. and trans. Bertram Colgrave (Cambridge: Cambridge Univ., 1968) 91.

8. Henri de Bracton, *De legibus et consuetudinibus Angliae*, ed. S.E. Thorne (Cambridge: Harvard Univ., 1970-77) 2.30, following Justinian, *Digesta* 50.17.32; Antoninus, *Summa Sacrae theologiae* (Venice, 1581-82) 3.3.6; Paul III, *Motu proprio*, November 9, 1548, trans. in John F. Maxwell, *Slavery and the Catholic Church* (Chichester: Ross, 1975) 75; Lugo, *De iustitia et iure* 6.2, *Disputationes scholasticae et morales* (Paris, 1899) vol. 8; Jacques B. Bossuet, *Avertissement sur les lettres du Ministre Jurieu*, in Bossuet, *Oeuvres complètes* (Lyons, 1877) 3.542.

9. Gregory XVI, *In supremo apostolatus, Acta*, ed. Antonio Maria Bernasconi (Rome: Vatican, 1901) 2.388. Bishop John England was at pains to explain to Secretary of State John Forsyth that none of the bishops at the Provincial Council of Baltimore thought that Gregory XVI's condemnation affected the American institution of slavery: see John England, *Works*, ed. Ignatius A. Reynolds (Baltimore: J. Murphy, 1849) 3.115-119. The Holy Office in 1866 ruled that the buying and selling of slaves was not contrary to natural law (Holy Office to the Vicar Apostolic of the Galle tribe in Ethiopia, June 20, 1866, *Collectanea S.C. de Propaganda Fide* [Rome, 1907] I n. 1293).

10. Kenrick, *Theologia moralis*, vol. 2, tract 5.2.6

11. E.g. Vatican II, *Gaudium et spes* no. 67, in *Decreta, Declarationes*, ed. secretaria generali concilii oecumenici Vaticane II [Rome: Typis polyglottis Vaticanis, 1966] 790 (*Constitutiones* 790).

12. Augustine to Boniface, *Epistula* 185, *PL* 33.803.

13. Thomas Aquinas, *Summa theologiae*, ed. Pietro Caramello (Turin: Marietti, 1952), 2-2, q. 11, a. 3 (death penalty; comparison of forgery); q. 11, a.4 ad 1 (Church "cannot imitate" God in reading hearts and so does not keep relapsed heretics "from peril of death" imposed by the state).

14. Lucius III, *Ad abolendam* (Dectetales Gregorii IX, 5.7.9).

15. John A. Ryan and Francis J. Boland, *Catholic Principles of Politics* (New York: Macmillan, 1940) 317-21. The same teaching appears in John A.

Ryan and Moorhouse F.X. Millar, S.J., *The State and the Church* (New York: Macmillan, 1924) 35-39.

16. Vatican II, *Dignitatis humanae personae* no. 2, Second Vatican Council, *Constitutiones* 55.

17. Lefebvre, Intervention, Sept. 20, 1965 (*Acta Synodalia Sancti Concilii Oecumenici Vaticani II* [Rome, 1976] 4.1, 409).

18. J. Robert Dionne, *The Papacy and the Church* (New York: Philosophical Library, 1987) 193.

19. *Dignitatis humane personae* 11.

20. See Karl Rahner, S.J., *Theological Investigations* I, trans. C. Ernst (Baltimore: Helicon, 1961) 41.

21. John Henry Newman, *An Essay on the Development of Christian Doctrine*, ed. Charles Frederick Harrold (New York: Longmans, Green, 1949) 28.

22. Consider as representative of recent work, Jan Hendrik Walgrave's *Unfolding Revelation: The Nature of Doctrinal Development* (London: Hutchinson, 1972). It has no discussion of moral doctrine. Jaroslav Pelikan's massive work, *The Christian Tradition: A History of the Development of Doctrine* (Chicago: Univ. of Chicago, 1971-1989) does not deal with any of the four changes used as examples here; in other words, the development of moral doctrine is no part of his comprehensive treatment of "the development of doctrine." A recent sensitive account of the history of moral theology offers no theory of development; see John A. Gallagher, *Time Past, Time Future: A Historical Study of Catholic Moral Theology* (New York: Paulist, 1990) But John Mahoney, *The Making of Moral Theology* (New York: Oxford/Clarendon, 1987) 320 observes that "the Church has a great difficulty...in handling the subject of change as such." Mahoney goes on to note that change is "an unavoidable element of human existence" and to suggest that change in moral doctrine is sometimes the right response to changed conditions (326-27).

23. See Owen Chadwick, *From Bossuet to Newman: The Idea of Doctrinal Development* (Cambridge: Cambridge Univ., 1957) 20 (Bossuet); 171 (Brownson); 25-44 (Spanish).

24. Newman, *Apologia pro vita sua*, ed. Charles Frederick Harrold (New York: Longmans, Green, 1947) 79.

25. Newman, *Essay on Development* 2.5.6, 186. Newman wrote as an Anglican but did not amend the quoted passages when he revised the *Essay* as a Catholic. On the analogies, see Chadwick 151, 155. Aidan Nichols sees Newman's fundamental metaphor as that of a seal cutting a design of wax (*From Newman to Congar: The Idea of Doctrinal Development from the Victorians to the Second Vatican Council* [Edinburgh: T.& T. Clark, 1990] 44).

26. See John T. Noonan, Jr., "The Philosophical Postulates of Alfred Loisy" (M.A. thesis, Catholic University of America, 1948).

27. Vatican II, *Dei verbum* 8, Second Vatican Council, *Constitutiones* 430.

28. Ibid. 8, 424.

29. Compare the criticism of Newman's metaphor by Ambroise Gardeil, *Le Donné révélé et la théologie* (Paris: J. Gabalda, 1910) 156, noting the difference between "la vie d'un végétal et la vie d'un esprit."

30. Newman, *Essay on Development* 1.1.6, p. 74

31. Ibid.

32. Ibid. 2.5.2, p. 167.

33. Pius X, *Pascendi dominici gregis*, Spt. 8, 1907 (*Acta sanctae dominici sedis* 40.632; Eng. trans. in *All Things in Christ*, ed. Vincent A. Yzermans [Westminster, Md: Newman, 1954] 117).

34. Vatican II, *Dei verbum* no. 8, Second Vatican Council, *Constitutiones* 430.

35. Bernard Haring, *My Witness for the Church*, trans. Leonard Swidler (New York: Paulist, 1992) 122.

36. Urban III treated the words of Christ on lending as mandatory (Urban III, *Consuluit, Decretalia Gregorii IX* 5.19.10, *Corpus iuris canonici*, ed. E Friedberg). Domingo de Soto is the first major scholastic theologian to challenge this interpretation (*De iustitia et iure libri decem* [Lyons, 1569] 6.1.1).

37. Cf. Louis Vereecke, *Storia della teologia morale moderna* (Rome: Lateran, 1979) 1.4-5 (moral theology is where the unchanged gospel encounters changing cultures).

38. See Thomas Jefferson, *Notes on the State of Virginia*, ed. William Peden (Chapel Hill: North Carolina, 1955) Query 18.

39. See Roger Williams, *The BLOUDY TENENT, of Persecution, for Cause of Conscience, discussed, in A Conference between TRUTH and PEACE* (1644), reprinted and ed. Samuel L. Caldwell, *The Complete Writings of Roger Williams* (New York: Russell & Russell, 1963) 3.3-4.

40. See Alexis de Toqueville, *Democracy in America*, trans. Henry Reeve, rev. Francis Bowen (New York: Alfred A. Knopf, 1945) 308-9; John Courtney Murray, "Governmental Repression of Heresy, *Proceedings of the Catholic Theological Society of America* 3 (Washington: Catholic Theological Society, 1948) 161.

41. Charles de Secondat, Baron de Montesquieu, *L'Esprit des lois*, in his *Oeuvres complètes* (Paris, 1843) 5.309.

42. See David Brian Davis, *The Problem Of Slavery in Western Culture* (Ithaca: Cornell Univ., 1966) 291, 333, 401.

43. Leo XIII, Catholicae ecclesiae, November 20, 1890 (*Acta sanctae sedis* 23.257).

44. See John T. Noonan, Jr., *The Scholastic Analysis of Usury* (Cambridge: Harvard Univ., 1956) 199-201.

45. Owen Chadwick, *Newman* (Oxford: Oxford Univ., 1983) 47.

46. Newman, *Essay on Development* 1.1.7, 38.

Part Five

THE CONTEXT FOR CASUISTRY TODAY

Science, Metaphor, and Moral Casuistry

THOMAS R. KOPFENSTEINER

INTRODUCTION

In spite of the ample criticism of the casuistry found within the neoscholastic manuals of theology, the casuist's art of applying principles and norms to concrete situations and problems is still a necessary part of the moral enterprise. The rehabilitation of casuistry will succeed to the extent that it is freed from the caricature of practical reasoning found in the neoscholastic manuals and contributes to a broader conception of the moral life. The goal of this article is to retrieve the casuist's art by situating it within an historical notion of science, and thereby to provide a new metaphysical basis from which to analyze the moral act. These two points can be described briefly before proceeding.

The moral casuistry of the neoscholastic manuals of theology was modeled on a modern notion of science. Using its criteria of rationality, casuistry was a *mos geometricus*, moving deductively from self-evident and unchanging principles to particular and contingent situations. Under such a conception of rationality, problem solutions could be presented with a great deal of certainty and were universally applicable. It is precisely the modern ideal of science, however, that has been undermined through recent studies in the history and philosophy of science. Shifting to an historical ideal of science opens an avenue to critique the casuistry found in the neoscholastic manuals on strictly epistemological grounds.

The historical ideal of science reflects a close contact with recent studies that have explored the relationship between ontology and language, especially the role of metaphor. A metaphor holds two terms, examples, or thoughts in tension with one another.[1] Metaphor is more than an element of linguistic style which embellishes what is already known; it is an element of linguistic invention. Metaphor has a creative role in the generation and growth of knowledge. The metaphysical commitments behind the metaphorical character of language will provide a new basis upon which to anchor the analysis of the moral act.

SCIENCE AND RATIONALITY

A modern notion of science cannot be divorced from the influences of the empiricists or early logical positivists. For them, the study of the human world was done against the background of the natural sciences. One or other of the natural sciences was taken as the paradigm of "scientificity" and the standard against which progress in the human sciences was to be measured. A major tenet of this commitment was that there is a unity of scientific method. This was understood in a way that, despite the differences among the various sciences, the methodological procedures of the natural sciences were equally applicable to the human sciences. More specifically, for the neopositivists the form and goal of inquiry was the same for both the natural and human sciences. Scientific investigation, whether of human or natural phenomena, aimed at the discovery of law-like generalizations that could function as premises in deductive explanations and predictions.[2]

Next to this methodological tenet stood an epistemological one: for anything to merit the title of scientific knowledge it would have to have a firm touchstone or foundation in the objective or empirical world. That world was simply given, "out there" to be observed directly.[3] Pure and immediate experience, prior to any interpretation, was the foundation for knowledge. In other words, the context of discovery or genesis was not at all relevant to the context of justification; scientific inquiry was interested only in the context of justification.

In contrast to the modern approach to science, there is an approach that takes the history of science as its point of departure. Beginning with how science is actually practiced has lead to the realization that there is no neutral or autonomous access to the world. Our knowledge of the world is in part due to the framework or context within which the world is perceived and understood. Such a conception of knowledge builds on the accepted insight of philosophers of science like Hanson, Kuhn, and others that we do not just gaze upon the world, we see it *as* something and not another. The interpretive or hermeneutical *as* is inseparable from the scientists' inquiry into what is. This is what they mean when they say that there is no pretheoretical observation; all observation is theory-laden. Or, again in the terms of the sociology of knowledge, this view of knowledge means that the context of discovery is no longer independent but constitutive of the context of justification.[4]

Consequently, if there is a unity of scientific method it is because the world is known through procedures not unlike those employed in the hermeneutical interpretation of texts.[5] In particular, hermeneutical understanding involves a "circle" of readings, a circle that cannot be broken by recourse to unvarnished experience or brute data. A reading can be corrected only by further readings. As a text never receives a definitive reading due to the shifting perspectives of its readers, the world is underdetermined—open to new construals and interpretations due to the shifting perspectives of scientific inquiry. There is an interminability (*ein Niezuendekommen*) to the hermeneutical circle. The hermeneutical circle, however, should not be characterized as a vicious circle. In light of the reciprocal relationship between theory and praxis, it is better characterized as a hermeneutical spiral.

Not surprisingly, these two conceptions of science carry divergent understandings of language. Within a positivist conception of science, language was a mirror or picture of reality. Scientific language was characterized by its precision in labeling the objective world; it had a univocal or literal character. Scientific language was limited by the empiricists' criterion of verification or falsification.

Within a postempiricist and historical view of science, however, language plays a different and richer role. Language does not merely report what is in the world; language is the medium through which we have a world. The things of the world are presented or disclosed through language. This means that the world is not given in an immediate or a naively objective way; rather, we interact with the world by means of interpretations.[6] In addition, language is not simply a product or tool of the individual; it transcends individual use and eludes a merely functional role. Language is a communal and historical reality. We are born into a language community; the language we learn initiates us into a living tradition and gives us access to a history by which our lives are shaped. Language forms us and our relations to the world. Language is also the vehicle for transforming how we understand ourselves and interact with the world.

The relationship between ontology and language has been developed through the study of metaphor, in particular the cognitive effects of metaphor.[7] Metaphors help determine our perspective on the world and how we situate ourselves in it. They help us unite situations, phenomena, or experiences by relevant similarities and differences. By teaching us to see and interact with the world in a certain way, metaphors induct us into an ordered network of cognitive relations. Metaphors access an epistemic horizon in which we reason and speak about particular phenomena. This means that metaphors help shape how we look at things, what issues we find pressing, and even which solutions are adequate to the problems we deem worth solving. Metaphors provide a direction for inquiry and research; how a problem is posed or framed determines the direction to go in search of a solution. Problem setting always precedes problem solving.

More importantly, however, language changes and grows through a metaphoric process. Metaphors play a role in changing the topography of an epistemic horizon. A change in metaphor will introduce an element of incongruity into discourse, cause a rift or tension within a particular field of meaning, and lead to a restructuring of the conceptual relations within that field. Following Ricoeur, the metaphoric process will effect a shift in the logical distance between one concept and another.[8] In other words, the inherent creativity of language impacts the conceptual relations within a discipline or research program. Metaphors are creative in that they enable us to "see" things which we had not seen before.[9] A change in metaphor effects the mutual accommodation of language and experience in a way that allows the familiar usage of language to be surpassed and the alterity of the world to unfold. Although the metaphorical sense eventually becomes established and the metaphor dies and language becomes univocal, we speak and reason anew about the world. Consequently, there is a difficulty in communicating with those whose topography of conceptual relations within a certain field of meaning differ from our own.

The most noted historical example of this kind of conceptual change is the scientific accomplishment of the astronomer Nicholas Copernicus. The metaphoric process changed the natural referents to the word "planet." In the pre-Copernican world the earth was the center of the universe. The planets—among which were the sun and moon—revolved in different fashions around the earth. In making the sun the center of the heavens, Copernicus effected a new understanding of the relations among the celestial bodies. By changing the way one saw the earth and its relation to the other celestial bodies, Copernicus effected a change in the conceptual topography of the heavens. The features of a planet were attributed to the celestial bodies differently before and after Copernicus. The earth was like Mars (and was thus a planet) after Copernicus, but the two were in different natural families before.[10] Any communication between a pre- and post-Copernican world must account for this change; for communication to succeed, language cannot be applied univocally across the Copernican divide.

CASUISTRY AND HERMENEUTICAL REASONING

Moral problem solving has been placed traditionally under the rubric of casuistry.[11] Casuistry is not exclusive to moral reasoning. Case studies are also an integral part of the educational process in the fields of law, medicine, and science. For the student, solving problems crystallizes the discipline's underlying matrix of abstract and formal theoretical assumptions. Through case studies, the student learns how theoretical principles and norms are translated into praxis. Problem solutions or case studies, however, have more than a pedagogical role; their use goes beyond explaining or teaching theories. Because of the unity of theory and praxis, problem solutions are a fundamental and irreplaceable part of science, playing a role that is *constitutive* of the theories they express. Theory and praxis are mutually dependent. On the one hand, the disciplinary matrix defines and organizes the relevant problems to be solved; on the other hand, problem solutions exemplify and perpetuate the basic commitments of the matrix.

Between scientific theory and practice or, in an analogous way, between moral norms and moral praxis, there is a balance or equilibrium which is achieved and maintained. This equilibrium takes the form of an intensional and extensional coherency. The former refers to the disciplinary matrix being present in a tacit way in the individual problem solutions; the latter refers to the family resemblance that is created among individual problem solutions.[12] There is a mutually conditioning relationship between a disciplinary matrix and the exemplars or concrete problem solutions of a science. A change on one level will have repercussions on the other; the reciprocity between the disciplinary matrix and the range of problems to be solved guarantees the historical and dynamic nature of scientific discourse. This has an important methodological consequence for a conception of moral casuistry. It means that individual cases can no longer be merely subsumed under unchanging general principles.

There is no doubt, for instance, that the moral casuistry of the neoscholastic manuals is part of the effective history of the Enlightenment. The neoscholastics' retrieval of the work of Thomas Aquinas was not naive; it was conditioned by their intellectual milieu. As Jonsen and Toulmin observe,

> any discipline wishing to be accepted as a serious field of study . . . was expected to develop its own body of abstract theoretical concepts and principles and to present them, if possible, in the form of an axiomatic system.[13]

At the time of the neoscholastics, the Cartesian demand for geometrical clarity set the standard for rational discourse. It was quite natural, then, that the neoscholastics viewed moral reasoning within the constrictions of modern science. Hence, the casuistry of the neoscholastic manuals was presented as a deductive system. Moral principles were likened to mathematical axioms; their meaning was thought to be univocal. Behavior that was allowed or forbidden was likened to necessary conclusions deduced from first principles; judgments about rightness and wrongness were universally applicable. Based on a modern scientific ideal, moral reasoning erected a coherent, ahistorical, and closed system of norms and precepts to guide everyday life.[14] Though this quasigeometrical system guaranteed that moral arguments received a high level of validity, it also gave the impression that history was no more than accidental changes around an immutable natural order.[15]

This deductive or geometric view of moral reasoning shares an affinity with the positivists' exclusive epistemological interest in the context of justification. It does not reflect, however, an ideal of science informed by the history of science. From the latter's perspective, there is an openness to the reasons and arguments that guide scientific activity. Any criteria for justification are embedded in and conditioned by a more original and genetic context. This allows for a dynamic and historical conception of moral reasoning to emerge. The reciprocal relationship between genesis (or discovery) and justification means that the moral norm is incomplete not only because the norm cannot anticipate all situations in advance but, more importantly, because the meaning of the norm shares in the effective history of moral insight and experience.

We gain insights through experience; experience stimulates insight. Moral experience, however, is conditioned by human freedom. Experiences are specified, ordered, and integrated by the legitimate expectations of freedom. In speaking of freedom, the analogous nature of truth must be kept in mind. In a moral context, freedom does not mean the ability to choose between a variety of objects. Freedom is the ability to realize the moral good. What is needed is a hermeneutical reflection that aims to uncover all the normative orientations preceding freedom's embodiment in single acts.[16] Further, the object in the moral sciences is not an empirical object but ourselves, individually and collectively! What is created through the extension of moral norms is not a range of knowledge about the world, but our moral reputation and character. Through our moral actions, we make ourselves into certain kinds of persons.[17] History takes on an autobiographical dimension; it is the accomplishment of insight and freedom.

Freedom, though, is not understood in a solipsistic sense. The exercise of freedom reflects and shapes the moral traditions in which we live. Being initiated into a tradition means learning what the tradition takes to be the legitimate expectations of freedom. So on the one hand, moral norms are interpreted from the point of view established by the tradition's ideology of human fulfillment; norms are interpreted in a way that will protect and promote the legitimate expectations of freedom. On the other hand, the limits and possibilities of freedom are tacitly present in moral action; moral action reveals the plausibility of the tradition's ideology of human fulfillment.

This conception of moral casuistry, or the application of the moral norm, has a hermeneutical character.[18] The application of the moral norm is not achieved *more geometrico*, but is achieved by insights into the legitimate expectations of freedom. This does not lessen the stringency or coherency that exists between moral norms and moral action; it means that there is a rhetorical relationship between them.[19] The linguistic formulation of the norm is ambiguous; it shares this character with all language. As a word's meaning depends upon the cognitive background against which it is used, the norm's application depends upon the legitimate expectations of freedom. Like a text, a norm's "reading" or application cannot be separated from our experience of the world. The prospect of a plurality of "readings" of a moral norm, however, does not mean that the norm is applied in a relativistic way.[20] The effective history of experience and insight reflects legitimate expectations of freedom behind which we cannot go and still hope to reasonably shape our moral lives. These achieved standards of freedom set the limits to communicable conceptions of the ideology of human fulfillment; they bear witness to the moral progress of the community.[21]

The idea of moral progress focuses on the creative impulse of moral reasoning. Moral reasoning is creative in an exploratory and constructive sense. Not only does moral reasoning apply a norm through the legitimate expectations of freedom, at times it is necessary to undertake an imaginative exploration beyond the limits and possibilities of freedom. Moral reasoning can acquaint us with a breadth of possibilities beyond those our tradition provides. This creates a vantage point to critically review our tradition; the breadth of possibilities forms a basis for contrast and comparison with our tradition.[22] This kind of reasoning is analogous to a "thought experiment" in the natural sciences. In a thought experiment, a set of traditional assumptions and intellectual commitments of the scientific community are temporarily suspended in the face of anomalous problems or aberrant data. Replacing or revising intellectual commitments within the disciplinary matrix results in a new direction and scope for scientific practice.

In a moral context, however, the impetus for this kind of thinking is a pressing need to resolve a conflict or a growing number of conflicts. This is a qualitative judgment and not merely a quantitative one. The introduction of a thought experiment is preceded by the sense that a tradition's possibilities are constricting; the loss of certain goods may be unable to be sustained or sustained only with diminishing plausibility. Both the limits and possibilities of freedom embodied in a particular moral tradition may begin to appear less reasonable; the tradition is easily cast into doubt. When this happens, the ideology of human fulfillment is open to criticism and critique.[23] Moral reasoning shifts its focus from promoting and protecting traditional standards of freedom, and projects beyond the tradition's legitimate expectations of freedom in the hope of creating better alternatives of human-being-and-acting in the world. In this way, though the linguistic formulation of a moral norm is unchanged, the legitimate expectations of freedom are raised, and new criteria guiding the *subtilitas applicationis* of a moral norm are achieved.[24] The present limits and possibilities of freedom will reflect a moral tradition's effective history of conflict resolution.

NORMATIVE NATURE AND METAPHOR

The historicity of the legitimate expectations of freedom has an immediate impact on the notion of the natural moral law. The normativity of nature is not reducible to human nature as it is given or in nature's facticity. The natural inclinations are necessary but not sufficient criteria for the determination of normativity. They are underdetermined in a normative sense. This does not mean that we can approach nature without constraint; nature is more than the raw material for normativity. While not immediately normative, nature is a limit in the sense that reason and freedom are always *in* nature. Nature is an indispensable condition of freedom and reason; we cannot be freed from nature.

As indispensable as nature is, however, normativity is not a property of nature; nature is only the vehicle of normativity.[25] Normativity results from nature being completed, transcended, or interpreted by the *ordinatio rationis*. Though both poles contribute to what is meant by normatively human nature, the rational order is the sufficient critierion for normativity. This is what Korff means when he writes that

> all human behavior remains universally determined by conditions which may not replace reason, since they need interpretation and to this extent do not present themselves as ethical norms, but which nevertheless eliminate arbitrariness from this behavior in all its realisations.[26]

Nature is not infinitely malleable; the order of nature is subordinated to the order of reason and freedom.

Within normatively human nature or the natural moral law a distinction can be made. There will be a principle of transcendence which is the rational and free nature of the person, and a principle of limit which is reason as it is situated *in* nature. There is a mutual accommodation between person and nature. Together they form an integral vision of human nature. This integral nature of the person (*nature intégrale de l'humain*) is what Malherbe labels *nature métaphorique* in the sense that the givenness of nature is assumed by and integrated into the rational order of the person.[27] In this way, normativity emerges out of an act of creativity.

The metaphorical structure of normativity underscores the fact that moral reasoning is not merely passive in the face of nature, but moral reasoning has an active role in fashioning individual human goods in the service of the ideology of human fulfillment. Similar to the meaning of a text being codetermined by the horizon of the reader, the ideology of human fulfillment is the hermeneutical key for the weighing of premoral but morally relevant goods.[28] The weighing of goods is never done in an abstract way, but always within the normative context that constitutes the legitimate expectations of freedom. The metaphorical structure of normativity will reflect the mutual accommodation between the two in a way that allows for truly new meanings of normativity to arise.[29]

The metaphorical structure of normativity reflects the influence of the recent epistemological discussion in the philosophy of science. The metaphorical structure of normativity embodies an historical ideal of science. The metaphorical tension between nature and person, however, does not entail a dualistic relationship between them. In fact, as the world is mediated through language, the metaphorical structure of normativity underlines the substantial but flexible unity between person and nature.

Further, the metaphorical structure of normativity reflects a necessary refinement of the philosophical tools needed to understand the natural moral law. This means that just as the metaphorical structure of language presupposes an historical ontology, the metaphorical structure of normativity presupposes a personalist and not an essentialist metaphysics of human nature. The neoscholastics worked with an essentialist understanding of the *natura absoluta et metaphysica hominis*. The effect that differing metaphysical commitments can have in moral casuistry is seen in the analysis of human action and the determination of the moral object. The metaphysics of the act is a cornerstone of moral casuistry.[30]

Under the influence of the modern notion of science and the legal–canonical categories of Alphonse Ligouri, the metaphysics of the act centered on the *finis operis*. The *finis operantis* was relegated to the psychology of action.[31] It could only effect the determination of the moral object in an accidental way. This was reinforced by the epistemological option of realism that was at work in neoscholastic thought. The concern was with the precision of analysis.

Although the neoscholastics' determination of the moral object was guided by an essentialist understanding of human nature, it frees them from the misplaced criticism of naturalism or physicalism.[32] It is one thing to have a reductive and ahistorical metaphysics; it is quite another to commit the naturalistic fallacy based on the positivists' separation of fact and value. Keeping this in mind will determine how we retrieve the past for the present.

The personalist metaphysics entailed in the metaphorical structure of normativity offers a new perspective from which to determine the moral object. The phenomenal aspect of the act is ambiguous because its object can take on a variety of meanings. The act receives its moral determination from the normative context within which it is interpreted. Like nature, the act is a necessary but not sufficient criterion of normativity. Within this personalist metaphysics, the *finis operantis* is no longer relegated to the psychology of the act, but constitutes the moral object.

The metaphorical structure of normativity and the historical ideal of science upon which it is based has important consequences for the analysis of the act. The analysis of the act is removed from a reductive normative theory and placed within the dialectical structure of insight and experience. There is a mutually conditioning relationship between the legitimate expectations of freedom and the moral object. A hermeneutical spiral is formed between them in a way that the determination of the moral object shares in the effective history of the legitimate expectations of freedom.[33] This means that the analysis of the moral act promotes and protects the legitimate expectations of freedom. As the breadth of possibilities of freedom expands through the creative and imaginative explorations of moral reasoning, the malleability of the act grows. As the limits of freedom are drawn in defense of certain goods, the interpretive potential of the act is narrowed.

CONCLUSION

This article has used the recent epistemological developments within the philosophy of science as a heuristic by which to critique the moral casuistry found in the neoscholastic manuals. The casuistry of the manuals was based on a modern ideal of science; rationality was measured by its correspondence to the axiomatic ideal of theoretical form. Any discipline worthy of the name "science" was to be developed *more geometrico*. The shift from a modern to an historical ideal of science offers the opportunity to explore the role of moral casuistry anew.

The changed epistemological terrain does not undermine the necessary role that problem solutions or case studies play in moral reasoning. Through problem solutions we are introduced into the effective history of our moral tradition. Problem solutions cannot be separated from the multifaceted commitments of the disciplinary matrix that they embody. Problem solutions serve as a kind of moral shorthand, normally bypassing the need to justify a community's normative commitments. In this way, problem solutions carry the presumption of truth in the community. Nevertheless, when those commitments are questioned and altered, problem solutions also share in the emancipatory history of moral reasoning. Under an historical ideal of science, moral casuistry is a hermeneutical art.

An historical ideal of science entails another consequence for moral casuistry in terms of the natural law and the determination of the moral object. The modern notion of science was the filter through which the neoscholastics retrieved the metaphysical tradition of Aquinas. In the shadow of the modern ideal, neoscholastic casuistry was guided by an objectivist and essentialist understanding of the natural moral law. This reductive understanding of the natural law had the effect of reifying the neoscholastic analysis of the moral act.

The rehabilitation of the natural moral law was done in an indirect way. The route to metaphysics was through language; language is the medium of experience. The way to history was through metaphor. Metaphor, as a process of transfer, assumes the realm of nature into a specifically human one. This means that there is a permanent hermeneutical tension between nature and person. When normative nature is seen metaphorically, there is a concomitant shift in the axis around which the analysis of the moral act revolves. The analysis shifts from one based on an objectivist and essentialist metaphysics to one based on a personalist and historical metaphysics. Finally, when the creative power of metaphor opens avenues for multiple interpretations of a human action as well as alternative solutions to moral problems, then moral casuistry becomes an instance of comparative hermeneutics.

NOTES

1. Paul Ricoeur, *The Rule of Metaphor*, trans. Robert Czerny (Toronto: University of Toronto Press, 1977) 7.

2. See for instance, Fred R. Dallmayr and Thomas A. McCarthy, eds., *Understanding and Social Inquiry* (Notre Dame: University of Notre Dame Press, 1977) 77-78. The best overview of recent epistemological trends is Richard Bernstein, *Beyond Objectivism and Relativism: Science, Hermeneutics, and Praxis* (Philadelphia: University of Pennsylvania Press, 1983).

3. Carl Hempel, "The Empiricist Criterion of Meaning," in A.J. Ayer, ed., *Logical Positivism* (Glencoe: Free Press, 1959) 109.

4. Thomas S. Kuhn, *The Structure of Scientific Revolutions*, 2nd ed. (Chicago: University of Chicago Press, 1970) 8-9.

5. The blurring of the traditional distinction between the sciences is discussed in John M. Connolly and Thomas Keutner, eds., *Hermeneutics vs Science? Three German Views* (Notre Dame: University of Notre Dame Press, 1988) 44-45; Richard Rorty, *Philosophy and the Mirror of Nature* (Princeton: Princeton University Press, 1979) 322; Charles Taylor, "Understanding in Human Science," *Review of Metaphysics* 34 (1980) 26.

6. The link between ontology and language that has been made in contemporary philosophy is detailed in James DiCenso, *Hermeneutics and the Disclosure of Truth: A Study in the Work of Heidegger, Gadamer, and Ricoeur* (Charlottesville: University Press of Virginia, 1990) 53-55.

7. George Lakoff and Mark Johnson, *Metaphors We Live By* (Chicago: University of Chicago Press, 1980); Mary Hesse, "The Cognitive Claims of Metaphor," *The Journal of Speculative Philosophy* 2 (1988) 1-13.

8. Paul Ricoeur, "The Metaphoric Process in Cognition, Imagination, and Feeling," *Critical Inquiry* 5 (1978) 143-59.

9. Josef Stern, "Metaphor as Demonstrative," *Journal of Philosophy* 82 (1985) 703-4; Thomas S. Kuhn, "Metaphor in Science," in A. Ortony, ed., *Metaphor and Thought* (Cambridge: Cambridge University Press, 1979) 418.

10. Ibid., 416.

11. Casuistry is by no means a univocal concept throughout history. See Albert R. Jonsen and Stephen Toulmin, *The Abuse of Casuistry: A History of Moral Reasoning* (Berkeley: University of California Press, 1988).

12. Klaus Demmer speaks of a vertical and horizontal coherency within a science. See his *Moraltheologische Methodenlehre*, Studien zur theologischen Ethik, 27 (Freiburg: Herder, 1989) 45-46. The unity of theory and praxis can be shown through the deconstruction and comparison of problem solutions. See the exemplary study of James F. Keenan, "The Function of the Principle of Double Effect," *Theological Studies* 54 (1993) 307-11.

13. *The Abuse of Casuistry* 275-76. See also, Bas C. van Fraassen, *Laws and Symmetry* (Oxford: Clarendon Press, 1989) 6-7.

14. John A. Gallagher, *Time Past, Time Future: An Historical Study of Catholic Moral Theology* (New York: Paulist Press, 1990) 98-119.

15. This trend continues in William E. May, *Moral Absolutes: Catholic Tradition, Current Trends and the Truth*, The Père Marquette Lecture In Theology (Milwaukee: Marquette University Press, 1989) 43-46, and Martin Rhonheimer, *Natur als Grundlage der Moral: Ein Auseinandersetzung mit autonomer und teleologischer Ethik* (Innsbruck: Tyrolia, 1987) 210.

16. There is a narrative character to our experience and knowledge of the world. This is clearly developed in Alasdair MacIntyre, *After Virtue*, 2nd ed. (Notre Dame: University of Notre Dame Press, 1984).

17. The retrieval of virtue has underlined the unity between a normative theory and a theory of action. This is argued in two particularly fine studies: James F. Keenan, "Virtue Ethics: Making a Case as It Comes of Age," *Thought* 67 (1992) 115-27, and Paul Wadell, *Friendship and the Moral Life* (Notre Dame: University of Notre Dame Press, 1989).

18. Application is constitutive of all understanding. Understanding, interpretation, and application comprise one unified process. See Hans-Georg Gadamer, *Truth and Method*, trans. Joel Weinsheimer and Donald Marshall, 2nd ed. (London: Sheed and Ward, 1989) 307-11.

19. Jonsen and Toulmin, *The Abuse of Casuistry* 293-94, 298; Sydney Callahan, *In Good Conscience: Reason and Emotion in Moral Decision Making* (San Francisco: Harper: 1991) 134-38.

20. For the general notion of "reading" as a hermeneutical category, see Werner Jeanrond, *Text and Interpretation As Categories of Theological Thinking*, trans. Thomas J. Wilson (New York: Crossroad, 1988).

21. Demmer, *Moraltheologische Methodenlehre* 145.

22. John Kekes, *The Morality of Pluralism* (Princeton: Princeton University Press, 1993) 99-107; Mark Johnson, *Moral Imagination: Implications of Cognitive Science For Ethics* (Chicago: University of Chicago Press, 1993) 202-207.

23. Hermeneutical reflection and ideology critique form two distinct but complementary functions of moral reasoning. Paul Ricoeur, "Ethics and

Culture: Habermas and Gadamer in Dialogue," *Philosophy Today* 17 (1973) 165-73.

24. Jean Ladrière, "On the Notion of Criterion," *Concilium* 155 (1982) 10-15.

25. Jean-François Malherbe writes, "En effet, bien qu'elle nous impose les conditions minimales de notre survie, la nature, entendue encore au sens biologique, reste absolument silencieuse sur la finalité de notre survie." He then gives this analogy: "La nature est à l'humain ce que la carte géographique et le véhicule sont au voyageur: conditions indispensable mais décidément silencieuses sur le but du voyage" ["L'Éthique entre nature et culture," *Le Supplement* 182-183 (1992) 320].

26. Compare Wilhelm Korff, "Nature or Reason as the Criterion for the Universality of Moral Judgement?" *Concilium* 150 (1981) 87, and Klaus Demmer, "Natur und Person: Brennpunkte gegenwärtiger moraltheologischer Auseinandersetzung," in *Natur im ethischen Argument*, ed., Bernhard Fraling, Studien zur theologischen Ethik, 31 (Freiburg: Herder, 1990) 61. Also Franz Böckle, "Nature as the Basis for Morality," in *Readings in Moral Theology*, no. 7: *The Natural Law and Theology*, eds., Charles Curran and Richard McCormick (New York: Paulist Press, 1991) 407-10.

27. Malherbe, "L'Éthique entre nature et culture," 321-22.

28. "Alle humanen Einzelgüter sind funktional auf die genannte Zielvorgabe hin, der Teil steht im Dienst am Ganzen" (Demmer, "Natur und Person," 61).

29. As Ricoeur writes, "a discourse which makes use of metaphor has the extraordinary power of redescribing reality. . . . But if we assume that metaphor redescribes reality, we must then assume that this reality as redescribed is itself novel reality" ("Creativity in Language: Word, Polysemy, Metaphor," *Philosophy Today* 17 [1973] 110-111).

30. Gerhard Stanke, *Die Lehre von den "Quellen der Moralität". Darstellung und Diskussion der neuscholastischen Aussagen und neuerer Ansätze*, Studien zur Geschichte der katholischen Moraltheologie, 26 (Regensburg: Friedrich Pustet, 1984).

31. Demmer, "Natur und Person," 65-66.

32. The clearest exposition is by Josef Fuchs, "Natural Law or Naturalistic Fallacy?" in *Moral Demands and Personal Obligations* (Washington: Georgetown University Press, 1993) 30-48.

33. This has been detailed in Thomas R. Kopfensteiner, "Historical Epistemology and Moral Progress," *The Heythrop Journal* 33 (1992) 45-60.

Contexts of Casuistry: Historical and Contemporary

JAMES F. KEENAN, S.J.
THOMAS A. SHANNON

HISTORICAL CONTEXT: DOUBT AND PROMISE

The essays in this collection illustrate how casuistry emerges historically out of a context of doubt and uncertainty occasioned by the prospect of extraordinary opportunity. The fact that doubt is the root cause of sixteenth century policy-making casuistry, for instance, is considerably ironic in that its seeds are planted in the midst of great daring and accomplishment and come to full bloom precisely when the Europeans enjoy considerable confidence based on extraordinary feats. As the European vision and presence expanded into the East through trade and into the New World through exploration and colonization, these experiences reinforced those tendencies for further expansion, exploration, and experimentation. This was an era of great promise and great risk, and the Europeans relished both.

Like today, when technology in all walks of life (e.g., medicine, communication, business) outpaces moral reflection, so too these sixteenth century European ventures outdistanced moral thought. Recent renewed interest in the person of Bartolomeo de las Casas, for instance, demonstrates convincingly the gap between what the Europeans did and what they should have done.[1] The European domination of the people of the New World testifies to the absence of any significant moral reflection on the question of the identity and moral standing of the people of the New World. Even when the question was addressed, it was abstract and lacked any experiential reflection that could have led to an appreciation of the communality between the people of Europe and of the Americas. Thus fascination with human capacities, whether in the sixteenth-century world of exploration or the twentieth-century world of technology, seems actually to have blunted needed inclinations toward moral reasoning.

Nonetheless, in the midst of this confidence, there was moral uncertainty—not about themselves, but about the validity of existing principles. At the beginning of the sixteenth century the economic and political institutions that followed in the wake of European expansionism stretched beyond the breaking point the moral principles that traditionally governed these institutions. The need to generate new capital to subsidize and guarantee these new ventures in trade and exploration forced the professors of the University of Paris to consider questions of maritime insurance, the triple contract, and other questions of financing. At the beginning of the sixteenth century there was a confidence in human reason and a willingness to determine what exactly constituted right institutional conduct. As merchants and explorers experienced confidence in their endeavors, so too did the university professors, who now reflected upon the new moral questions raised by these same endeavors. These experiences then led to doubt, not about whether or how to proceed, but about the validity of existing principles acting as guides.

These determinations of institutional guidelines for moral conduct continued into and throughout the Reformation. In fact, scholars generally agree that interest in and a need for these new guidelines for emerging capitalist institutions and structures were at least compatible with, if not actually an outgrowth of, the critical insights of the reformers themselves.

If confidence characterizes those considering the institutional uncertainties of the sixteenth century, anxiety describes those facing personal matters of faith. The reformers' message that one is saved by faith actually made many uncertain Christians even more fearful and perplexed about salvation. The spiritual renewal in sixteenth-century Catholic life likewise led to a radical reexamination of one's own moral, particularly sinful, state. These experiences on the part of both led to profound doubt about the fundamental status of one's self before God. This fundamental doubt was coupled again for both British Protestants and Catholics with the urgent practical concerns that they faced on matters like truth-telling, self-preservation, and the protection of others.

The context of casuistry for institutional life is clearly more confident and academic; the context of casuistry for personal questions of salvation is less confident and more ministerial. In both contexts there is the willingness to entertain a tremendous amount of new moral and empirical data: the former because of existing confidence in both the institutions and the families that led them;[2] the latter because of the need to confront the profound heartfelt anxiety about personal salvation and sinfulness. To understand how both contexts engaged that new data, we need to examine circumstances, consciences, and principles as centrally related to the concerns of these casuists.

CIRCUMSTANCES

In light of the ineffectiveness of existing principles, this willingness to entertain new data, not being supported by a deductive method of moral reasoning, turned to more inductive methods. This turn led to the use of the case, not as a substitute for principles, but as a source for moral guidance more foundational than the principles ever were. Those who turned to the case were seeking original moral insights. The case provided a method for teasing out the nuances inherent in both institutional and personal situations. The case method furnished a framework through which concrete individual circumstances were regularly entertained. It provided freedom from the existing moral principles that set an agenda in which the true is general, unvarying, and essential, and which by nature excluded specific, concrete, and practical circumstances. The case method hungered for them, for it thrives when it engages the new, the specific, the concrete, and the personal. Whereas the principle codifies an agenda, the case breaks the agenda open.

Circumstances highlight the uniqueness of one situation from all others. But as newer cases are considered with their attendant circumstances, a connectedness among cases emerges precisely through the circumstances themselves. These congruencies prompt the casuist to depend upon the resolution of one case through its analogous relationship with others.

Certainly the academy tended to casuistry (as Jonsen and Toulmin demonstrated in *The Abuse of Casuistry*) because of its ability to entertain circumstances in institutional matters, but ministers more urgently and desperately inclined to the same method because it could address and resolve the variety of concerns and anxieties that their communities' members suffered.

This ministerial context for casuistry served the institutions of preaching and confession. The content of this casuistry, however, differed according to the communities: Continental Catholic casuistry considered sin and forgiveness, British reformed casuistry focused on salvation and ordinary life. The former was so open to circumstantial possibilities that, as O'Malley notes, Jerome Nadal recommended that Jesuit confessors study cases an hour daily.[3] Though this casuistry considered the object of (sinful?) activity, the method always engaged circumstances, particularly the intentionality of the agent. British reformed casuistry, however, was tied to neither confessors nor the confessional, but sought to assist the individual directly in answering her or his perplexities about salvation and ordinary life. This was casuistry par excellence: training the laity to be their own casuists, not about sin alone, but about the whole of life. The circumstantial possibilities were limitless.

Conscience

Teaching the lay person accountability through exercises of moral reasoning depends on a recognition of the person's conscience as *locus authoritatis*. That recognition was already achieved by the Reformation's insistence that the individual's conscience was at once judge of one's sinful unworthiness yet called by faith to salvific freedom. For the reformers, the conscience of the individual both consented in faith and governed ordinary life. In a similar, albeit restrictive way, sixteenth-century Catholic probabilists (recalling Thomas' defense of the primacy of conscience[4]) promoted greater freedom for the individual to resolve doubts and to determine right conduct. In both communities, then, the casuist is more enabler than judge, more instructor than arbiter.

This wholeness that centered authority in the individual's conscience is complemented by a vision of Christian life that does not distinguish the ascetical from the moral. Like the preachers who preceded them, the casuists (again the reformed more than the Catholics) demanded that the moral task be identical with the spiritual task: to fully live out one's vocation. Thus, though the method always entertained the uniqueness of an individual's situation with a variety of circumstances, it always aimed at extensive integration. Perkins showed, for instance, how reflection on one's situation must be integrated into the whole of one's life. Mair and Taylor also demonstrated that one's particular vocation can never be isolated from the whole of one's community of faith. The willingness to entertain the specificity of the matters of an individual conscience never endorsed solipsism, but rather aimed to analyze as objectively as possible all the morally relevant details making claims on an individual's daily life.

Principles

Finally, with the abandonment of high casuistry in Catholic continental circles in 1660 because of the devastating attacks of Blaise Pascal and in British Protestant circles in 1690 because of attacks on Taylor, moral reasoning returned to principle-based reasoning. Ironically, these principles which replaced the case method were among the effects achieved by high casuistry. Though the lack of principles prompted the need for the case method, casuistry eventually provided new principles and general rules to replace the outdated ones. These new principles were both formal, methodological ones (double effect, cooperation, toleration) and material ones (human liberty, human dignity, just credit). These principles became codified into the manual tradition of Catholic theology.

During high casuistry both types of principles derived their genesis and validity from the congruency of various cases; similar insights developed into patterns that were eventually articulated into these methodological or material principles. The context for interpreting the validity of the new principles referred to the original context of the cases that engendered them. In the context of manualism of the last two centuries, however, principles enjoyed an unexamined validity. For manualists, principles were not historically formed, but rather universally given. Ironically, they were used to measure new cases, while their casuistic roots were forgotten. Likewise, circumstances were no longer morally determinative, but were rather standardized or, worse, excluded from the cases measured by these principles and rules. Moreover, the principles usurped the certitude that once belonged to right reason and to the conscience of the one exercising it. The assumed validity of the principles, no longer noted as rooted in the successfully resolved cases, was furthered by their successive appearances in the texts of manualists, accepted by their peers and by ecclesial authorities. For two centuries this ahistorical understanding of principles supported their acontextual claims and application: principles were above and beyond circumstances and conscience.

Still, the ahistorical claims of principles and rules that are found in the manualist tradition are challenged from within its own tradition in two ways. First, as Curran notes in his essay, though Sabetti generally presented already perceived determinations by a deductive application of a principle to a case, whenever he needed to resolve an uncertainty not yet contained in the manuals, he used the inductive case method. Moreover, at these moments, Sabetti was free not only from an agenda that the principle sets but from the Roman authorities who had not yet resolved the new and perplexing case. Thus, in the case of ectopic pregnancy he sought to understand the uniqueness of the circumstances of the particular case as determinative for the resolution. That resolution was eventually codified into a rule for resolving all other cases of ectopic pregnancy but the historical solution itself, which later became the rule, remains recorded. The manualists cannot ultimately deny the need to attend to particular circumstances to find successful resolutions.

Second, the nineteenth- and twentieth-century manualists cannot deny the historical contingency of a newly minted rule. Though they assumed that the principles were immutable and timeless, in fact they were historical expressions of case resolutions from sixteenth- and seventeenth-century high casuistry. The principle of double effect is a case in point; it derived from seventeenth-century high casuistry.[5]

As propositions, all principles are historically conditioned. In his essay Noonan shows through four case studies that principles thought unchangeable were reconfigured to respond to the changing moral demands of the day. Similarly, Kopfensteiner argues that every deductive application of a principle to a case is itself an historical moment. That is, when a principle is applied to a new case, even if it excludes the circumstances and all other determinative particularities, nonetheless the application itself changes the understanding of the principle. The actual expression of the principle or rule may seem to remain constant, but in reality its understanding determines its meaning. Thus even though manualists and their supporters may foster the mistaken belief that these principles are ahistorical, they cannot avoid the claim that the application of a principle to a case always occurs in history, is determined through history, and is thereby reappropriated to the tradition.

CONTEMPORARY CONTEXT

While it enjoys extraordinary achievements in technology, the contemporary world is simultaneously characterized by a high degree of moral relativity. This relativity is in part a reaction to the ahistorical (and therefore nonobjective) application of rigid principles to contemporary situations. Additionally, the authority of these principles, not acknowledged as rooted in the historical exercise of the case method, is found in the status of the figures who espouse their validity. The authority of the principles then is largely extrinsic, not intrinsic, to their expression. Moreover, the authority of the exponents of these principles is being tested today, both by those who want a more intrinsic notion of certitude to prevail and by those who deny any legitimacy to moral authority at all.

Certainly, the inflexibility of these principles is not the major cause of moral relativity today, but it is the major cause of their ineffectiveness. When principle-based ethicists and other authorities deny the moral relevance of circumstances through their insistence on the primacy of ahistorical and acontextual moral principles, then this deductive method cannot successfully respond to the need many people have to reason rightly in the face of new problems embedded within a rapidly changing social matrix. Moreover, this ahistorical approach aggravates and furthers the growth of relativism. Inasmuch as this age witnesses to a return to the subject as moral arbiter, it also witnesses to a subject making moral decisions without an objective method for moral deliberation.

The need for a new method of moral reasoning must attend to the needs for an objective method for the twenty-first-century subject. But this need must attend to the claim we made in the introduction, that casuistry itself is not context free, but context dependent. That is, if we appropriate casuistry today without any particular set of presuppositions or without any fundamental context, there is no guarantee that the conclusions derived from the case method would be objective. Jonsen and Toulmin's ability to use the case method in Washington reflects, we believe, the fact that despite differences among the members, they all shared enough of a common context to arbitrate cases without entertaining relativistic claims.

Casuistry in the hands of a laxist or a tutiorist is equally effective. Casuistry has no purposes intrinsic to its logic or method. The context in which it is employed provides the purpose. Thus casuistry never stands free of its context or its practitioners. Though the method of casuistry may have been the same for John Mair, Jeremy Taylor, William Perkins, Thomas Sanchez, or Danilo Concina, the effects and insights achieved were always different.

In light of this finding, we close with a proposal for a context for casuistry that may be effective in meeting the needs of many who are looking for an inductive method of moral reasoning, while avoiding relativistic tendencies.[6]

As virtue was the context for the casuistry of many British reformers, virtue could provide again a framework for the morally responsible exercise of right reasoning through the case method. This claim is made based on certain merits of virtue ethics that are compatible with the insights of casuistry. We attend to those merits briefly. First, the virtues can be rooted in claims for an objectively based moral foundation. Notwithstanding the culturally relativistic claims endorsed by some, Martha Nussbaum, among others, argues for the nonrelativistic nature of the virtues while at the same time arguing that they are culturally sensitive.[7] This allows for a systematic foundation that provides the attractiveness of an objectivity that transcends borders without being historically detached.

Second, Jonsen and Toulmin noted that the failure of high casuistry resulted in part because casuistry became excusatory instead of directive. This shift, they argued, resulted from a lack of moral idealism. Unfortunately as high casuistry developed in the institutional arena, attentiveness to the mean was often at the cost of neglect for the goal. Likewise the dynamism of the casuistry of the early British reformers like Perkins, Ames, and Hall, who advocated the virtues, collapsed in the legalistic context urged later by Taylor. Virtue ethics is by definition teleological in its essence, determining the mean precisely in relation to the goal. The need for moral idealism is caught well by an ethics that challenges all to *become* just, temperate, brave, and prudential.

Third, this teleology likewise complements the developmental traits of the casuistry of the seventeenth-century British reformers. Just as the reformers tried to develop prudence in their listeners so that they in turn could become self-governing, virtue ethics itself is based on the belief that who we are and who we are to become are separate questions and that the moral task is to determine what exact steps we must take to achieve the latter.

Fourth, in the turn to the subject, moral truth must be found in the person. We need to develop what Kopfensteiner calls a "personalistic metaphysics of human nature." Here human reason is not passive in the face of the given, but "has an active role in fashioning individual goods in the service of the ideology of human fulfillment." That quest for human fulfillment in a Christian context is not arbitrary, but rather conditioned by the gifts of human freedom and right reason, lived out in the reality of human community. Thus virtue ethics affords us an anthropological vision of truth in the concept of prudence and sets the framework for a responsible turn to the subject as arbiter, but not as arbitrary.

Fifth, in this same turn to the subject we need an account not only of right reasoning, but of rightly ordered persons. The cardinal virtues provide in particular an anthropological foundation for this personalistic metaphysics. These virtues may not necessarily be the same as those first articulated by Plato and long held in the classical tradition. Indeed, we may have difficulty articulating exactly the name and number of the cardinal virtues; we may not fully express a complete anthropological model. But naming some virtues provides us with some heuristic insight into both who we are and who we ought to be. Moreover, they provide us with an insight into the character needed for one to reason rightly.

The right reason (or prudence) of virtue ethics finds in casuistry an attentiveness to detail that appreciates the uniqueness of the situation and the surrounding circumstances precisely in order to obtain right resolution. In a virtuous context we could address objectively the particularities that the case method demands and promotes.

This proposal is admittedly nascent. However, virtue ethics is in need of an inductive method of moral reasoning that high (or early) casuistry could provide. Similarly, the personalistic metaphysics that contemporary casuistry needs could be expressed in the teleological anthropology that a virtue ethics promotes.

This proposal for a contemporary context of casuistry, like our investigation into the historical context of casuistry, is heuristic. But we believe that renewed interest in the virtues and in casuistry is not coincidental. Nonetheless, hitherto there have been only rare moments of entertaining the two. Though the epistemological method may find internal compatibility with an ethical context that is anthropologically driven, we believe that there are four other, external, reasons that make our proposal additionally attractive.

First, the unstated presuppositions that drive those interested in casuistry eventually need to be surfaced. Jonsen and Toulmin's claim, that case resolution provided the national commission with a context that allowed them to find moral solutions without entering into the fundamentally diverse moral presuppositions that the members held, needs serious reexamination. Were there really no shared beliefs? Were the members really so disparate in their moral presuppositions? Could not some beliefs have been articulated, expressed, and discussed? If casuistry is not as context free as Jonsen and Toulmin claimed, then certainly the fact that the commission members achieved consensus on several matters suggests greater congruency in moral beliefs and presuppositions than supposed. Rather than articulating those beliefs in the form of principles, could not the virtues provide a broader and more nuanced expression for airing what precisely those presuppositions are?

Second, for Christians the return to the virtues and the return to casuistry may signify a renewed interest in preaching. Preachers like Bernardino and Perkins both found that the virtues they highlighted were best expressed through cases. The immediacy of the case engaged the congregation and helped them understand practically their response to the Word. But those cases were always given in the form or context of virtues and vices. The genre of the moral sermon may finally provide a way to see the practical responsibilities that the Scriptures call us to exercise.

Third, moral teaching can be better communicated by a virtue-based ethics coupled with the case method. For instance, the National Conference of Catholic Bishops' letter, *Economic Justice for All,* may have enjoyed greater reception if virtues and not principles had been the instruments to express the excellent insights therein and if the case method had been used to determine the rightness and wrongness of emerging policies. Are principles the proper medium for expressing the call to Christian conversion found in the gospel? Are they the proper medium for providing preachers with suitable language for addressing the real needs of the congregation? Would not a dependence on the virtues and the cases have been more attractive to preachers?[8]

Finally, moral theology is at the crossroads. As it looks forward it seems also to be looking behind. A reawakened interest in its history appears in works cited throughout this book by Mahoney, Vereecke, Noonan, Gallagher, as well as Jonsen and Toulmin. But the legacy of moral theology from Augustine and Thomas to today often was expressed not in hard fast rules or principles but in the more supple virtues. As Thomas writes in the preface to the *Secunda secundae,* all of moral theology comes down to the virtues. Nonetheless, Thomas did not have the benefit of a legacy called high casuistry. Still, the casuists we saw borrowed Thomas' contribution on the virtues. We conclude by suggesting that we appropriate the insights of both: the epistemological ones of high casuists and the anthropological ones of the best of scholasticism.

NOTES

1. Bartolomeo de las Casas, *The Only Way*, ed. Helen Parish (New York: Paulist Press, 1992); Gustavo Gutierrez, *Las Casas: In Search of the Poor of Jesus Christ* (Maryknoll: Orbis Books, 1993); Reginaldo Iannarone, *La scoperta dell'America e la prima difesa degli indios: i Domenicani* (Bologna: Edizioni Studio Domenicano, 1992).

2. John T. Noonan, Jr., *The Scholastic Analysis of Usury*, (Cambridge: Harvard University Press, 1957) 171-192, 194-195, 199-201.

3. John O'Malley, *The First Jesuits* (Cambridge: Harvard Univ., 1993) 147, see also 136-152.

4. Thomas Aquinas, *Summa Theologiae*, I. II. 19. 5 and 6.

5. See James Keenan, "The Function of the Principle of Double Effect" *Theological Studies* 54 (1993) 294-315.

6. This proposal reflects primarily the perspective of James Keenan. Thomas Shannon hesitates to endorse totally the proposal because he believes that casuistry could be appropriated in other contexts such as those that proportionalists and other revisionists highlight.

7. Martha Nussbaum, "Non-Relative Virtues: An Aristotelian Approach," *Ethical Theory: Character and Virtue*, ed. Peter A. French, Theodore E. Uehling, Jr., and Howard Wettstein (Notre Dame: University of Notre Dame Press, 1988) 32-53 at 36.

8. John Barrett, *"Economic Justice" Through the Eyes of an Ethics of Virtue* (diss: Fordham University, New York, 1994).